SAGE was founded in 1965 by Sara Miller McCune to support the dissemination of usable knowledge by publishing innovative and high-quality research and teaching content. Today, we publish more than 750 journals, including those of more than 300 learned societies, more than 800 new books per year, and a growing range of library products including archives, data, case studies, reports, conference highlights, and video. SAGE remains majority-owned by our founder, and on her passing will become owned by a charitable trust that secures our continued independence.

Los Angeles | London | Washington DC | New Delhi | Singapore

CORRUGATED SLICES

CORRUGATED SLICES
The Social Jalebi

Shombit Sengupta

www.sagepublications.com

Los Angeles • London • New Delhi • Singapore • Washington DC

First published in 2015 by

SAGE Response
B1/I-1 Mohan Cooperative Industrial Area
Mathura Road, New Delhi 110 044, India

SAGE Publications Inc
2455 Teller Road
Thousand Oaks, California 91320, USA

SAGE Publications Ltd
1 Oliver's Yard, 55 City Road
London EC1Y 1SP, United Kingdom

SAGE Publications Asia-Pacific Pte Ltd
3 Church Street
#10-04 Samsung Hub
Singapore 049483

Published by Vivek Mehra for SAGE Publications India Pvt Ltd, typeset in 11/14 pts ITC Century Book by RECTO Graphics, Delhi and printed at Saurabh Printers Pvt Ltd, New Delhi.

Library of Congress Cataloging-in-Publication Data Available

ISBN: 978-81-321-1770-4 (PB)

The SAGE Team: Sachin Sharma, Neha Sharma and Anju Saxena

For my grandchildren,
Sreeya and Ariyan Sengupta

My profuse thanks to
Prahalada Rao
S.R. Prakash
Robin Raj
Amitava Chattopadhyay
Renee Jhala

Thank you for choosing a SAGE product! If you have any comment, observation or feedback, I would like to personally hear from you. Please write to me at <u>contactceo@sagepub.in</u>

—Vivek Mehra, Managing Director and CEO,
SAGE Publications India Pvt Ltd, New Delhi

Bulk Sales

SAGE India offers special discounts for purchase of books in bulk. We also make available special imprints and excerpts from our books on demand.

For orders and enquiries, write to us at

Marketing Department
SAGE Publications India Pvt Ltd
B1/I-1, Mohan Cooperative Industrial Area
Mathura Road, Post Bag 7
New Delhi 110044, India
E-mail us at <u>marketing@sagepub.in</u>

Get to know more about SAGE, be invited to SAGE events, get on our mailing list. Write today to <u>marketing@sagepub.in</u>

This book is also available as an e-book.

CONTENTS

LIST OF FIGURES

FOREWORD

Corrugated Slices: The Social Jalebi is the third book in *The Jalebi Trilogy*. Going through it, I certainly learnt more about heterogeneous India than I have experienced in my four years of managing an Indian company in Mumbai.

The book offers market and marketing insights from an astute market researcher who travels the world and India to learn about priorities of life, lifestyles, and purchasing processes of multiethnic, multireligious, multistrata societies. You can share the extraordinary life of a great contemporary painter from his humble start in West Bengal to the heights of becoming a world-renowned business strategy consultant and brand creator in many business sectors.

Using the same incisive ability of managing his artist's brushes, Shombit Sengupta portrays India's societal evolution by highlighting how business houses should approach billion-peopled markets differently from a westernized focus on million-peopled markets.

Behind a simple narrative, Shombit shows you how we can be alert to societal evolution with an open and respectful mind. The book teaches the importance of being humble but determined to apply your brain and not to blindly follow the incumbent fashion without a critical approach. And what is more important, I got provoked with an overwhelming infusion to learn much more.

The book clearly and straightforwardly deals with very sensitive aspects of contemporary society, from homosexuality to the previous Catholic Pope's involvement with Nazis. Going beyond an uncritical, common approach, Shombit constantly stimulates the reader to further dive in for more robust understanding.

It is not easy to constrain the book within a *genre*: management book, sociological book, autobiography book? Probably, all of these! It's a rich experience that helped me understand both India and Europe from a different perspective.

Perhaps I may be the perfect target for the book: Caucasian background in desperate need to understand India. In general when I buy a book, if I do not immediately understand from the title what the book is about, which may be the case here, I try and go through a few lines to understand in 30 seconds whether the content attracts me. Most of the time, a few lines make me decide to buy or not, rather in an emotional approach as books are my hobby, I have almost 12,000 of them! When you start reading this book, you will experience the right mix of personal understanding in different countries/cultures, management/marketing ideas, provocations on politics and religion. The "story" can evoke the need to agree or challenge the author, it triggers the mind with its uncommon approach. Overall, the book can be enjoyed by different age groups in any corner of the world.

Reading the book gave me much more than pure emotion: I got knowledge, new ideas to mull over, uncomfortable disconnects with my own belief, and, therefore, challenges to validate my belief, as well as deeper understanding of societal aspects relevant to my job in India.

Dr Giorgio De Roni
Chief Executive Officer, GoAir

PREFACE
Wavy Slivers of Life

As long ago as 1642, Frenchman Blaise Pascal invented the mechanical calculator, the precursor to computer technology. But until it suddenly descended upon us, no scientist, philosopher, or politician had accurately predicted how the digital impact would turn every moment of our lives upside down merely by activating our fingertips. Except, of course, physicist Albert Einstein (1895–1955) who said, "I fear the day technology will surpass our human interaction. The world will have a generation of idiots." Of course, the *jalebi* (sweetmeat in slurpy sweet syrup) was invented much earlier, in the 13th century. Due to its juicy, tasty, undulated character, the jalebi has comfortably remained in India and the Middle East, century after mouthwatering century.

The last millennium saw many inventions and discoveries such as radio, TV, antibiotics, rocketry, nuclear energy, automobiles, airplanes, internet and personal computers from developed societies. These fructified to initially make the world's developed countries either symbols of advancement or superpowers. Developing countries were impacted much later.

Up to 1991 there was a time lag between inventions. But at the cusp of the 21st century, digital technology democratized the world. Suddenly every new digi-tech product or service is being launched simultaneously across the world. Moreover, there's barely any time interval between such inventions that are happening every fortnight, if not earlier. This has changed everything, in particular, human behavior of whole populations that have bypassed the mechanical era to enter the digital one straight from agrarian lifestyles. Today, all forms of art, culture, science, literature, and sports are pulsating to keep pace with the incredible new that's overpowering everything across the world. Most significantly, human behavior is continuously changing too.

Twenty years ago we could not imagine that the most advanced, all-time-requirement human companion device would be the mobile phone. From now onwards, this mobile device will become the critical industry of the world for human needs. Currently this industry is totally dominated by the 50-million populated South Korea, the global lord of the mobile phone.

I have sometimes wondered if this digital trend is hype like the mechanical to electrical to the electronic eras that boomed at the start and then stabilized. Not everyone could enjoy the electrical or electronic eras at the same level due to cost discrepancies. But the digital era is growing in every aspect of life, industry, and culture.

In the last 20 years we have not witnessed any stagnancy or hint of its obsolescence. The mobile connection line cost being the same for all has reduced rich and poor divide, only the hand device has a range of prices. So this indeed is a sparkling era.

The advent of virtual social networking globally is shaking up even politicians. Whether they bribe someone or have a love affair, they cannot escape the court martial verdict, snide remarks, and admonitions from people they will never know or meet. This is today's armchair revolution. All these convoluted happenings are interlinked like syrup. We have to keep our eyes open for 24 hours a day lest we miss out on the new that is zipping in. Just as life's many happenings break up or interrupt every instant, in the same way you cannot eat a whole jalebi at one shot. That is why it is sliced and corrugated. Yet, just as a jalebi has syrup, so will life's bloodlines always be connected.

Let us consider the feelings the jalebi evokes in us in this third volume of *The Jalebi Trilogy*. The interactive world has been truncated into micro-tales by text messages, Twitter, and Facebook. In the same spirit I am not burdening you to read a long book to extract a story. Here are 63 shivering mini-tales slicing up the straight and narrow route, confronting the discomfiture that a jalebi-like twist brings. Sans predictability of what to expect in the next mini-tale-slice, just be assured that you will be treading a corrugated path.

We have already gauged the jalebi's positive aspects in the first book, *Jalebi Management: All Stakeholders Can Enjoy a Bite*. We consumed the not-so-straightforward jalebi in the second book, *Strategic Pokes: The Business Jalebi*. Today's altered socio-psycho-political dimension has taken on the parallel character of the syrup-saturated, yet crisp, jalebi. Sometimes the societal trend gives us a delicious roll on the tongue, at other times life takes an awkward turn, like when you sink your teeth into an oversweet jalebi.

Every aspect of our times has radically changed, and is changing continuously, since 1991 when digital technology kicked in, bringing us to this third book, *Corrugated Slices: The Social Jalebi*. It is like a blog with numerous iffy happenings in the world that teased my mind's eye from my practical experience. I have toyed with them, been engrossed in them in laughter, pain, shock, or anger; so let me bring you these wavy slivers of life.

India's sub-30 generation is not the Indian societal archetype of the 20th century that was veiled from global trends. They are different today from their elders in every aspect, such as taste buds, education, handling jobs, friendship, sex, and relationships. So unleashing the potential of these Digital Zappers could add substantial growth to India's economy tomorrow. They hide nothing. Provoking them to actually ideate outside the box can prevent society's jalebi from snapping their innocence and ingenuity. Their intermittent irrational and rational behavior can be combined in unpredictable ways. Liberating this generation from the comfort of conformity is imperative to tackle tomorrow's digital technology world.

In the 63 mini-tale-slices on the pages of *Corrugated Slices: The Social Jalebi*, let us dissect life's odd asymmetries. Let us chew on how the delectably sugary and unstraight jalebi ways have added to our undiluted craving.

1

INDISCOPE

When in real life you are mired as though you are inside the flanks of a *jalebi* (sweetmeat in slurpy sweet syrup), how would you feel? In this situation, does "thinking" even exist? Is it not mere fuzzy vapor? After all, an idea materializes from stimuli that hit us into action. So "Does thinking exist?" is how Indiscope is going to enter your mind space.

Aside from relegating thought to the tectonics of brain cells, Indiscope is about different slices of action I have picked up from across India. In managing daily struggles, the poor have to extricate themselves from jalebi-like twists. I remember how the refugees from East Bengal, whom I grew up with in a refugee colony outside Kolkata, seemed to accept poverty like a religion. But to exit that jalebi maze, I sincerely believe that only individual effort and gumption can break the bondage of poverty.

In the individual mini-tale-slices in the following pages you will find my personal experiences intermingling with observations on subjects I am obsessive about. It is a cloudy jalebi I masticate when subtlety and aesthetics are missing in our behavior and actions. It is an ugly jalebi I gnash between molars when hygiene and civic responsibility are missing, particularly in public places.

What ignites my passion is the sub-30 generation that constitutes the largest age cohort of decision-makers. I call them Zappers. The first two books in the *Jalebi Trilogy* mention them too. They decide what to buy, when to buy, where to buy, and how to buy, with money they have earned or their parents have earned. They can crunchily enjoy a jalebi or disgustedly crush out its juice in a fistful of aggression and throw it away. Their impetuousness, openness, and flexibility can be disciplined to be incredibly creative and productive.

Whether we are the Compromise (born between 1965 and 1980) or Retro (born before 1965) generation, we too want to experience the dynamism of ideation from Indian youth, which is extremely heterogeneous and cannot be compared to that of any other country. Let us dive into that opportunity while nibbling at the differently flavored mini-tale-slices in this chapter.

DOES THINKING EXIST?

What's thinking, does it exist? Is it not infinite hazy vapor until an idea materializes? Being a metaphor of an intangible human aspect, it is very difficult to realize the corporeal material of thought.

Materializing imagination

Could thinking be the escape of intellectuals to place selected people at a higher societal level? The birth of a human being is probably the most valuable instance happening in the universe, but the exact time and date of conception is mysterious, and comes from not thinking. "Don't think." In the normal course, nobody can predict life's end.

So life's beginning and termination are within a boundary beyond control and thought. So don't think, push the act, and let imagination take over.

The towering thinkers of the world we eulogize materialized their thoughts very rationally. They used forms such as writing, painting, singing, designing, drawing, playing music, writing music, inventing. What made them do what they did is a big question mark. People often analyze a famous inventor's ingenious thinking process merely to rationalize it. But that is simply an interpretation without truth or tangible base.

Reacting to stimuli

When you say "I'm thinking," in reality you are being impacted by stimuli that you physically react to. By default, people absorb happenings around them, bounce with stimuli, get conditioned, or are stimulated to imagine. Unlike animals, people act with conscious or unconscious judgments that shape them.

Can thinking exist without stimulus from society, nature, or the universe? Closed in a box with no stimulus whatsoever, would someone be able to think? Would he not become a vegetable? An inspiration spurs him to act, but thinking, not being a stimulus, may be frigid.

The higher up in society we go, the more people talk of thinking. Does the problem of underprivileged people struggling for their next meal get solved by thought or by action? If in spite of poverty they hit the limelight, it is because they chose to respond to stimuli. They reached what is unreachable within their means, not by thought but by friction provoked by stimulus.

In the crossroads

In 1984, I encountered a big predicament. Should I continue to work successfully for others or should I create my own enterprise? Thinking, scribbling, thinking, and more thought was stifling me. I wanted to break away from Parisian life for a few days, think about my future.

I have often loitered around the beautiful Loire valley 204 km from Paris. I would weave into villages, castles, farms without any travel agenda, with unrestrained thinking. Sometimes, sitting by Loire river's beautiful picturesque French countryside, I have watched people cycling hurriedly, being intimate, old people playing the typical French pétanque game, others just walking, kicking up dust. The serene landscape and vibrant action before me has filled many a drawing book with sketches, as brushes, colors, palette, and canvas are my constant companions.

On this thinking tour, as I was crossing Rue Victor Hugo, from the river bank into the narrow village lane in Amboise where the road sharply takes an L-turn, I saw a small, old castle. It had an old man's gravure poster. Written on it was "I am a genius." This intrigued me; I recognized the words uttered by Leonardo da Vinci when he was 39 years old. Somehow, in spite of being well versed in art in France, I had bypassed this place.

Goose pimples suddenly ran through me. I realized that I had stumbled upon Leonardo's home. This incredible shock was the stimulus that kicked me hard. And what did I discover? In 1516, King François Premiere had invited Leonardo to Amboise, providing him Clos Lucé to stay and work in. A famous painter, engineer, medical scientist, and inventor from Italy, Leonardo arrived with three of his paintings, *Mona Lisa*, *Sainte Anne*, and *Saint Jean Baptiste*, and lived here until he died on May 2, 1519.

Visiting Leonardo's mansion, I found powerful stimuli that stopped me in my tracks. Framed on the wall were his words: "A day with a full load of work gives better sleep; only a life totally covered with work gives a tranquil death." People refer to Leonardo as the Master Thinker, but his personal statement put action above everything else. This made me understand that thinking may just be sophistication, to distance the elite from the masses. In actuality, the world moves with stimulus–action.

So, on my return to Paris, I resigned from my post as one of the highest-paid creative directors in France in the most famous design consulting company there. I founded my own company from scratch. Leonardo da Vinci's 600-year-old words were my life-changing stimuli. If you go into his mansion you will see his kitchen, living room, and bedroom, which can really bring you closer to the Master. This experience revealed to me that the right stimulus in the right atmosphere and at the right time of life makes you act, to take breakthrough steps.

How business uses thought

Thinking is considered an intellectual prerequisite in the world of business. It probably means buying more time to be impacted by multiple stimuli. It's possible that people choose various provocative ways to force themselves to create something new. Perhaps how, using figurative and physical stimulants, you prepare ingredients for your imagination is more crucial than thinking. You may need different types of stimuli at different times in life according to your individual character.

If you are recognized as a genius, your brilliance was not nature's endowment. You would have chosen to imbibe strong stimuli that transformed you exceptionally for society to distinguish you. Not everyone can receive extraordinary stimuli. The common person's life may be boring, with no stimuli that allow imaginative juices to flow.

The mastermind generates a provocative stimulus that whirls into his/her mind's eye. Responding to an incomparable stimulus will obviously empower the unearthing of new dimensions, creating something perceptibly different. Without analyzing this, people say a person is a thinker. But that is no compliment, as mere thinkers contribute nothing to society. So, don't think, choose stimulus, act!

Action is inventive

Was the two-time Nobel Prize–winner for physics and chemistry, Marie Curie, a thinker or a hard worker confronting laborious stimuli? For four years she and husband Pierre boiled, stirred, poured, and distilled tons of pitchblende to produce a tiny amount of radium. That turned out to be among 20th century's best discoveries. Leonard da Vinci's contribution is not fuzzy thought but actual engineering models and scientific anatomical drawings. These propel us to this day.

This mini-tale-slice is all about endless imagination beyond thinking. When you don't think, imagination fills your mind space, thrilling you with free-flow connect-to-connect-to-connect. Are people not tired of thinking? The more exceptional the stimulus that stimulates your imagination, the more creative, industrious, or uniquely different your resulting act will be.

So, don't think. Get hit by stimulus. Act to create the shock-of-the-new to change the world.

STIMULUS LEADS TO ACTION

Stimuli make human beings act differently; thinking is mere fuzz. Each one of you has plenty of examples of spectacular stimuli in your life; you just need to open your past and savor them. Let me demonstrate this with my personal experiences.

Turning points with art

Examples of my stimuli are nothing exceptional, but from the beginning of my life they emanated from art and became turning points. In my childhood of extreme poverty in a village in Bengal, living just 500 m from our bamboo-hay-mud house was Subhinoy *Kaku* (uncle). A graduate painter and artist, he worked as a clerk in the Electricity Board. From when I was five years old, he was my biggest attraction, as he would paint and sculpt. I learnt art from him, but he always cautioned me against following in his footsteps. Art was his bad addiction, he said, it earned him no money.

Incidentally, my father did once mention in passing that he had seen an English film of a poor Dutch painter whose painting became bright after he migrated to France. He did not remember the artist's name, but knew that his paintings fetched no earnings in his lifetime; he only became famous later. Subhinoy Kaku's powerful artistic expression remains my exceptional, propelling stimulus. My well-wishers in our neighborhood could never understand why I enrolled in the Government College of Art & Craft in Kolkata in 1971. They called it a "zoo" because inhabitants there have no earning capacity, they are just watched.

Our art college professor divided the class into groups for sketching outdoors. My group had a student from an affluent family. I needed mental preparation to converse with her, but her appreciation of my artwork broke the ice. She allowed me to work with her imported Winsor & Newton artist colors and brushes, something unimaginable for a refugee-colony resident like me. I owe her generosity a debt. One day she wanted to take me to the American Library. I refused, saying I could not afford it. She insisted it was free, but I could not make her understand my intimidation at stepping into such a sophisticated place.

In that plush, air-conditioned library, the first glossy art book I picked up had Vincent van Gogh's gloomy *Potato Eaters*, painted in Holland in 1885. As I turned the page, the brilliant *Sunflowers* stared at me. Van Gogh had painted this on reaching Paris, in 1888. I immediately recalled my father's words. Witnessing this dramatic change in painting style kicked a big stimulus into me. From that day I became desperate to go to France.

Materializing a reverie

With circus-like trapeze and tightrope walking, this unreachable dream somehow materialized. My mother sold her marriage bangles for my ticket and also scraped together US$8, with which I left India without finishing college. Reaching Paris on a cold November day in 1973, I had no idea where I would spend that night. I knew nobody, spoke no French. My only faint chance was a Bengali scientist I had heard of.

Among the hurdles of leaving the airport was finding the scientist in a directory available in those days. I found his research laboratory, 103 Boulevard Raspail, and arrived there. The French receptionist did not understand my accent, so I wrote "PYNE." She squinted at the paper and beamed, "Ah Peeenn...!" When Dr Pyne arrived, I began narrating my story: "I've come to become an artist in Paris, I'm ready to work anywhere, how can I stay on after my 3-month visitor visa expires?" He looked totally at sea. Having set eyes on me for the first time in his life, he was bereft of a response. He just scurried me away from the reception.

In his laboratory I quickly dipped into the big handbag I was clutching. I pulled out my sketches and paintings. That is when my art buffeted me with the next big stimulus. When Dr Pyne saw my paintings, without hesitation, he announced I could stay with him until I found a job. His spontaneous munificence is my life's unforgettable stimulus. Looking back, late Pyne *Da*'s (elder brother) largesse, which was prompted by my paintings, was the stimulus that has chiseled me today.

Job-hunting

After two months I met Jacques Gourdon, and sought a job at his famous lithography print shop 10 km from Paris. The world oil crisis occurred in 1973, so there was no question of immigration. He said I could not be recruited without a work permit. By instinct I had carried my big black bag of sketches, watercolors, and paintings. When Mr Gourdon saw my art, he seemed astonished. He wanted to give me an opportunity. Paying 500 Francs per month from his own pocket, he hired me as a sweeper. France's minimum salary then was 3,500 Francs, but during my dire straits, my art was my savior stimulus.

Artists who frequented the lithography studio buoyed me up as a fellow artist. They bought my paintings so I could attend classes in fine-art and graphic-design schools. In 1976 the print shop closed. Renowned painter Yves Brayer, whom I had met at the print shop, gave me the address of Navarre & Associates.

Patrick Navarre was surprised when I showed up suddenly. It was quite unexpected in those days to see an Indian looking for a job in an ad agency. Giving me no chance to open my art portfolio, he started talking of a cultural gap between India and France. Suddenly the phone rang. As he took the call, I dared to reach for the paper and pencil on his desk and drew a sketchy portrait of him. He was taken aback by my sketch. He commented, "Incredible." He hired me on the spot at 4,000 Francs. Art as stimulus gave me entry into the communication world. Art increased my earnings from 500 to 4,000 Francs.

Stimuli always paved the way

Since then, art has been my driving stimulus in corporate work projects globally. I have used art as a central pattern and stimulus to strategize corporate culture change, brands, industrial design, and retailing. I have established that execution and activation will make my clients achieve their objectives.

Art as stimulus paved my path from a refugee colony in Shahidnagar to Paris. Without thinking, I pursued Subhinoy Kaku. It was not thought but gentle nudging that made me enter the American Library. I did not think of where I would stay, what I would do when I flew into Paris equipped with US$8. Dr Pyne did not think, but spontaneously welcomed me with no reference check. Nor did Jacques Gourdon think of legalities when he compensated me. Patrick Navarre gave me a break as a paste-up artist without thinking of my capacity for communication arts.

So today, should I think or should I act on a stimulus?

THE OPIUM OF POVERTY

Karl Marx wrote, "Religion is the opium of the masses." My personal experience, not from thinking but from being born into a poor family, is that acceptance of poverty is also opium in our highly tolerant Indian culture.

The poor are dependent

"Amra gorib lok" (We are poor people) is what I heard over and over again in my neighborhood throughout my childhood. It amounted to, "We should not dream too much as that would paralyze us." To act like poor people was like a religion. Having a watch in your hand, or wearing Bata shoes or sunglasses, was a sign of the bourgeoisie. If any of us in my locality had one of these three things, it was a discussion point. The acceptance of poverty has left large numbers of our population below subsistence level. My obsessive thought since those days has been about how the poor can break the shackles of poverty with dignity, shine in life, and change the world.

Western society regards poverty as a kind of defeat. Those who do not have enough, work very hard to get rich. In contrast, it is very difficult for Indians with a scarcity mindset to emerge from it. The affluent support the persistence of poverty through charity works. NGOs try uplifting the poor. But how effective such an activity is in changing the plight of the poor may be questioned.

"The inevitable consequence of poverty is dependence," said the English poet Samuel Johnson. It is human inclination to exercise control over people, so keeping the poor dependent is a ploy to feel powerful. The real mission for tomorrow's India should be to activate the economically weak so they are no longer dependent. The only help they need is to learn how to earn and how to enjoy life. Otherwise this huge visible difference in equality will continue to grow.

Only individual effort can break the bondage of poverty

I had to take a breakthrough step to release myself from poverty. When we were underprivileged, my parents' stringent discipline banned me from seeing Hindi films, possibly to avoid my adopting Bollywood fantasies. I remember stealthily accompanying school friends at age 14 to *Around the World with 8 Dollars* at Lakshmi Cinema, Kanchrapara, my native town. These backbencher school friends showed me many prohibited areas. When followers of my father, who was a well-known proletariat leader, sometimes caught me in a forbidden act, my grandmother had to save me from severe punishment.

I have been witness to pitiable situations like wage workers of the Kanchrapara railway workshop getting completely drunk on payday, returning home, and beating up their wives. One of these drunk "uncles" would regularly say, "*why comesou.*" We would laugh, imitate him, but nobody could figure out its meaning. When our village folk got drunk, they would spontaneously speak incomprehensible English. This remained a mysterious memory for me until, arriving in France, I discovered *soûl* means drunk. So uncle's drunken speech had superseded English and transformed into French even without his knowledge!

Subconsciously though, I have never since enjoyed Hindi films and do not drink alcohol in spite of having worked for several alcohol companies. I do watch popular Hindi films today but only for a short period in cinema halls to observe and understand public enthusiasm.

In early life I was poor both in India and France. Here's the difference. In keeping with India's caste-ridden structure, poverty becomes another social layer. Poor people are afraid to take opportunities. The proof is my mental shivers when my rich fellow student at Government College of Art & Craft in Kolkata insisted I accompany her to the air-conditioned American Library that was freely open to all.

In contrast, in my first job as a sweeper in a lithography print studio near Paris, the owner would introduce me as a fellow artist to all the famous artists who got their lithography prints done there. In my experience, the acknowledgment of equality is the biggest driver of personal ambition and performance. It demonstrates that when you do not want to compromise with poverty you can radically change your situation and see your life differently. It is definitely possible for all poor people, not only me, to take opportunities.

Employ tech advancement

Let us look at how industrial auto-mechanized machines can help remove poverty. Inventions through auto-mechanization have changed the poor in the West. Six hundred years ago Leonardo da Vinci made unbelievable mechanical inventions much ahead of his time. His principles of flying machines, bridge building, functioning of the human anatomy, have changed the way we operate in modern times. Yet he had to hide his ingenious inventions as they went against religious dictates of his time.

Feudal lords, in association with religious authorities, totally opposed development for mass benefit. That is because it would deprive their use of human labor to slave drive the interests of the aristocracy and the power of religion.

Historically, economic growth has led to poverty reduction. Britain's Industrial Revolution spread to Europe, led to overall development, and eliminated mass poverty. In 1820, 75 percent of humanity lived on less than a dollar a day; in 2001, only about 20 percent did. The World Bank says three quarters of the world's poor live in the countryside; so fighting poverty should begin there.

To fortify the livelihood efforts of poor people like two-acre-owning farmers, porters, and daily-wage earners, practical invention of machines is required. People in India are working on innovations for affordable, effective commercial transportation. But the challenge is to convert them for mass-scale use, with sustainable quality for the poor to get off the dependence ride.

From human labor to mechanization has been a significant shift that society has had to accept. With deeper injection of democracy in political systems, the mechanical aspect is gaining ground in reducing human effort. Having transformed to auto-mechanism, it has now become digital auto-mechanism, fuelling a productivity chain that is prompting the masses to work, earn money, and then spend.

Take courage

There are no religious barriers today; the fundamentals of invention exist in the world. Courage is all the poor need to change their mental acceptance of "slavery." To empower the underprivileged, an inventive assembler can digi-auto-mechanize devices relevant to our country's need. Merely growing the information technology (IT) sector and developing software for foreign companies will not take us anywhere in reducing India's poverty line. Digi-auto-mechanized machines in different working class layers are the most crucial devices India needs to uplift the masses at large.

IS INDIA INCREDIBLE?

During my research with the chairman of a global insurance client, a Scotsman operating from Japan, I visited the homes of consumers who earn ₹5,000 per month in different states in India. We micro-detailed their ideas and lifestyle, went into their kitchen, bathroom, bedroom, and puja room to understand how they live and respond to the environment. This India has not been branded "incredible" by anyone.

High contrasts

On Sunday morning we were in North Kolkata's Hatibagan weekly bird market, and the flower market under Howrah Bridge. We could barely walk for the crowd, the slippery mud, and multicolored birds in cages. Then we went on to the outstanding, Western-standard, South City Mall and saw people spend ₹25,000 on a single branded garment. "Shombit, this India is really incredible. Within a few kilometres you can see extreme poverty, folklore, to highly Americanized modernity."

The tourism ministry's "Incredible India!" advertising arouses curiosity about traditional India. But when people see copycat Western malls and cars, they see modern evolution, which they dub Americanization. That is why we need to make India incredible in another aspect in the near future, India has to be disruptive rather than folkloric.

Century after century, India has been renowned for her trading business. Today business is driven by body shopping, and meeting the basic low-cost-to-intelligent manpower needs of developed countries. A new culture has recently emerged, that of downloading. When will we ever become an inventive society that uploads on the Internet, and not merely downloads?

"Innovation" has become an industry buzzword, used as a business tactic in quarterly results to satisfy shareholders. In developed countries, physical inventions are uploaded on the Internet as e-information. Those who can afford a computer in India take the opportunity to download this fruit.

Take a lesson from the US

Evolving from being conquerors to cowboys to inventors, Americans have made their country rich and famous. Their inventions have changed people's working and living standards through functional betterment of human life, mass-scale consumption, high-end lifestyle, and unbelievable entertainment. The US has become an economic power to reckon with, aiding all-round growth and commanding the world.

Just take 10 American companies, GE, Bell, IBM, Coca-Cola, McDonald's, 3M, Xerox, Microsoft, Apple, and Nike, which have become the world's biggest brands. Their initial initiative was invariably inventive. These brands acquired power, but not through media hype or investing in advertisements using film stars. They had fundamental innovation at inception. This made them authoritative enough to stay in the customer's subconscious mind as indispensable requirements for a better life.

There may be heavy criticism of the US encouraging mass consumerism. But nobody can deny that mass consumption has democratized human rights in developed countries. Painter Andy Warhol, who made pop art famous, said that America is great because, "the richest consumers buy essentially the same things as the poorest. You know the President drinks Coke, Liz Taylor drinks Coke, and you can drink Coke, too. All the Cokes are the same and all the Cokes are good."

Undoubtedly, access to money led to consumerism, but the industry's approach to improve American life has always been inventive. A basic American family cannot afford a Trump Tower restaurant in New York's Fifth Avenue. But a few dollars will buy this entire family a sumptuous meal at McDonald's near the Trump Tower. Chains like McDonald's invented quality processes in sourcing, manufacture, service, and globalization. There is complete predictability in what they offer, no matter where in the world they are located.

Need for upgradation

In India's unequal society, the biggest chunk of population earns below ₹10,000 a month. Our $millionaires or $billionaires earning from transnational companies and living in Western-style comfort may need no invention. But everyone else in India needs inventions injected with the flavor of India's soil, just like Americans invented for American people. Several American inventions, even those by today's richest, such as Bill Gates, seem to have started in the garage.

Perhaps India's inventions will happen in slums. Can we think that by 2020 the minimum wages of an individual will become ₹25,000 per month as per today's monetary valuation as they fulfill eight hours of efficacious work? If that becomes feasible, we will realize the Indian government's vision of becoming a developed country by 2020.

Most Indian companies target the populous "bottom of the pyramid" to sell their products. However, they pay scant attention to how poor people will afford these low-priced goods. People have to earn first. Only when their buying power improves can there be a robust pyramid of human society.

Three idea examples

To achieve the status of being a developed country, India needs culturally relevant invention. What does this mean? Here are three idea examples that India specific invention has to achieve:

1. The yearly income of a farmer owning two acres of land has to increase from about ₹40,000 today to ₹300,000.
2. Porters should get an auto-mechanized device to transport heavy loads without expending their manual labor like bullocks do. This will power their everyday working efficiency to earn ₹25,000 per month.
3. A totally molded, minimally mechanized, and service-proof four-wheeler vehicle with very low cost of ownership can be created. This will be used for transportation of commercial goods and as necessary for the family's lifestyle.

From the 1760s, Britain's Industrial Revolution mechanized everything; it facilitated high productivity with reduced labor. People's living style improved. For India to really become incredible, we absolutely need a revolution in India-centric invention of auto-mechanized devices for

70 percent of our billion+ people. That would rid us of poverty too.

Do not deprive what is due

To represent India as a developed country, a certain homogeneity is required between the poor and rich. Comfort in life at both the workplace and the home is every individual's human right. After that, merit can take a person far into boundary-less achievement, depending on every individual's drive and caliber.

The West has proved that functional devices can end slavery and improve human life. Privileged Indians should help abolish the unofficial "slavery" that the underprivileged face. Workers in unorganized sectors, like migrant construction workers and domestic staff, are paid sub-minimum wages. Servants should be treated as service people.

Charity with money makes the poor dependent. We have to equip them with an instrument for personal growth. In other words, no free fish, give them a fishing rod to catch fish every day. This is the way incredible India can really fall in place. To change India's inequality we need INDIA to be an acronym for Innovative Nation Driving Inventive Action as I had mentioned in the first book of this *Jalebi Trilogy* called *Jalebi Management*. Such disruption of the usual order will make India incredible in its essence.

SAGA OF UNPREDICTABILITY

For foreign visitors, there is an exotic charm in India being unpredictable in multiple senses. To start with, the most unfathomable is poverty and how to cope with it.

Finding a reference

Developed nations that are "Oh! So boringly predictable!" are hard pressed to find a reference for developing business in India. Business people from the West, Japan, or even China plan strategy from five-star hotels or high-rise corporate houses. Armed with their global success statistics, they try to fit the same frame around India. Economic reform in highly populated countries is considered excellent for the future business growth of global companies. But at the foundation of their business rationale, very rarely do they measure the instability and unpredictability prevalent in such societies.

Predictability woes

In my 35 years of global experience, I have found the West to be highly predictable. People even plan their own funerals, selecting before they die the quality of marble to be placed in the graveyard. Thousands of years of the inventive European mind has been based on how to bring in predictability to improve the quality of life. The most vivid example is in medical science where predictability has changed people's lifespan. Two hundred years ago the average lifespan was less than 30 years, today it has risen to 67 years. By 2050, it is projected to increase to 75.6 years.

Extreme predictability can have a negative effect too. A while ago, to discipline road traffic, the French government hung cameras at strategic points to catch motorists not respecting the road code. Often the radar pictures captured the driver in compromising positions with the opposite sex. Many extramarital affairs were exposed when the photographic evidence of violation of traffic rules, with the love affair being incidental, reached the home. It led to such public revolt that this manner of discipline had to be done away with. Instead, the government had to change its policy and decided to photograph the back of the vehicle only, recording the time and date.

Tracking the traffic offender has become highly predictable now, but car owners are still not satisfied. The penalty will now fall on the owner's driving license even if somebody else, a son or friend, made the mistake on the road using the owner's car.

Volatile existence

Let us check out unpredictability of India's poor. The Planning Commission has accepted the Tendulkar Committee report that 37 percent live below the poverty line (BPL). The NC Saxena Committee reports that 50 percent live below the BPL, while the Oxford Poverty and Human Development Initiative found 650 million people (53.7 percent) living in poverty. The Arjun Sengupta report states that 77 percent of Indians live on less than ₹20 per day. Whatever may be the actual figure, from our research across India's rural hinterlands, we have found that farmers owning two acres of land live from hand to mouth. They have little knowledge or capacity to cultivate their small landholding to make it high earning and profitable. And should their bullocks die unexpectedly, the crop goes for a toss, as they cannot afford a tractor.

In contrast, when I was doing some research in Sacramento, California, to strategize on farm equipment in the US, I met a hobby farmer with two acres of land who produces heirloom tomatoes. He said he earns more money farming these tiny button tomatoes than from his regular profession as an architect in the city.

Suppose you have got into the habit of buying fruits from a fancy modern air-conditioned retail outlet in India. Suddenly one day you see the same fruit of similar quality being sold in a cart in front of that sophisticated retail store at half the price. How will you react? Will you not buy it outside? So you can imagine the dilemma the modern organized retailer is facing. In spite of having invested in an extraordinary ambience and expensive supply chain, a seller with a cart unpredictably snatches away its customers. The problem, of course, is that the tough route of unpredictability has been totally ignored. Most of India's organized retail business is run on the theory of statistics.

Actually, unpredictability runs in our culture, and Indian industry has no grip on it. I do not think business seriously considers the gates of unpredictability, let alone apply tactics to overcome them. To give an example, a logistics-and-supply-chain company I was working for committed an unrealistic time to the client for door-to-door delivery. Nobody had taken into account the many kinds of problems the driver who takes the merchandize faced on the long route. The result? Unhappiness for the customer, anxiety for the service provider, and overall delay.

Can technology stabilize the system?

Of course, resolving the unpredictable cannot be entrusted to the private sector, the government has to take responsibility. The excellent mission of unique biometric identity cards for all Indians appears an apolitical drive to reduce Indian unpredictability. People can change names or look different with plastic surgery, but fingerprints and eye scans will reveal their identity. Brazil is successfully using biometric traits for governmental assistance programs. Identification increases the dignity of people, certifies their economic situation for being helped if necessary. It can reduce corruption, provide protection against terrorism, and aid forensic work. The whole country should wholeheartedly support this most noble and pragmatic fieldwork for the country's growth in future.

I am sure the homeless people will be counted as well. This will provide us the first semblance of predictability.

Advances in technology and auto-mechanization are created to reduce unpredictability. A professional Airbus 320 pilot I was traveling with confessed to me that he prefers to pilot a small plane with propellers, the way he used to when he learnt flying. It is more thrilling when everything is controlled by him. It seems Airbus guarantees that its extremely modern aircraft is 99.9 percent risk-free. A chain of action can occur with modern technology without too much human interface in the cockpit. So, he says, he is not a pilot any longer, but a cockpit operator.

Statistically if you look at how many planes fly in the sky today, the number of disasters is marginal. The aviation industry has worked in such a way that every system has been automated and everything is predictable. Except, of course, the human factor when pilots go on strike, unpredictably bringing everything to a grinding halt.

PARADOX OF BILLION VS. MILLION

I have often visited India accompanying many CEOs of Western clients who want to understand the Indian market. In 1993, Victor Sherer, the CEO of Grand Metropolitan Corporation, where I was engaged in a global project, had come with me to check out opportunities post India's economic reforms.

Color hides poverty

Accustomed to everything being linear and predictable in Europe, Sherer was fascinated by India's haphazard, colorful ways where subtlety was missing. The bargaining practice thrilled him. When I warned that it is difficult to get hard discounts in the organized retail stores, but very possible with hawkers on carts, he was effusive: "Such vibrancy within just 10 metres!" Neither did he understand Kolkata Gariahat's potholes, and invariably fell into them while ogling beautiful sari-clad women who exuberantly exposed their midriffs.

"Poor people wear colorful clothes to overshadow their poverty," was Victor Sherer's exotic view on India. His conclusion that color hides poverty continued to intrigue me. It took almost 10 years for me to get the answer, after I had worked on a few projects that addressed very low-income people. On my consumer interactions during home visits and roadside meetings, people said color signifies that some extra work has been done to make the product worthwhile, even when the price is low. In the psyche of India's masses, color brightness is the payoff.

The same tuberose for life and death

In 1995, Jacques Vincent, the outstanding CEO who transformed Danone into a global dairy leader, asked me to help him evaluate business potential in India. Having worked to create and renovate 175 brands of the Danone portfolio in multiple countries, I was eager to showcase my own country's real picture. I arrived in advance from Paris to organize for us to visit urban and rural markets and consumers' homes.

Jacques met me at Kolkata airport at 11 p.m. He skimmed over the five-day agenda I gave him. Before checking into his hotel, he chose his first dinner option to be the Bengali food my mother had cooked at home. After dinner we went to Keoratala crematorium at 1 a.m. This prelude to his next day's business schedule was to show him how life ends for eight million Indians who are cremated every year. The activities connected to death made a huge impact on a Catholic European where death is a silent ceremony. From electric incineration to the wooden burning ghat, Jacques was hallucinated experiencing reality play out. He exceeded the 30 minutes' stay I had planned by staying up to 4.30 a.m.: "Death also has an angle of festivity," he commented.

At a marriage ceremony a few days later, the tuberose garlands took him by surprise. He had seen tuberose at the crematorium too. That our culture allows the use of the same flower in marriage and in death is totally alien to Catholic society.

Train-travel ways

Being absent from India since 1973, I started to see the country with a new eye developed by French and European culture. On the way to the refugee colony I had spent my childhood in, I was shocked at people hanging out of the open doors of high-speed suburban trains. My father reminded me that I had traveled exactly this way when going to my art college. I immediately recalled how people sometimes hit the electric bar outside and died. In fact, as per Mumbai statistics, 824 people fall off trains every year, and every day four people die and four are injured in railway-track accidents.

Working for a French industrial design consultancy in 1979–1980, I became involved with some very advanced design for SNCF, the French national railway company. I learnt that electric train doors could not be kept open when in running condition. Electric trains first started in India in 1925, and later there was collaboration with SNCF for new technology. Western companies are habituated to the mores of sparsely populated nations. It dawned on me that it might not have occurred to them to deliver products to overpopulated countries to suit the recipient's culture, discipline, habit, population, or respecting their values.

I have heard that India's electric train doors did close initially. But closing doors would limit passengers to 250 instead of the required capacity, 500 passengers during the peak period. So the mindset of servicing a billion people is not to reduce passengers per train, but open the doors for ventilation. This, of course, is a completely wrong solution for using this product.

From this example I knew that to work for my native country with my European skills, I had to first address our myriad cultural skews that are not comparable to those of any other country in the world. China may have a billion people but we have multiple nuances among our billion people. The stark paradox of million-versus-billon-people countries came alive to me here.

The billion require functional benefits

For developmental projects in different industries, India often takes professional expertise from developed countries. Their execution may be sophisticated, but they may also fail to register relevance to the Indian masses. Take our several new airports with world-class aesthetics. Their insufficient security-check systems can still detain flights. At that place where people have no patience, it is always a push to get through small toilet doors that simultaneously block people inside from coming out. For the sake of the haphazard billions, would not two doors, one for entry and the other for exit, solve the problem? New airports have no space problem, but five years down the line they could become obsolete or congested if space planning for the future is not done.

In sophisticated housing layouts in the metros, children are growing up in protected atmospheres in Swiss-style homes. They defy relevance to reality that's visible just 100 m outside this cocoon. This closed environment may be good for expatriates to keep their families from intermingling with the unknown, but how will these Indian children adjust in later life? While making such layouts private, is it not possible to induce some real Indian cultural elements, like hygienic versions of open bazaar and flea market environments such as Mumbai's Chowpatty, Delhi's Daryaganj, Bangalore's Chikpet, or Kolkata's Gariahat, to change its clinical ambience?

In aspirational areas our ideation process is overly influenced by the culture of the Western millions. We proudly showcase Indianness with the tricolor on our faces at cricket matches, but neglect to build on the charm of being a haphazard billion-people country. Innovative designs that respect this culture can create a benchmark for the world.

While being within the system of a billion people with diverse cultures, religions, languages, and habits, it may be difficult to transform or modernize every public area with sophisticated hygiene. In all our designs we need to inject many functional advantages that emphasize the requirements of a billion people. That way we get an aspirational global look, yet become radically different from the million-mindset frame.

FOGGY SUBTLETY

Subtlety resides in the subliminal private garden of every person. Even individuals in countries with a billion+ population need an injection of subtlety to introduce an element of elevation into their lives. Subtlety contributes to a civilization's refinement. Empowered sections such as entertainment, politics, journalism, industry, and religion that help form and influence public opinion usually need to exercise subtlety to gain credibility.

Entertainment

Participating in different creative seminars in the West I have had occasion to mingle with film directors, cameramen, effects men, actors, and actresses. I have always heard them say that technique is a mere slave of the storyline, that subtle expressions or an undisturbed narrative is more memorable than in-your-face use of effects. Yet their motion picture industry has undergone immense innovation in effects to create gripping suspense and spectacular drama.

Bollywood and TV serials drive the common man's entertainment. So they bear a certain moral responsibility to induce knowledge that can improve or contribute to people's ideation process. Bollywood's "angry young man" theme connected in some way to the situation of unavailability of everything in the pre-liberalized era. But today's films spend so much money on effects and foreign locations that it is unclear whether they are made for Indians or nonresident Indians (NRIs) who want exotic melodrama not seen in Western films, from the country of their "native roots," enacted by performers they can identify with.

Today's young in India have this motto: "Earn more, work more, enjoy more." The entertainment media takes them on escapades replete with effects and décor, but when the workplace is shown it is actually an advertisement camouflaged as part of the plot. For example, a particular insurance company may be used as the hero's office and those insurance products specifically named in the film. Where is the subtlety that the mass entertainer should be exercising to uplift society?

Politics

Most politicians often forget to address subtlety. TV captures them holding forth abrasively against an opponent, or very irresponsibly, just switching off when someone else is talking. I have observed male politicians tend to make chauvinistic and snide remarks about women politicians, harshly disrespecting societal codes of conduct while addressing women. This sets disgraceful examples of lack of subtlety in a modern democracy.

When François Mitterrand was France's presidential candidate for the second time, he and Jacques Chirac were competing in a final TV debate. Chirac, who had served in President Mitterrand's government as the prime minister, suggested that for the TV debate the two candidates should address each other by their given names, not by their official titles. But Mitterrand continued to address him as "Mr Prime Minister." Respecting the establishment norm of using titles helped clinch the closely fought presidency for Mitterrand as the French appreciate the subtlety of decorum. The whole of France still talks of how Chirac's insensitivity made him lose, that he was indifferently looking at the ceiling when the president was speaking.

Journalism

French comedian Coluche, famous for his irreverent sense of humor, said, "In a dictatorship you're told: 'Shut up!' In a democracy it's: 'Keep talking!'…" But the media in India, the world's biggest democracy, need not have taken that literally during the Mumbai terrorist attack in 2008. In the scramble for TV rating points (TRPs), Indian TV was at high pitch, initially describing live every move of the Indian security forces to halt the terrorists. There was huge competition among the TV channels. Why can't the media distinguish between a reality story and dangerous happenings affecting national security?

TV also kills subtlety and devalues "breaking news" by reporting the mundane and the extraordinary in the same mouthful of air. What is worse is playing a chirpy advertisement after exposing news of some tragic disaster. The program's TRPs may be high, but if you ask viewers their reaction to seeing such an ad at that time, you will definitely find a negative flurry. Perhaps subtle discretion is required about when to air different ads if the news content is shocking.

The impact of the Internet and electronic media has taken the print medium to another dimension in the West. Reading newspapers has the authentic value of everyday life so the printed daily continues to be valued as a strong opinion leader. India's young generation already reads less, and with newspapers led more and more by brash advertising rather than the news subtly inducing ideas, will the cyber and ephemeral world take over tomorrow?

Industry

Industry spends heaps of money on advertising, finding superb locations, hiring the best cameramen and trendiest film stars, but when the brands reach the retailer's shelves, how do they present themselves? Our advertising skill is blatantly copied from the West, but with hazy subtlety. Almost 100 percent stores there are self-help supermarkets, whereas in India only 3 percent of selling outlets are organized retail, the rest are individual or mom-and-pop (*kirana*) shops. Here you will find food products jostling with detergents, rice, dal, and loose oil in large containers being totally susceptible to, and probably infested with, cockroaches and rats. There is a total disconnect from the TV ad and the condition of sale.

Will the consumer remember the product's advertisement when he or she goes shopping? Ads create a brand's awareness and pull, but if the marketer lacks the subtlety of elegant display at the point of purchase to jog the shopper's memory, chances are the shopper will purchase whatever the kirana retailer recommends.

Religion

Every individual has the right to worship through any religion, and I respect all religions. But in the name of god, when almost all religious houses blare prayers or religious songs over public loudspeakers, is it not mass disturbance and total noise pollution? When will we become sensitive enough to not impose on the privacy of others? At the end of the day, this becomes another form of lack of subtlety.

ALL YOU NEED IS THE BALANCE OF ELA

Traveling with MindTree's gardener, Subroto Bagchi, reminded me of a tea-break tête-à-tête almost two decades ago when we had met in Bangalore for some work. It seems I had said something not quite subtle: that whatever business strategy or best thing in life we may come up with, if an ELA problem arises, existence becomes hell on earth. He remembered that as powerful truth.

What is this ELA balance?

It is crucial for living life, irrespective of country, politics, religion, or economic condition.

Eating, the **E** factor of ELA balance, is surely our most important priority. Popular French singer Alain Souchon made famous the song, "On est foutus, on mange trop," meaning We are f…ed, we eat too much! But while some control food intake to retain their body beauty, those suffering illnesses have genuine eating problems. I hope 21st century's technology advancement will abolish the disadvantages of the world's 963 million underfed, so food truly becomes a human right.

In India, taste overpowers any trepidation about food not being hygienic and healthy. Let me illustrate from my professional work. Visiting kirana stores across the country I was shocked to find 76 percent of edible oil being sold loose in tins or plastic jars that consumers bring in. Retailers use the same large, sometimes open, containers with taps and funnels, year after year, in their overcrowded small shops infested by rats and cockroaches. It is deplorable that three-fourths of Indian consumers, their doctors and nutritionists, are oblivious to this unhygienic use of oil in daily cooking.

A renowned doctor explained that Indian medical studies do not factor in dietetics in the curriculum. So there exists no structured knowledge of diet in the doctors' recommendation. There is some government regulation like ISI, Agmark, and various laws on how food can be sold and stored. In developed countries there is a nationwide program for the upkeep of people's health. But in India the inspectors are paid by interested parties to ignore the rules and write out their no-objection or compliance certificates. When will we develop the pleasure of eating hygienically?

Let us enter **L** for the love factor through the unpredictable distances Indian truckers cover in their everyday life. Our first priority should again be to ingrain hygienic sense in them. Here is why.

Lorry drivers largely stay long days away from home while covering every corner of the country. They have to weather badly engineered trucks, miserable roads and weather conditions. They catch naps on highway *dhaba* (eatery) string cots, try to meet impractical deadlines, and eat in cultural regions they are unused to. On this harrowing journey, a trucker's only pleasure is engaging a sex worker. But he lays down a condition: he will not use a condom. His reason? "When I pay full value, why should I compromise on fulfillment?" The sex worker agrees for fear of losing this on-the-spot earning when there are starving children at home.

The Centre for Media Studies indicates that almost 40 percent of India's six million truck drivers are infected with the AIDS virus, and only 18 percent use condoms. Of the 18- to 45-year-old truckers surveyed, 80 percent were married. So they bring the fatal disease back to their families.

India has the world's third largest population suffering from HIV/AIDS (South Africa and Nigeria have more). So the challenge of Love, the central factor of ELA balance, is to first make the trucker want to use a condom when making love. As a designer I am yet to observe easy availability of condoms and systematic communication that is symbolic, aspirational, and noticeable in economically backward areas to train people to change their mindset and enjoy love with protection. Surely poverty and lack of education cannot take away the human right for love?

To touch upon the **A** (for ablution) of ELA balance, I will take you to a senior management leadership program I had conducted. It was on creating a sustained emotional connect to a brand. I asked the participants, who had 18–20 years of work experience in different industries, how they liked ablutions, their every morning toilet ritual of what the body expels. There was stunned silence. Is this something for discussion? Do they enjoy it personally? Would they love to hear more about it? In that sophisticated Harvard-school type conference room in Hyderabad, nobody knew what to say. "Will you have the passion to create branding that is relevant to ablution?" I asked.

Everything that has inner value can be branded, I told them. This inner value should have some benefit that consumers can see, experience, and enjoy. I then introduced Japan's Toto, the sanitary-ware company that inspires employees to ideate and dream in the context of excreta in order to innovate incredible products. Toto has teamed up with Daiwa to develop a bathroom that lets users monitor their health. It analyzes urine samples, measures blood pressure, and checks body fat even as the user is sitting on the "throne." Toto's Internet representation has pictures of posteriors of different colored people, each adorned with the drawing of smiley human face.

When working for a food giant in Greece, I happened to meet a super-rich Greek at Piraeus beach near Athens. He loved India, became a good friend, and started calling me Frenchie-Indian. Over dinner with his beautiful 35-year-old wife, he invited me to accompany him to Doussikou monastery, built by St Vissarion in 1522 near Salonika. Women are not allowed there. A 10-m high wall encircles this three-storied northern Greece structure comprising 366 cells. Reservations do not easily fructify in this exclusive holy place that commandeers people into regimentation, to live in prison-like cells without electricity, wear in-house robes, and not talk. I became curious about the affluent struggling to experience an exotic, if degraded, lifestyle.

Returning to Greece on work a few months later, I met my 60-year-old friend when his wife had just left for the US. He said he had already visited the monastery twice and insisted I come. Seeing my hesitation, he suddenly started crying.

He confessed:

I live in this palatial home, have untold wealth, but my life is wretched. Work pressure tension has deteriorated my health so badly that my restricted diet allows me nothing I enjoy, and I've become unable to satisfy my lovely wife. She loves me but I have to free her for affairs with young boys. My worst suffering is the terrible hemorrhoids. You can't believe my hours of pain at the toilet everyday. Believe me Sen, to escape from all these troubles, Doussikou Monastery has become my most pleasurable place. There I am commanded to abandon all greed, love and passion.

This, since 1994, has been my real learning; that ELA balance is vital for every life situation, whether you are rich, poor, or possessed of whatever characteristic, inherent, learnt, or acquired.

JOKE'S ON THE NRI, THAT'S ME

Flying in from Paris to New Delhi in the wee hours of a January morning in 1998, I was greeted by a chauffer waiting to drive me to my destination in the outskirts of Lucknow. I had come for a five-day market visit and some research on consumers for an Indian client. My research team had already reached the day before to make preparations.

Search for Tiger

Team members of the agent who recruits respondents for my research work were always very good to me. That day in particular, not only was I was coming from faraway France, but I had driven 500 long kilometers to be on time to animate the research with consumer groups. So they were ever-indulgent, trying to satisfy me, which I could only appreciate. Before beginning the research, they asked several times if I needed some food or refreshments. In fact, they insisted I eat or drink something, as the research would last about four hours. Even though I was not very hungry, I gave in and asked them to get me some Tiger.

After quite a few hours the recruitment company manager came to meet me, looking very dejected. She apologized that they could not get Tiger anywhere in the city. I was shocked. Just the week before I had received the report from Britannia that Tiger, the biscuit we created for them, was booming in the market, and that it had even reached rural markets. So I immediately called my client in Bangalore to enquire what the problem was. Why was Britannia's distribution not effective enough to ensure that Tiger biscuits were available in and around Lucknow? Within two hours the Britannia area manager came to meet me at the city's outskirts. He said the problem had escaped him, and took me to kirana shops just outside the research venue. And sure enough, there were plenty of Tiger biscuits.

The confusion was cleared up when my recruiting agent sheepishly confessed she had misunderstood. As I was an NRI coming from Europe and had asked for Tiger, she said she naturally assumed it must be some alcohol I was looking for. She had heard of Tiger beer. They figured there must be some drink called Tiger, so they immediately combed every liquor store in the area to satisfy me. I then understood that I was carrying the image of a stupid NRI. Even though the all-new Tiger brand had become very popular at that time, they could not connect this Tiger to an NRI. The NRI connotation is more with alcohol, not biscuits. The irony of it is that I am a teetotaler, and I just wanted to enjoy the brand I had created.

Choice of Mandeville Garden

One of my life's biggest dreams was to give my parents a certain level of living comfort. My joint family had suffered a great deal of hardship migrating from East Bengal. The refugee colony they had, perforce, settled in was dark, and life in our subsequent rented homes outside the refugee colony, in search of electricity, was no song. So when I could afford it, I asked my friends to find them a very decent locality in Kolkata as I personally had no idea of Kolkata's good areas. When I had left the city at the age of 19, I did not have the means to frequent such places.

On the suggestion of friends, I bought an apartment for my parents at Mandeville Garden in 1991. In the winter of 1992, I came to India to spend a few days with them in their new home. One day at about 11 a.m., as I took a walk to discover the neighborhood around our Mandeville Garden apartment, I was thrown off balance. In fact, I remember being totally disconcerted about how my friends could advise me to come to such a place. At every corner of the environs I was walking in I could find mostly young, well-dressed women, sitting, chatting, laughing, and gossiping in front of different houses or on the steps and footpath curbs.

I rushed back home, hot-headed, and enquired of my mother why we had chosen such surroundings to live in; did they know that we were actually in a red-light district? Several Kolkata relatives had come to visit us, and none of them could understand what I was fuming about, why I was carrying on about prostitutes.

I immediately marched all of them out of the apartment to show the stylish girls standing around in street corners. They burst out laughing; they just could not stop. It turned out these were young mothers who had come to pick up their tiny tots from school. There is a famous school called South Point adjacent to our apartment. As the children come from distant places and their session lasts just three hours, their mothers do not return home after dropping the children off. They either do their errands nearby or wait patiently to collect their children after school. I did not understand that. That was clearly another NRI stupidity I had displayed.

NRI connect to India

An NRI Bengali friend recounted a heart-rending story of how he had instilled in his two sons a great love and sense of belonging for Bengal. They were born and brought up in France, but they knew Bengali. Once, on an Indian train, they had started talking a few words in Bengali, but when fellow passengers continued the conversation they could not answer, and looked at them foolishly. Later my friend overheard the passengers whispering and laughing about the "two stupid NRI guys from Paris." He was heartbroken but tried to hide his emotions by making it a joke.

There are NRIs who stay connected to India by watching Bollywood films. My granddaughter Sreeya was going to ballet class in London when she was 5 years old. When I'd ask her to show me a dance, she'd open YouTube and do a gyrating Bollywood cinematic number while singing, "Tum hi … meri Sonia…!" in a cockney accent.

ZAP86 TRENDING TOMORROW'S INDIA

Whether it is unwanted girls or pampered boys, it is increasingly becoming obvious that connecting to today's India you have to factor in the dynamic surge led by the ZAP86 generation. Young Zappers could be setting a lasting trend in society's collective consciousness.

What is a trend?

Mirroring society's uncommon micro-movements, often rebellious, and their effects boiled in a sociological cauldron creates a trend. Unlike the steady social evolution that occurred before World War II, perhaps the horrible effect of this first atomic war gave rise to several rebellious factors in the West. From American baby boomers to Elvis-the-Pelvis, Beatlemania, hippies, punks, skinheads, among others, all drew powerful, defiant trends on society's canvas. They engraved their outstanding impact for all time. Such trends have influenced literature, music, science, philosophy, invention, and art, embedding their differences to become references of history, not the past. To enter India's ZAP86 generation, let us take a snap historical perspective.

3rd century BC to 21st century AD

There was a great rise in culture and trade from the third century BC until 15th century AD. The new influence of Muslim culture from the 16th to the 18th century saw integration and further boosted the economy. British colonialism from 1757 to 1947 made Indians subordinate, but created one India. Freedom turned to instability in the protected economy between 1947 and 1991. It led to the downfall of moral fiber, with growth in corruption, and negligible public benefits or upliftment of the downtrodden as expected in independent India.

A sudden technical change took place with economic reforms being introduced in 1991. The ratification of the World Trade Organization (WTO) treaty and TRIPS compliance in the 21st century led to a new departure. Investment came from American and European multinational companies (MNCs), and corporate India very innovatively took the opportunity to translate that into phenomenal GDP growth, from 3.9 percent in 2003 to 9.4 percent in 2007.

ZAP86

When the liberalization of our economy started in 1991, a new generation could be identified in those born in or after 1986. As five-year-olds by 1991, these children were old enough to consciously influence purchase decisions. The rolling economy opened up their parents' purse strings. They had no idea of India's savings mentality, of the scarcity of choice in a protected economy. I call them ZAP86. Zappers flit from subject to subject, the way they zap TV channels. They are totally cut off from the Retro generation born before 1965 or the Compromise generation born after 1965.

The Retro generation has characteristics of savings, sacrifice, routine. Retro feels more secure in a government job, and suppresses thoughts of sex. The Compromise generation is Westernized but with Indian values. People of this generation are good listeners and learners, investment-oriented, and thoroughly dominated by their demanding ZAP86 children.

ZAP86 have global thought and knowledge, enjoy speed of technology, and sexual liberation. They flirt with jobs, speak in code language, and have no role models. They influence all purchase decisions in every home. Their flexibility is visible in the tremendous success of call centers in India. A 22-year-old Zapper, who speaks Tamil at home, speaks "Hinglish" with her cosmopolitan Indian friends. But in the BPO, her entire physiology and expression change. Before commencing any business conversation, she can warm up her client by chatting away in an effortless American accent about the basketball game in Cincinnati the evening before.

In a research project with about 100 metro Zappers (girls and boys), we showed them a Dolce & Gabbana advertisement where a girl is willingly portraying her sexual desire toward a man, while three other men look on desirously. Of the ZAP86 girls, 60 percent had no problem fantasizing about participating here, but in real life they preferred the absence of the watching men. All ZAP86 boys wanted to be in there, and thought the scene had nothing wrong in it. But the Compromise and Retro generations viewed the picture as vulgarism, violation, or rape, and did not appreciate this trend of open sexuality.

Trends boost business

Business can exploit trends. The hair-grooming industry changed dramatically following the rebellious 1970s punk movement. Because civilized human society could never think of sporting multicolored hair, the nonconformist punks revolted by using vibrant colors in their hair. They used boiled sugar syrup to create various styles. When cold, the syrup kept the hair shiny and upright.

This creative punk achievement, with no scientific lab, was ingeniously taken forward by L'Oréal. With masterpiece research and development (R&D) and marketing, L'Oréal created hair color as fashion that replaced hair dye, and unisex hair gel, where earlier lacquer was used, and only by women. Skillfully translating trend into business L'Oréal took this punk product invention to market as an art form. They connected it to Piet Mondrian's authentic neoplasticism values, the painting style of flat, bright colors that this famous modern painter created in 1930. The branding of L'Oréal's StudioLine gel and hair color reflected Mondrian's art. Today, even formal office wear accepts color-streaked hair, and applying gel or styling mousse is a style statement.

The billion-people trend?

As trends change people's mindset on sociocultural aspects and give rise to business, India can take the opportunity of generating a Zapper trend. This generation can become tomorrow's trendsetter.

There is a way to cultivate trends. It is a multi-profession engagement in society with several activities to grow the trend. Graffiti, for example, continues to grow as an art form, from the time of ancient Greek and Roman empires until today, in spite of prohibition against defiling public wall space. Even established governments give credence to rebellious wall messages, as did French cultural minister Jack Lang who nominated graffiti as real art to be put in museums. Americans have supposedly declared New York metro graffiti to be a form of art. Contemporary music, culture, and entertainment have had origins in street art, but not the graffiti of political banners. Graffiti is not about political messages but reflects a wayward, rebellious creative character.

India's ancient architecture and culture, multi-community celebrations, and profusion of mix-and-match colors in fashion are treasures not yet exploited as trends to bequeath to the world. Instead, Western trends have smothered us, without us having been a part of that trend's genesis.

Harness Zapper trends

India's new departure after economic liberalization, WTO, and ZAP86 has created several social breaks. But current brands and products are driven by, and targeted at, the Compromise and Retro generations. Foreign companies like Sony, Apple, and Samsung try to connect to ZAP86 by importing Western trends, increasing their zapping mentality. Harnessing the aspirations of ZAP86 can drive Indian trends. The scope for industry to fill this gap ranges from automobiles and two-wheelers to beauty products, fashion, food, music, literature, art, and advertising, all of which can identify, portray, and define Indian trends emanating from ZAP86.

The Retro and Compromise generations have connived with India's socio-eco-political circumstances to create ZAP86, who are poles apart from them. Today's 12-year-olds are born to technology; seven-year-olds teach their parents how to google. This future of the country needs fostering at both the workplace and society to unearth the radical new. Will you not give them space to craft the billion-people trends for the world to emulate tomorrow?

HAZY AESTHETICS

Looking the same is a major crisis, especially when people have money. The first response is to differentiate in lifestyle. Whether you are a boy chasing a girl or a girl guarding her independence, individuality has to be exposed.

For industry, differentiation in deliverables is essential to increase net worth. The culprit in making all the world's bricks look alike is digital technology. That is when a sense of aesthetics can make a difference.

Women inspire aesthetics

Indian women have had an inherent, exceptional sense of beauty from time immemorial. Their ornamentation is the most spectacular, from the nose ring, bindi, *alta* and mehendi on the feet and hands, anklets, finger rings with chains ending in bracelets, bangles matching every dress, earrings that reach up to accentuate hairstyles, and jewelry on the hips.

Women's hips are so universal in aesthetics that strokes from Western masters, from Leonardo da Vinci to Pablo Picasso, have eulogized them in paintings. I have never found two women on Indian roads to have the same design of saris. Chewing pan was an ancient practice used by women to give sensual appeal to their lips. Even today's young glocal Indian girls fuse Eastern and Western wear to make beautiful fashion statements.

However, there are a few of the very affluent who distinguish themselves from this cultural fiber with hotchpotch combinations, and lose the glamour of Indian women. In general, it is amazing how Indian women from all walks of life are conscious about aesthetic art in their looks.

Men oblivious to aesthetics

But for most Indian men, aesthetics is "wot's dat?" A while ago, waiting for a flight confirmation at Mumbai airport during Mumbai's cyclone I was just opposite a toilet when suddenly a man in a white *lungi* (sarong) emerged wet from the toilet, shivering as though he had taken a dip in the Ganges. In the corridor between him and me, travelers were passing by, beautiful air hostesses pulling trolley bags, foreign tourists and Indian executives all proceeding for security check.

In full view of this traffic, the man lifted his lungi, took out blue boxer briefs from his bag, and jumped around alternatively on either foot trying to draw them up. When successful, he swung the lungi away in a flourish, and in swift movements continued to use it as a towel to wipe his body and hair. He then wore a shirt and trousers, took out a mirror and combed his hair, getting ready to board the plane.

As I enjoyed this scene, I was reminded of rural railway platforms with only a tap, and was surprised that even the security guard failed to send him inside the toilet. What a contrast in aesthetics, the man was totally oblivious to everyone's curiosity!

Take a look at a man's shirt pocket: all kinds of papers bulge from it, plus modernity participating in the form of the mobile phone. Handset aesthetics have undergone a sea change, becoming sophisticated and trendy, as also the retail outlets of service providers. But check out how they are junking public eye spaces with ugly telephone towers in the city or outskirts, without maintenance, other electric and telephone wires hanging out, sometimes becoming like a net on the road.

Cities need professional planning

Mushrooming real estate in cities and small towns may have presentable décor inside, but its public view has no character, just unbecoming sanitary pipes and exposed electrical transformer gadgetry. Old skyscrapers with cracks filled with putty create designs. Is that because most of society's decisions are taken by men?

Western Europe after the world wars had to opt for quick housing and bring immigrants to construct their roads and buildings. These badly made 1950s and 1960s buildings with poor aesthetics and sanitation became horrible ghettos that created problems of corruption and delinquency. So they were ceremoniously bulldozed in the 1980s. India's current architecture may face this same problem 20 years from now.

Paris is considered the world's most beautiful city

Paris attracts the largest number of tourists, 85 million in 2013, larger than France's population of 64 million. The tourism revenue France earned that year was €77.7 billion. In contrast, just 6.8 million tourists came to India of 1.2 billion people, and spent €29.4 billion (₹2,283 billion) in 2013. Culturally and historically I do not see that we have any deficiency that we cannot attract tourists like France does.

Paris was planned to become beautiful and modernized. Napoleon III commissioned Georges-Eugène Haussmann to renovate the city. From 1852 to 1870, the Haussmann plan redesigned Paris with broad streets for trains and better traffic flow, public utilities like water, drainage, and sanitation, and buildings in homogeneous architectural wholes that unified the urban landscape. Over 20,000 houses were destroyed, slums cleared away, and over 40,000 houses rebuilt. Huge controversy was raised by writers like Emile Zola, accusing Haussmann of corruption, and architects like Charles Garnier, deploring the "suffocating monotony" of monumental architecture.

But 145 years later, Haussmann's work is the most valued heritage property and his buildings the most expensive in the world. In fact the city plans of London, Moscow, and Chicago have borrowed liberally from Haussmann.

India does not have a renovating culture

If you come from south Mumbai on the Santa Cruz flyover, just look to your left. Below eye level are the unfortunate slums. This always bothers me, as I too was underprivileged in early life and wish for this terrible situation to end in the 21st century. Just move your eye up, and you will miss the building balconies for all the people's dirty linen washed in public, or rather, clean linen, shirts, trousers, bras, panties, and saris hung out to dry in full public view. Actually aesthetics for buildings have completely given way to rods, grills, air-conditioner boxes, and paint that has become moldy over time. Without renovating all these buildings you suddenly find new construction being sold at exorbitant prices.

In Mumbai I found a new type of décor in the staircases of apartment buildings, pictures of gods and goddesses in ceramic. I admired this very interesting move until my client told me it was to prevent people from spitting pan juice in staircase corners. What a clever idea, I thought, as god is highly respected in the country. But lo and behold! In another public staircase, the gods were stained with thick red spit. What is it that can instill the aesthetic sense in us as a people?

CRACKS IN HYGIENE AND CIVIC DUTY

Before aesthetics comes the fundamental factor of hygiene. About 2.5 billion people in the world have no access to safe sanitation, and half of South Asia suffers the indignity of open defecation. This lack of hygiene facilities is a fundamental cause of disease, leading to 1.5 million children dying every year as per UN figures.

Can India's 2020 promise to become a developed country free from poverty be fulfilled without improving our hygiene and civic responsibility?

Hygiene

Landing in Amritsar international airport I felt really proud that India's B-class towns are becoming so advanced. High-rise structures in modern glass and metal architecture; even the new baggage belt looked better than the latest German engineering. This thrill was knocked out by the foul-smelling toilet, with insects running around.

On a routine market-observation visit, a newly built public toilet in Delhi's Malviya Nagar looked good from the closed car window. But on stepping out, its sharp stink immobilized me. On its left, a permanent store was selling fresh flowers. I wonder how people differentiate floral fragrance from the toilet's ammonia or feces smell.

Most spectacular is Mumbai's Rolls Royce showroom, just 500 m from Worli Gutter, a putrid garbage drain that joins the sea. Just imagine this ambience when buying the world's most expensive and sophisticated car. New Delhi's up-market South Extension displays the latest Japanese and Korean electronic products in neon-lit splendor, but their toilet on the floor above is ugly, dirty, and reeks. The purpose of a high-flying lifestyle escapes me when the fundamentals of better living are far from being in place.

Civic responsibility

When people sweep their own premises, it may not occur to them that they are gifting dirt to their neighbors. This aptly reflects our complete lack of civic responsibility as a people.

Incidentally, India has developed an excellent hygienic habit in the jet washer in modern public toilets. This is undoubtedly superior to Western toilet paper that keeps the body unclean all day. Until you see water spots in the toilet seat, you never know if its water from the jet washer or a human body. The question is, how do you educate people?

I remember when I left for Europe in 1973, the toilet-cleaning method I was accustomed to in my refugee colony was specified people carrying away drums of human excreta on their heads every day. I feel ashamed that this disgraceful practice still exists in India. Later at Kolkata's art college I learnt of the Indian-style sanitary toilet. But it was on the plane to Europe that I first saw an English-style commode.

In the student hostel in Paris we used a common toilet. A Greek friend knocked on the toilet door one day, but I did not reply. So he climbed over the open top and found me with my feet on the toilet seat, in the Indian traditional style. I did not even know that I had to put the seat cover down and sit on it as in a chair. It took me nearly six months to actually learn and get used to this Western toilet culture.

In practically every street in India you'll find a man or two turning away from passing people and cars. He's enjoying turning on his personal tap water, very confidently makes jerking body movements and then turns around relieved to continue his walk down the street. Neither he nor the public appears offended by this act. When women can control such uncivil behavior, why are men devoid of civic sense?

While working for a supply-chain logistics company on how frontline staff should be customer sensitive with their package delivery system, one of our researchers followed a globally reputed company competitor's delivery van with a camera. The van stopped outside a customer's gate, the man got off, first relieved himself on the customer's wall, and then went in with the package!

In every urban corner you will generally find overflowing, odorous dustbins. Before India joined the WTO, our public dustbins mostly had Indian products; now they also have beautifully designed, non-bio-degradable plastic wrappers from famous multinational brands. A few responsible Bangalore citizens took the initiative to collect garbage from homes for bulk disposal in large black plastic bags. The other day I happened to drive through greenery in Mutkur village off Varthur lake and suddenly saw mounds of black plastic bags dumped alongside the village walkway. Vultures and poor children were rummaging through the garbage, breaking the bags to find some surprises.

Sanitation started in India, but...

India's poor hygiene situation was not always so. The earliest recorded covered sewers are in the Indus Valley Civilization cities. In 2500 BC, the people of Harappa in India had water-borne toilets in each house, linked to drains covered with burnt clay bricks. They considered sanitation an important public-health measure essential for disease prevention.

Today's lack of hygiene and civic responsibility is damaging the aspirational value of all business. Whether an industry is in manufacturing or service, the real delivery to customers' hands is from the shop floor or frontline people. Did anyone check the difference between the factory workers' toilet and the corporate office one?

The factor differentiating organized retail from wholesale, mom-and-pop or commodity markets, is housekeeping. But housekeeping is totally alien to those hired to maintain cleanliness, so the retail store soon looks disheveled. Inside an American fast-food outlet in New Delhi's Greater Kailash, the dustbin was being cleaned next to people enjoying their chicken. You may mistake the car park behind the market as a garbage store yard, but it is puzzling that even globally renowned companies mushrooming in India make no move to clean up the environment. Perhaps as part of 2020 development, the government should create a separate ministry for hygiene and civic responsibility to take serious action together with MNCs and Indian companies.

Hygiene derives from Hygieia, the Greek goddess for preservation of good health and disease prevention. Let us take her blessings to modernize India, teach people basic hygiene as an initiative in civic responsibility, to better everyone's body and mind for work and enjoyment.

CHRISTMAS *DIL KI DOYA* (COMPASSION FROM THE HEART)

"Christmas puja is what the Santa Claus cap is for," explain the beggars-turned-salespersons at traffic jams. Without considering hygiene factors, Kolkata footpaths are piled high with plum cakes ranging from ₹20 to ₹100. Indian Christians decorate their homes with *diya*s (earthen oil lamps) to welcome the birth of Christ, just like some Hindus welcome Ram, Sita, and Lakshman from their 14-year *vanabas* (exile) on Diwali. This is co-opting the million-mindset culture in the environs of the billions.

Driving commerce

The way McDonald's, KFC, and Maggi noodles are becoming the Indian national standard, Christmas drives commercial avenues just like Dusshera, Durga or Ganesh puja,

Ramzan, Onam, Pongal, and Bihu do. But it is the top money-spinner as it is celebrated worldwide. In Europe alone, total Christmas sales are expected to rise to €313 billion, equivalent of 16 percent of annual retail sales in 2012. Of this, 10.3 percent will be online sales, with average sales per household being €590.

Pre-Christmas festivity is very strongly visible nowadays. From across the US, UK, Canada, Bangladesh, East Timor, Germany, Jordan, France, Pakistan, and different parts of India, Loreto Shillong girls came for a reunion in the manicured lawns of a colonial south Delhi home. When I walked into that event, surrounded by choir music on a chilly early December evening, I was not sure if I had arrived somewhere in England. The fervor of the Loreto alumni singing their traditional jingle, "To East and West of that Fair Isle [meaning Ireland], Where the first Loreto stands, Loreto's banner now doth fly in many distant lands ... Loreto's name each girl reveres, And holds it ever blest..." displayed the tremendous strength of their old-school tie.

Versatile moods

Suddenly a beautiful, trance-inducing voice singed the cold air. A Baul singer, a wandering spiritual Sufi musician from Bengal, strumming his *ektara* (stringed instrument) belted out in a Bengali dialect, "Din duniyar malik khoda, Tomar dil ki doya hoi na" (God, you are the owner of the world of the poor, Have you no compassion in your heart?). From the Christmas atmosphere we unexpectedly entered the itinerant flavor of life on the road. His Loreto Shillong wife accompanied him devotedly, with small Bengali cymbals called *kortal*. I knew her from Paris where they are part of the world music scene. Here they were, disrupting the Irish

Catholic atmosphere with a mystical, nomadic culture more than five centuries old.

Then without much ado the Loreto women enthusiastically joined in for "Jingle Bells." This made me imagine India's Yuletide spirit some 70 years ago, transcending the British Raj legacy. After some time, the alumni started to sing and dance with their husbands to favorite European pop and disco numbers from the 1970s. That was the time I had left my poverty-ridden life in India. I now saw how familiarly the Loreto girls were enjoying what I had seen only on arrival in France. At that time I could not imagine that there existed a certain social class in India who had the same type of opinion and living as in the West.

This very hands-on alumni party proved to me their versatility. They are comfortable celebrating the Catholic origin of Ireland and the rollicking dance steps that Abba induced, and switching to pay rapt attention to minstrel Baul music.

X'mas to Burra Din

A certain higher class, and of course all Christians, celebrated Christmas with our colonial masters. Today Christians decorate banana or mango trees and fill churches with red poinsettia flowers. With economic development, Christmas now puts everyone in a festive mood, irrespective of religion.

I made another discovery when one of my American friends in Bangalore invited us to a Christmas party on December 11. There were several people, with 5- to 10-year-old Indian children very adeptly singing Christmas carols on karaoke with American accents. My pre-Europe Kolkata experience was Burra Din on December 25, but in Europe I learnt that Christmas means the night of December 24, not before or after, and it is always family-reunion time.

Celebration with friends is on December 31. But easy-going Americans have elongated Christmas to month-long entertainment with friends, colleagues, and family. Their marketing efficiency makes Christmas typically account for up to 25 percent of the retail industry's annual sales.

How did Christmas carols originate?

According to Clement Miles, author of *Christmas Customs and Traditions*, Christmas hymns started in fourth-century Rome. The 13th century saw Christmas songs originate in the French, German, and Italian languages under the influence of Francis of Asissi. The carols we recognize today were originally communal songs sung during celebrations such as harvest tide.

It is recorded (in.answers.yahoo.com) that ancient European pagans celebrated the midwinter and other festivals long before Christianity ever existed. Babylonians celebrated the feast of the Son of Isis by eating, drinking, and gift giving, and the goddess of fertility, love, and war. The church, under Pope Julius I, declared that Christ's birth would be celebrated on December 25 in AD 350, which fructified in AD 378. Scandinavian countries celebrated Yule, honoring Thor.

Yule is synonymous with Christmas, a usage first recorded in AD 900. In Germania midwinter celebrations had 12 wild nights of eating and drinking. On December 25, the Romans celebrated their god Sol Invictas. Wikipedia says the earliest known reference to December 25 as the nativity date is found in the *Chronography* of AD 354, an illuminated manuscript compiled in Rome.

According to missionislam.com, several cultures recognize December 25 as their gods' birth date, such as Mithras of the Persians, Osiris, god of the dead and underworld in Egypt, and in Greece, Adonis and Hercules, son of supreme god Zeus. The website www.islamweb.com says a Muslim is neither allowed to celebrate Christmas day nor allowed to congratulate non-Muslims on their festival celebrations. Yet Christmas is a very big festival in all GCC countries where schools, colleges, and offices declare it a holiday, malls and shopping centers decorate and promote huge sales and even a few local Arabs, pressurized by their children, put up a Christmas tree at home.

On my way back from New Delhi on December 23, I reached the airport two hours ahead, and was subjected to the grating boringness of "Jingle Bells" in continuous repetition. This is another innovative American characteristic. They have created a standard song and internationalized it as entertainment for a certain period, which everybody seems to follow. Go to malls and hotel lobbies, you will hear nothing else. The expression "Happy Holidays" in place of "Merry Christmas" originated in America as many controversies surround the inception of Christmas. But the spreading power of Christianity has reached modern mobile-phone-using youngsters who are forwarding up to 500 SMSs accompanied by "Jingle Bells."

DIGI-TECH PROXIMITY

Aside from age-old festivities like Christmas, digital technology is now bringing the world closer. The day after the iPad was launched, I was working with my small four-by-nine-inch laptop computer while having dinner at a Bangalore restaurant. A seven-year-old girl, not even old enough yet to send 500 SMSs to her friends as all youngsters seem to do, was returning from the washroom to her parents a few tables away.

Swamped and united by digi-tech

Suddenly, the seven-year-old spied my computer, got distracted, and rushed to our table. Her eyes lit up, staying glued to my Sony Vaio laptop, she asked, "Is this the new iPad?" It totally disappointed her that the little computer was not an iPad. She said she had seen the new iPad on Google. She and her friends were already chatting about it on Yahoo. She confidently said she was keen to use the functionalities of iPad immediately. She did not talk of a print advertisement or TV news; her reference was the Internet.

iPad had definitely done something really special, much beyond traditional advertising. On only the second day of its worldwide launch, a seven-year-old Bangalore girl was awaiting it with bated breath.

Adolescent users of mobile phones all across the world do not use them for talking but for social connect, SMS, and MMS with video streaming. This generation has adeptly devised and used a new telegraphic type of text language. With the mobile phone and the Internet totally connected, video streaming, watching movies, and accessing YouTube are an important part of their lives. While on research in rural Kerala last year, a young boy wearing the *mundu* (sarong), T-shirt, and earphones was intently watching a regional film on his mobile phone. Simultaneously he was keeping an eye on the cattle he had brought out to graze.

Internet social networking

Marketing departments of companies are naturally thinking of cyberspace as an alternative media for brand promotion. But calling this space Internet social media is a misnomer. It is in fact social connect through cyberspace, Internet social networking (ISN). It would be a mistake for advertisers to consider it another medium for communication without customizing their connect beyond the advertising message.

I would divide groups on cyberspace into different age groups for social connect. The children's group of 5–12 years, the adolescent teenager, the 20- to 30-year-olds, 30- to 45-year-olds, and the 45+ group. In addition, there are different social groups. However, the main zone where social connect happens is below 30 years of age. To reach out to these groups, each message has to be in a different tone and manner.

Cyber social platforms present a completely new opportunity to instantly deliver messages to millions of people. Its first efficient use in Barack Obama's presidential campaign records its tremendous potential. Every company is trying to enter this space to connect to the 3 billion people who are active on the Internet, but these "advertisements" remain ineffective because one-on-one conversations do not happen. The brands remain faceless. Giving the same message to everyone all at once may spell the death knell of organized, traditional advertising as we know it.

The sub-30 group does not care about what you want to promote. You just have to leave it there for them, be provocative, and give a disruptive form or message. Do not sell the obvious, make them decode what they want using their own intelligence. ISN is clever as it is interactive, private, and non-lucrative.

Privacy is a big issue, and, of course, there can be abuse too. The new generation counts virtual connections as real friends. People are very familiar and "talk" endlessly to like-minded people they have met over the Internet. In fact, such friendships have often resulted in marriages.

During recent travels, I have found the mentality of the boy from Mumbai or Bangalore to be the same as that of a New Yorker or Londoner. That is a big change from the 1970s, when as a 19-year-old I arrived in Paris and found nothing in common with a French boy my age.

If only the Internet had arrived earlier...

I became friends with Bernard Offen, a Polish survivor of the Nazi death camps, through email. At my request he included me in his Auschwitz-Birkenau concentration camp tour where he explains his horrible experience of the Holocaust. To ensure that this brutality is not obliterated from history, he said that the Supreme Commander of Allied Forces, General Dwight Eisenhower, had ensured that photographs and films were taken to record the death camps because somewhere down the road, someone would say this never happened.

In an email to me, Offen wrote:

> The UK debated whether the Holocaust should be removed from its school curriculum because it offends a certain section of the population who claim it never occurred. It is not removed yet. However, this is a frightening portent of the fear that is gripping the world and how easily each country is giving in to it.
>
> Six million Jews, 20 million Russians, 10 million Christians and 1,900 Catholic priests were murdered, raped, burnt, starved, beaten, experimented upon and humiliated

while the German people looked the other way. How many years will it be before the attack on New York's World Trade Centre [*sic*] "never happened," because it offends some community in the US?

The life of Offen and others in the death camps would have been different if the Internet had existed at that time. Someone could have as easily sent this personal message addressing millions of people across the world.

BITTEN BY BUG

Years ago, India's famous music director S.D. Burman sang, *"Dheere se jana khatian me, O Khatmal."* Its literal meaning is, Bedbug, move unhurriedly on the bed (toward your stealthy purpose of sucking her blood is implied). There was a lateral meaning too. In those days, romantically approaching a young girl was taboo. The song figuratively indicated that the man creeps slowly, invisibly, like the bedbug that society does not see, and bites her tactfully, but does not get caught, the way you never catch a bedbug.

Digital disturbance

But today's bug mania is digital, so open discussion on it can connect everyone, bringing them closer. It is a virus caught through the Internet on your computer. American capitalism empowered the open economy; similarly, digital bugs have democratized society with multiple meanings, interpretations, and options. What you would analyze as bad could be good for me and her, what is ugly for me is good for him, bad for another.

Clearly the eclectic nature of digital technology delivers BUG mania, B for bad, U for ugly, and G for good. The bug in your computer is an error, flaw, mistake, fault, or failure in the system or software, but BUG mania is our obtuse digitalization of human foibles.

B = bad

Disturbs privacy. Earlier, you would handle landline calls adroitly. If your father received the call and suspected hanky-panky, the situation would roller-coaster into family chaos. The mobile phone has changed the privacy code. Is prostitution declining? No longer do hookers saunter the streets petulantly, lipstick and mirror in hand, obliquely keeping tabs on male movements behind them. In fact, escort agencies have taken over, escort solicitations now secretly land on your mobile handsets or emails or stare you in the face in print advertisements.

Grandmothers have lost happy moments of narrating fairy tales. With a click, the Internet takes children to unimaginable wonderlands, pornographic sites, and violence videos. Does that make technology bad? Remote-controlling their lives, tech-born kids visit virtual farms, clean animal pens, and feed the goats every day. They start blogs for their pet dogs, exchange cyber conversations with other dogs. They multitask on the computer, take no phone calls from numbers they do not recognize, and send endless SMSs. When they write they expect automatic digital correction because, "Is spelling more important or the expression?" Is social networking bad for making us unsocial, ignoring spelling mistakes, giving us access to exploitation through pictures, negative propaganda?

Should the terminology for "adult at 18 years" be changed? With Freud's Oedipus and Electra psychological complexes at the back of their minds, and hands gripping mobile phones, hide-and-seek about sex may have misplaced relevance for children. Notwithstanding amorous sexual depictions as religious culture in Khajuraho and Konark temples, Indian adults want to hide sex under the carpet or ignore its phenomenal impact on children of the age of 12 and over. This is not to criticize digitalization ruling our lives, but its analysis is not black and white.

U = ugly

Revolting political mudslinging on our liberalized electronic airwaves. The public is fed up with political debates with no code of conduct or ethics, screeching fights where nobody can understand anything. Take another technology-enabled ugly scene, the MMS disclosing sexual intimacy between lovers. Cuckolded husbands or ditched boyfriends often, and quite disgracefully, take secret revenge on the woman by circulating such an MMS on the mobile. Everyone enjoys this sharing point save the not-so-innocent victim.

When a TV channel encourages people to send videos by MMS, of their instant newsy experiences for telecast, it uses such material to raise the channel's TRP, and so cashes in on more advertisements. But does it not also excite people to fabricate antisocial horrors? Remote Indian villagers buy higher-GB SIM cards only to get blue film downloads integrated inside. Of course they will justify the higher spend on watching feature films or songs.

Insensitivity can be ugly, like a minister's tweet on traveling cattle-class. Perhaps a playful aside of upper-class arrogance, but it exposed how condescendingly politicians treat their innocent, underprivileged electorate. It also exposed Twitter's online power of disruption.

Another "U" bug is haggling to buy sportsmen. "It's not cricket" was an expression understood to mean unfair, ungentlemanly practice. India's IPL 20/20 has blown the lid off such sophisticated aspects of cricket. Reigning today is a mentality akin to commercial transactions with slaves, animals, or women in ancient Middle Eastern bazaars. So Shah Rukh Khan has every right to invest in an appropriate player-purchase, but Kolkatans went crazy that their star item for sale fetched zilch. When that is shown on TV, were they not devaluing their hero instead?

G = good

Digitalization has widened society's mind sphere. Sitting anywhere you can interface anything virtually, yet be personalized. It is particularly thrilling when, after 40 years, you suddenly discover, through ISN, a childhood woman friend whose face and name has changed after marriage. Ranjeet and Bonita subscribe to a matrimonial website to satisfy their parents, but actually they use it to find dating partners. The obsession is for multiple options. Sometimes they meet only once, sometimes many times. Aside from aiding romance, technology enhances careers too, giving you the opportunity to quietly change jobs at the click of a keyboard.

Comfort and convenience are good in digitalization. It makes even complex government processes transparent, efficient, and predictable. It is so easy to complain about service deficiencies and get instant responses, create awareness on critical issues, generate mass following to save the tigers, help the girl child, or buy movie tickets. Twenty years down the line you will only have Kindles or iPads, no physical book library at home, the way vinyl records have vanished, and cassettes and CDs are fast disappearing. Digitalization enables global peace and harmony, people of all religions text each other on festivals. The banyan tree took hundreds of years to download its roots, but within nanoseconds the Internet creates a human banyan tree.

The BUG's bite

Digital technology established BUG mania, where bad, ugly, and good aspects happen simultaneously. Today's below-30 Zap generation absorbs and enjoys this incomparable BUG trend, but older generations segregate the bad, ugly, and good. That is where the chasm invisibly bites, like the bedbug, resulting in attrition at work, or switching off from talking to parents at home.

If you can cuddle into contemporary lifestyle and ideation, embrace BUG mania to feel young again, you may enlarge business too like L'Oréal did (see mini-tale-slice 'ZAP86 trend is India's future').

THE REALITY BOOM

You may enjoy the failures children experience as part of reality television, but unconsciously, like antibiotics, you absorb the frequent advertisements at the pauses between reality shows. That is big business being conducted, complete with BUG (bad, ugly, good) characteristics, but you are oblivious to it.

Criticism in the name of encouragement

When a child or earnest youngster is highly criticized for his/her imperfect performance, tele-spectators find vicarious fun in it, although most do not admit it. It is comparable to the excitement that stung the Romans when watching gladiators rip each other apart. Or the excruciating thrill Spaniards feel when they roar as the bullfighter or bull dies in the ring during every bullfight.

Let me restrict the impact of reality TV to children as they are the most vulnerable. Why do "brilliant" judges think they are entitled to criticize youngsters the way they want to in front of millions of tele-spectators? Have they thought about the future career of these aspirants? While enjoying the defects and defeat of striving young artists, save the winner, you, the tele-spectator, are endorsing the total success of the program's producer for getting high TRPs for the channel.

The reality boom hit the US at the turn of the century with shows such as *American Idol* and *Survivor*; earlier shows like the *Miss America Pageant* never made the big time. India's highly proliferated native cultural societies, copying the Caucasian American, seems a mismatch. Look at the US' evolution, from being invaders on a continent to embracing the cowboy culture. Their selling–marketing attitude made them take big risks and gambles, and led to their becoming outstanding inventors of all time. American inventions have changed the way the world thinks and works, with the rapid advancement of digital technology. All such disruptive consequences may have created American society to be forever agitated.

Gun-toting mentality

In the US, every citizen is allowed to carry a gun. It is for self-protection and defense because of the supposedly high crime rates. As gun-toting people, their mental makeup becomes totally skewed toward being daring and don't-care-a-damn. It is incomparable with India's culture that has transcended from ancient traditions, which encourage an attitude of compromise.

Let me illustrate with a personal experience of the disconcerting American social order. I once accompanied an American client of mine from New York City to his suburban home in New Jersey after working hours. There was a bumper-to-bumper traffic jam that could be seen for miles. My client suddenly switched on a device atop his dashboard which had programmed inside it different kinds of irritating sounds. The one he chose was the machine-gun shot.

In the middle of this colossal traffic jam, he attacked all the cars in front with gunshots, as though he was taking part in the film *The Terminator*. I watched amazed, feeling stupid, as I had never experienced this in Europe. He laughed, saying this way the time would pass faster, and we would not feel bored. By the time we reach, he said, we would have killed so many vehicles that this, he finds, has become his best stress-busting tool.

On another occasion, in a friend's car, I noticed an unsettling program that he activated in his car. He put his car radio in the auto-scan mode so that every 30 seconds the radio station changed, and he ended up listening to a medley of songs. These are anecdotes of disquiet in the American way of life, which is a unidirectional society.

American entertainment has its own history since the last 60 years. It is far removed from Indian entertainment that runs on outstretched fantasy. But India is imitating

America's hybrid culture without evolution, just jumping from fantasy to reality in a short span of time. Americans have become tired of blockbuster Hollywood films and scripted TV shows like *Dallas* and are now turning toward reality TV. I have no complaints against American culture, I love their Barbie doll and hamburger ethnicity, but when India blindly follows this culture, authenticity gets discounted. And originality all but dissipates into merely collecting money from TV advertisements.

Spare the children

Indian reality game shows and voyeuristic people-watching programs are good for boosting TV ratings. However, when young performers have to take barbs from so-called guru and *maha*-guru (great teacher) judges, their morale gets completely destroyed.

In this century, only a handful of artists have emerged from such national and regional channels, less than 10 at the national level. I find it quite amoral and inhuman the way children are harassed by judges on TV shows. When the prestige and confidence of debutant artists break, can it result in producing artists from the masses, as is the purported objective of these entertainment programs? The performing arts cannot be taught while facing a public forum; doing so intimidates the children.

Famous silver-screen actors and playback singers are often the judges. Actors have the advantage of shooting take after numerous take until the correct scene is captured. So in the released film, the public never sees their shortcomings and flaws. In today's practice, singers dub using modern technology, recording line after line, multiple times and in multiple tracks. They sometimes do not even see the musicians. All voice imperfections are corrected with digital technology. Even in front of an audience on stage, the musicians have to manage a singer's mistakes. The public is never privy to the professional artists' kitchen.

But when these artists become reality show judges, it is amazing how, sometimes with sugarcoated words, they feel free to bombard the young ones with high-definition censure. Undoubtedly, reality TV has helped underprivileged people express themselves, earn money and fame, but criticizing them on TV is a totally anti-artistic solution.

As a tele-spectator you enjoy the defeat of hapless children artists. They do not exactly get physically killed as the barbaric gladiator competitors did in the Roman emperor's arena, but such reality shows can kill children's self-esteem. Incidents have already occurred, where they have become severely unwell, such as becoming paralytic with the shock of defeat. It appears that the National Commission for Protection of Child Rights is enquiring into the long hours, remuneration, and working conditions of children in reality shows, especially since employing a child under 14 is a crime.

ROMANCING BOLLYWOOD

While engrossed in a scholarly discussion, not on idiot-box small talk, with my professor friend, Dr S Raghunath, the phone rang. "Bhavna has invited us all to see a Hindi movie," his wife Usha announced. How could we refuse their beautiful teenage daughter? I promptly blurted out to Usha my one-frame résumé of 65 years of Bollywood potpourri: "Suresh! *Tumne mujhe dhoka diya (you have jilted me)!*" Does this not capture the poignant scene of betrayal the heroine suffers at some moment in every film?

"No, no, it's very different nowadays…" Usha said, so without further disagreement we went to see *Shanghai*, the latest *dhamaka* (hit).

My contention is proved!

At halftime, the near-dead hero's wife came from Delhi to take her husband away, only to discover a girlfriend attending to her husband in hospital. So my argument that "Suresh! Tumne mujhe dhoka diya" is Bollywood's single-point focus was proved! Experiencing Bollywood extravaganza after many years has inspired me to list the clichés I have absorbed. With utmost respect to the millions of spectators who enormously enjoy these delicious films, let me give you a list of the typical sensational ingredients that churn out box-office hits.

Social melodrama to kick off the movie

Older films portrayed the underprivileged in the opening frames and focused on the social situation or family complex; now it has acquired a Western flair. After all, children of Indians born in the US, UK, or abroad elsewhere, have been added to the original large audiences based in India. They may speak with local Yankee or Cockney accents, but their migrant parents keep Indian culture vibrant at home. That "culture", for millions settled abroad, happens to be Bollywood mores.

To cater to such good custodians of Hindi films, directors do not stubbornly stick to old winner scenarios; they create Indian family dramas outside India too. There are only a few dozen storylines, with myriad permutations.

Heart-rending themes include rich girl running away with poor boy, long-lost relatives, high-class boy in love with low-caste girl, slum dweller forced to become gang leader, then discovering he is not an orphan but the son of the merciless industrialist his trade union is targeting to destroy. The tragic death of a loved one at the film's kick off establishes the cause of revenge. Most of all, the presentation has to touch very raw nerves, bringing tears to spectators' eyes.

Dance song

Songs comprise the film's core, determining the success formula. Everyone knows that actors only lip-sync. Playback singers were earlier associated with certain actors whose voices tallied with their harmonious renditions. Some actors used one playback singer's voice for their whole career. Only if you are excellent at playback singing can you become a famous singer in India. I remember in our young days a song would be released, made into a hit, and subsequently the film would ride piggyback on its success. The electronic media has made singers better known today, but their public fame is appended to the hero or heroine, and the film's performance.

The hero has a crooner's role, teasing a girl, who plays hide-and-seek, to show that she is shy and unwilling-but-actually-willing. Rarely would heroines start romantic overtures. Sometimes, reminiscent of Lord Krishna's soul mate Radha and her *gopi*s (cowgirl friends), the girl dances with village belles in colorful *lehenga*s (long skirts) in front of wheat fields. Or the passionate couple prances around in some forest, garden, mountain, snowfield, or beach with staccato head-and-body movements.

Foreign sites

From such natural locales, Hindi film songs have shifted to the streets of New York. The inspiration seems to be from Broadway choreography for group street dancing from the 1961 comedy musical, *Westside Story*, composed by Leonard Bernstein. You can distinctively spot the romantic couple in Bollywood versions as they are dressed differently from the backdrop dancers performing the perfect aerobic routine.

Suddenly, dancing on foreign streets has almost become mandatory. You see foreigners gaping askance on the sidelines sometimes, but the couple is oblivious to the surroundings, as people in love are. Dancing to songs builds up the crescendo, so whistles of high excitement come ferociously and in quick succession at Indian theaters.

Crime

Villains are must-haves. They are the salt and pepper of Hindi movies. Dialogues of powerful, *paan*-juice (betel nut and leaf) spitting bosses are memorized for real-life play-acting by imitative fans. Sometimes they become Robin Hood, stealing from the rich to save the poor. Such villains get heavy applause at movie halls.

Political drama

The plot always features some direct or indirect political corruption. The public is disgusted or jealous of the politicians' ill-gotten wealth, yet has no voice to check them. So when Hindi films portray politicians being punished for their scandalous corrupt crimes, it thrills the public.

It's still the trend to show the law-and-order machinery backing the right cause, whether that is true or not. The police station has both good and bad policemen, but the ethical ones always prevail.

Fight

The spiciest of all is the fight. Initially the hero does not win, but you can be sure he will come back to win. The fighting hero is a handsome dude with gleaming biceps. He has the power to fight multiple villains, mixing techniques of wrestling, judo, and karate. The villain is bad, bad all the way. He has crooked teeth or false glass eyes, ensuring no girl can fall for him.

A gunfight is okay, but it is physical *dhishum-dhishum* (returning blows) fighting that brings every spectator to the chair's edge. The way you await dance sequences, moving your sitting torso and lips in rhythm, the fight gets you involved, perhaps more so. You mentally feel a punch, physically crouch on your seat, quickly take in your breath, exclaim, or narrow your eyes. A girl may squeeze her partner's hand and hide behind his shoulder when the scene gets too graphic. That, of course, is the boys' bonus pleasure of watching fight scenes at the movies.

Intermission!

Hindi movies never finish so quickly. What about footage on hate, love, foreign tours, betrayal, lecturer's dialogue, happy end, value-for-money technical effects, trend influence, mother–son affection, all so essential to complete a real Bollywood format? Coming up next…

IGNITING EMOTIONS

Igniting diverse emotions in us, Hindi movie plots cover star-crossed lovers, sacrifices, angry parents, siblings that fate separated, rapists, rebirths, mistaken identities of twin brothers, one innocent and the other stomping the underworld. Continuing the saga of "Suresh! Tumne mujhe dhoka diya!" which summarizes Bollywood fantasy for me, let us get into themes beyond the melodramatic kick-off scenes, dance songs, crime, political dramas, and fights.

Hate

Bollywood storylines can flow to establish extreme jealousy, greed, and passion. The hate factor apes the West. Absolute bad and/or good are not culturally prominent in India. Even our mythological stories convey that something bad for one could be good for another. In contrast, the Catholicism that the West largely follows clearly demarcates good from bad. Hindi films have adopted hate, so the hero or heroine, villain or some side actor, has to choke over hate, as though it is food stuck in the gullet.

Love

Triangular love is a much-used theme. Different men can show overbearing love or secret attraction for the heroine. But a woman cannot openly have many boyfriends, as is the social reality among today's young generation. Depicting that would make her a whore. It seems a few movies tried that with no overwhelming acceptance. The girl should love the good man, never the villain.

Foreign tours

Foreign tours were always a kind of windfall in Bollywood movies. Sitting in India spectators enjoy a visit to exotic foreign countries. In this era of globalization, an overseas setting has become obligatory. Shooting abroad makes the film relevant for the extended audience of foreign-born Indian-origin children. Experience shows that a scene shot in a developed country upgrades the film both in terms of its acceptance status and production quality. Consider it Bollywood's quality development or showcasing of the producer's power.

Betrayal

Betrayal anchors more or less every movie. The emotional corruption of betrayal can happen between the hero and heroine, with two friends, within the family, in business, among gangsters, in politics, or also shown through a death. When the betrayer is caught and punished, there is great applause in the cinema hall.

A lecturer's dialogue

This is an all-too-frequent Bollywood attempt at education. One character talks directly into the camera as though preaching to or teaching society. The cameraman zooms into the actor's face without stops and commas, so the *gyan*-giving (lecture) session can become one long shot. This translates as the film director's social conscience, or do-good idea of teaching ethics or philosophy to society.

Happy end

Most Bollywood movies have the happy-end format so as to not dissatisfy spectators or leave them in inconclusive situations. Of course films with sad endings do make an exceptional entry, but the payoff comes from what we would all like our lives to be: happy. As Bollywood cannot afford to disturb its paying public, composed of the underprivileged population and NRIs, the formula of every puzzle being solved at the end is the success factor.

Value-for-money technical effects

Technical effects established exuberantly, never subtly, is the icing on the Bollywood cake. The most advanced art effects are dramatized and shown as part of the storyline. New camera techniques, glamorous never-seen-before-in-Indian-films props, use of advanced digital effects and artistic modus operandi like slow motion, fast forward, morphing, traveling shots, crazy animations, are embedded or interwoven into films. They prove that we are no less than foreign films, and flesh out as a bonus for spectators.

Trend influence

The influence of Western trends was a little late in coming to Bollywood, but the gap has narrowed now. For example, bell-bottoms took forever to be seen in Hindi films, but torso-revealing, hip-hugging jeans made it in instant digital time.

Mother-and-children affection

After listing my observations on Hindi films, I checked with Aravinda, who Professor Raghunath says is the most careful driver he has met. I asked whether I had missed anything. Aravinda very often gives me social imagery that I may not so easily see. He promptly answered that I had totally overlooked the mother–children affection chapter. Mother is the moral foundation of Hindi films, the mother–hero relationship is very intimate. Bollywood makes it obvious that Indian society values sons over daughters. The hero is invariably the best son a mother can have, and vice versa. Mother–son bonding against all odds leaves copious tears in the eyes of cinema-hall audiences.

Telling statistics

Bollywood is top-of-mind but it is actually the South Indian film industry that currently generates 75 percent of all film revenues in India. Of the 1,274 feature films that went to the Central Board of Film Certification in 2010, there were only 215 Hindi films. Southern productions totaled 631, with 202 Tamil, 181 Telugu, 143 Kannada, and 105 Malayalam films. Among other regional players were 116 Marathi and 110 Bengali films.

India ranks first, followed by Hollywood and China, in the number of films produced. As per statistics from the Motion Picture Association of America, India produced 1,014 films in 2002, sold 3.6 billion tickets and collected revenues of US$1.3 billion from theater tickets, DVDs, television, and so on. In contrast, Hollywood made 739 films, sold 2.6 billion tickets but generated revenues of US$51 billion.

These statistics make quality versus quantity evident in the silver screen. Perhaps Indian movies need a disruption of universal appeal, away from the "Suresh! Tumne mujhe dhoka diya!" fantasy, while still being relevant to India and Indians. Indian films go to 90 countries, but it is the Indian diaspora that lap them up. They have never become box office hits for natives of these nations.

Showcasing India differently

India's diverse salt, sugar, and pepper culture with multiple gods in one religion is unique in the world. Portraying a storyline outside of clichéd fantasy can create another dimension. For example, there is tremendous history from just 258 years ago when Siraj-ud-daulah, Bengal's last nawab, lost the Battle of Plassey against the British in 1757. Just imagine, if this untold story could be presented Hollywood-style, like Ridley Scott's film *Gladiators* in ancient Rome, what an incredible film that would be for the global market and India's reputation.

FRAGRANT POTPOURRI WORLD

Aside from motion pictures, diverse unconnected news waft in digitally, through electronic media, mobile phones, text messages, social networking, when traveling. As I was struggling to put some form to the recent happenings in the world, my wife was changing the potpourri in a wooden bowl near my writing table. The word I searched for streaked in, potpourri!

Fragrant concoction

Any collection of miscellaneous, diverse items is potpourri. English, Spanish, and French have the same meaning for pot, while *pourri* is French for rotten. Since the 17th century, fresh flowers and herbs are gathered in France through spring and summer, dried, and sea salt is added. The concoction that ferments or moulds is stirred, spices and scent-preserving fixatives added in autumn, and the mixture put in perforated pots. The benefit of rotting flowers is room fragrance; a potpourri of happenings delivers undulating emotions, both cheerful and cheerless. Let us travel for a potpourri of global happenings.

Greek TV slap

Greece is economically, politically troubled. Having worked for a Greek company continuously for 24 years, I greatly admire lovely Greece and the Greeks. As I switched the TV on, extreme-right politician Ilias Kasidiaris, was lunging forward, throwing water at Syriza Party's Rena Dourou across from him. He then stood up and repeatedly slapped Communist Party's Liana Kanelli during a political debate.

Bewildered at how two women were physically attacked, I turned to my Greek friend Theodore. He messaged back, "Greeks invented democracy, but it cannot be applied to modern Greeks. Politics is a derby race today. Every Greek acts, explains and translates democracy for himself, not for common public welfare." He added, ironically, "I definitely prefer enlightened dictatorships like Cuba's Fidel Castro and Venezuela's Hugo Chavez to democratic anarchy."

Bengali TV

Turning on a Bengali channel threw me off balance. Prominent, beautiful TV news anchor Moupia was talking very seriously, confidence combined with embarrassment in her voice, about Pinki Pramanik's "*lingo pariksha*" (sex examination). Indian woman athlete Pinki, winner of gold medals and several Asian and Commonwealth Games honors, was arrested when her female live-in partner exposed her to be a man. The arresting West Bengal police officer said the victim alleged that Pinki continuously raped her, promised to marry her but later refused. The gender test conducted on Pinki on June 20, 2012 was inconclusive and Calcutta High Court quashed all criminal charges against her on September 12, 2014.

Just after Pinki's news came the commercial for *japani tel* (oil of Japan). A snake charmer, accompanied by typical music arouses a sleeping cobra and sparks fly, very graphically indicating a kind of Viagra medicine. I have observed these ads come on regularly after political controversies, disaster, or entertainment programs, and only on Bengali TV, not elsewhere. Does japani tel's heavy media investment mean the product is working so well in Bengal?

Zapping to another Bengali channel, I witnessed an "anchor hunt" show. It undoubtedly had an innovative format. Very surprisingly, highly regarded senior members of different political parties were the test subjects for aspiring young TV anchor candidates. A jury comprising silver-screen actors and an existing TV anchor judged them. This new exam format may be good for TRPs, may expose media-hungry politicians too, but should candidates be humiliated in public? Will jury members like being badgered the way they criticized future TV news anchors?

Uncertain first lady

The absolute majority that French President François Hollande's Socialist Party won in the legislative elections allows him to govern independently, but it is his political love triangle that global media was abuzz with. The most important candidate he had openly supported lost the election. That was his party's 2007 presidential candidate, Ségolène Royal, who is also his ex-partner and mother of his four children. She was ahead in a triangular fight but the run-off saw dissident Socialist Olivier Falorni get 63 percent of votes.

Royal's backstabbing defeat is traced to Hollande's partner at that time, journalist Valérie Trierweiler. Taking a public swipe at Royal, she tweeted, "Courage to Olivier Falorni who has not been unworthy, who has battled alongside La Rochelle residents for so many years with unselfish commitment." This created havoc. Prime Minister Jean-Marc Ayrault advised Trierweiler to "know her place." The president's children have allegedly refused to speak to her.

Valerie finally capitulated, admitting she "made a mistake." After her electoral defeat, Royal felt "murdered" by Trierweiler's "violent blow" and quoted French writer Victor Hugo: "Traitors always pay for their treachery in the end." Perhaps that happened when Hollande's affair with actress Julie Gayet became public and Valerie left the Presidential Palace in January 2014.

Media's fixation

The liberty to carry a gun perhaps keeps Americans in a perpetually agitated state. So, making a criminal courtroom the venue for spectacular drama, with high media attention is their forte. Jerry Sandusky's trial in June 2012 for serial child molestation found him guilty on 45 out of 48 counts of sexual abuse. This could get him 422 years of imprisonment. What a weird sentence! Are Americans inventing some new drug to make prisoners survive that long?

The media always keeps political parties in high pitch, but do common people understand this potpourri in spite of being voters? Do 480 million BPL people in India care who, for example, is the president living luxuriously in the world's largest presidential residence? Surely it will not make any dent in their livelihood possibilities?

Real potpourri is preserving natural fragrance in fermented dried flowers. Modern potpourri is as colorful but artificial, yet retaining pourri's real meaning, which is rotten. I wonder if all these episodes above are real or artificial potpourri?

2

MY POLITICAL WHIFF

The political knowledge I grew up with was watching my father working for the betterment of the downtrodden. Having become a refugee himself after compulsorily forsaking his family's home and vast farmlands in what was East Bengal then, he became an activist for the poor, as they did not know how to express themselves.

A childhood memory from that squatter refugee colony on Kolkata's outskirts where I was born and raised is a movement my father started during the 1959 food crisis in Bengal. He mobilized thousands of underprivileged people into the Sarbohara Mukti Parishad, loosely translated as the council to free those who have lost everything, in search of food, with the typical slogan, "*Inquilab Zindabad*" (Long live the revolution!). The refugees, however, would respond, "*Inquilab Zhinga Bhat.*" *Zhinga* is a ridge gourd, and *bhat* is rice. The only expectation of those who had lost everything during their forced migration from East Bengal was an assurance of basic food, of rice, and of vegetable.

Upon hearing people shout the wrong interpretation of Inquilab Zhinga Bhat, I once laughed out loud. I will never forget how my father immediately gave me a hard slap in front of everyone, saying, "Never disrespect the hunger of poor people."

This subject grew in my mind. Irrespective of the banner of any political party, my father's leadership was different, rooted in people's actual requirements. He roused the core emotion of society by identifying and focusing on matters of immediate significance to them. I can say that this gave me a sense of the politics relevant at that time. That may have helped me to become a mass communicator through branding, and in ensuring the end-customer connect in my profession.

Politics today is synonymous with many things, governance of corruption included. It has become a jalebi, a googly that is quite unpredictable, yet it is part of the air we breathe. So we cannot but take a whiff of it.

In this chapter you will get jalebi slivers of how captivating life can be when entwined with politics both in India and in my adopted country, France. Common people are primed to get highly involved at election time. They want to bite into the shiny jalebi, to swim in a democratic system that leaves them to happily munch tasty slices of undulating life.

UNFURLING THE FLAG PUZZLE

It is so refreshing to see bright, trendy faces painted saffron, white, and green cheering India at international cricket matches. That young Indians are proudly patriotic is admirable. During our young days, for those of us underprivileged, leaving India for a better life or job was necessary. That is why I found my way to Paris in 1973.

Confusion in similarity

Today, using the national flag during various events to express pride is a growing trend. But is not the horizontal display of saffron, white, and green creating confusion between India's flag and the Indian National Congress (INC) party's flag? Taking advantage of our pride in being the world's biggest democracy, let me touch upon our flag's history.

Historians must pardon my not being an official historian, and others should not take my comments as criticism. I am reflecting on the democratic code. As branding is among the domains in which I have expertise, my observation is related to the authentic symbolic expressions of political parties. We need both ruling and opposition parties for the perfect balance in democracy. Can the political party that was at the forefront of India's political independence bequeath its party flag to become the national flag? Was it done to fuse the idea of the INC with the idea of India, to make it the idea of the nation?

Congress volunteers in Nagpur, commemorating the Jallianwala Bagh massacre, hoisted the *swaraj* (self-rule) flag on April 13, 1923. Pingali Venkayya, an agriculturist from Machilipatnam, Andhra Pradesh, designed this when, in 1921, Mahatma Gandhi proposed that the INC have a flag. The flag had red for Hindus, green for Muslims, and a manual spinning wheel (charkha) to symbolize Gandhiji's call for India's economic self-sufficiency. To include other religious communities, the design was modified with a central white stripe, and later red changed to saffron.

Charkha to chakra

Before India's independence, a committee headed by Rajendra Prasad and consisting of Maulana Abul Kalam Azad, Sarojini Naidu, C. Rajagopalachari, K.M. Munshi, and B.R. Ambedkar deliberated to find a national flag. They recommended the INC's flag after replacing Gandhiji's charkha with the chakra to represent the wheel of law of the Mauryan emperor Ashoka from the third century BC. Was this a quick-fix solution for lack of time or lack of ideas? Or was it a deliberate, forward-looking strategy of freedom fighters to transcend Gandhiji's legacy in the future? With or without understanding the consequences, did they impose the INC as the nation's representative?

The Indian and Irish flag colors are the same, but Ireland's is in reverse vertical green–white–saffron order. Is there any connection? Apparently not, but the fact is that Annie Besant, president of the INC in 1917–1918 was proud of her Irish origin. The INC, founded in 1885, notably upon A.O. Hume's initiative, did not initially oppose British rule. When Britain needed its empire's support during World War I, Besant echoed the Irish nationalist slogan: "England's need is India's opportunity." As editor of the *New India* newspaper, she attacked the colonizers, demanding India's self-rule.

In 1916, Annie Besant launched India's Home Rule League using the Irish model. The League became India's first political party to fight for change through public meetings and agitations. In June 1917 Besant was arrested. To show defiance, she flew a red-and-green flag in the garden of the house she was interned in. Both the INC and Muslim League protested her arrest, which created an opportunity for them to come together for India's independence. Such joint agitations forced the British government to free Besant and announce Indian self-government as its ultimate aim.

It is paradoxical that both Ireland and India had nationalist, anti-British feelings, and same tricolor. Could it be that Pingali Venkayya was inspired by Annie Besant's red-and-green flag of 1917? Could it also be that Besant's flag-flying act of protest was borrowed from Irish separatists' anti-British reactions?

Much ado about colors

No democracy other than India has a national flag that is similar to that of a political party. Only in communist China does red dominate both country and party flags, although with different symbols. Erstwhile USSR, where communism originated, had a single red flag from 1922 to 1991. When Mikhail Gorbachev dissolved the Soviet Union 1991, Russia returned to its 1883 flag of white, blue, and red colors, although Russia's communist party flag remained red.

Large numbers of Indians are unlettered, and generally people only associate and register colors with political parties. When the masses see the INC tricolor, they can believe they are being patriotic, recall those colors when casting a vote, and consider that they have voted for their country. This is unfair benefit that one party has over others. Breaking away from the INC in 1967, the Congress (Indira) party had to perforce change its symbol from the charkha. The colors of the national flag were retained, but was the change to a palm considered a breakthrough?

Gandhiji had always called for change. Following his ideology, should not the INC radically modernize the party? Where is the sense for economic growth to be associated with Gandhiji's charkha today? It was a tactical idea fit for a passive movement during the freedom struggle. It was not meant to be visionary or encourage innovation. The real INC has to cleanse its image from having taken undue advantage of the tricolor, from the legacy of Gandhi to Nehru, Indira to Sonia to attract the youth.

Keep the flag unique

Let us not tamper with our national flag, it builds our pride. Our people own those colors and symbol, and are happily flaunting them inside cricket stadiums. Just as India's Government has enacted laws on flag usage, they should prevent political parties and other brands from appropriating national symbols and colors to cash in on the accompanying sentiments. An appropriate timeline can be given to make the changeover. With their own different ideologies, other political parties too can find powerful identities that are not dependent on the national tricolor.

Then "Brand India" can proudly promote its tricolor while racing to become the world's number one economy in 2050, as predicted by the financial services group, Citi. India wants to invite the young generation into politics, which is essential for nation building. This calls for fundamental changes in promoting national symbols and colors in today's era of digital technology, which is driven by globalization.

ART OF MASS CONNECT

With a national flag we become an united nation, but in reality, do politicians know how heterogeneous our country is?

Choice. That is what free economy and competition give the masses. Unlike in politics, hyper-emotion is heavily encouraged by fast-moving consumer goods' (FMCG) brands in particular. Female consumers declare in jest that they cannot change husbands, so they compensate by changing brands. What she likes today could be totally different tomorrow. Nobody disturbs her decision; there is no social discrimination here.

Let us look at politics through the branding perspective, as that is intertwined with mass preferences. To achieve brand loyalty, brands engage with people's psychological aspect; poverty and affluence are not the factors at play here. When you buy Pantene shampoo, as a consumer you do not care about P&G's enterprise culture, who does its R&D, marketing, operations, or the CEO's name. The first benefit you single-mindedly seek is quality. Does it clean more efficiently, ensure lower hair fall, better hair growth than others? For the brand, repeat purchase is all that matters in the free economy's humungous competition. Will consumers remain loyal to the brand after three purchases? Will consumers continue to purchase it even after several years of use?

The common man on the street looks at political parties exactly like he checks Pantene shampoo's performance versus that of competitors like Dove. Do political parties understand that?

Connect to the lowly paid and up to billionaires

A consumer-product brand cannot enjoy market monopoly when choice is aplenty. Sony was top-of-mind for electronic products for 25 years. Almost overnight Apple ate up its market share. Then LG and Samsung became more talked about than Sony and Philips. Should Indian political parties take a lesson from how brands conquer the masses?

It is easy to connect to the few millionaires and billionaires who have mutual political interests. But politicians need to pull in mass support. Brands have no caste consideration, but category differentiation can be created. Everyone consumes Britannia's Tiger biscuits, but Mercedes is not for everybody.

The masses are no longer passive spectators awaiting the once-in-five-years voting festival; they are participating activists. Political leaders may lead a Mercedes-driven lifestyle, but their mass representation has to be Tiger. In the free economy in the digital technology era, they need to connect on a global platform to all, the lowly paid up to billionaires alike. Just as brands try understanding society's micro-nuances, political parties have to co-opt changing trends in this triangular focus by coping with (*a*) three conflicting generations, (*b*) the micro-judgment of people of eight socio-behavioral clusters, and (*c*) the crunched distance from rural to metro, as Figure 2.1 shows.

Figure 2.1 In Today's Global, Digi-tech, Free Markets, Appreciate Behavior to Reach Everyone—Rich, Poor, Urban, Rural

Source: Author's original illustration.

Three conflicting generations

Do industries, parents, and political leaders pay heed to the existence of three conflicting generations, Retro (born before 1965), Compromise (born between 1965 and 1980), and Zap (born in 1986 or after)? The digital-technology Zapper mindset is attuned to globalization post India's economic liberalization. When those in the Zap generation reach 40 or 50 years of age, they will be mature Zappers, with mindsets different from their Compromise and Retro parents.

You know the landline, but have you experienced the mobile homeline? During research in Maharashtra's deep rural areas, an 18-year-old took me to his congested, single-room, 13-member, joint-family home. He wanted to show me how he changed his poor family's economic condition. From a central pole, a mobile phone was hanging. He said he had to fight family elders to buy the phone. It now helps him coordinate rates in nearby small towns and sell his family's meager farm produce for the best price on offer. His family is addicted to the hanging homeline so he does not carry it himself. Zappers, irrespective of income, and regardless of rural or metro residence, have this same enterprising mindset. Are political leaders engaging with their enthusiasm?

Why are small and medium enterprises (SMEs) complaining that Zap children are not interested in the family business? Take a leaf from Germany's tremendous success in outperforming other European countries. Agile German SMEs are the backbone of the country's economy; they have competitively grabbed business across the globe.

Indian SMEs have difficulty professionalizing their enterprises or inspiring their Zap children, who think differently. In fact, even during higher education Zappers are not taught the three pillars of entrepreneurship:

1. Focus on domain expertise from an early age to digest the domain's nitty-gritty.
2. Develop management skills to activate teamwork.
3. Cultivate the capacity to sell. Entrepreneurship needs to be driven by daring, passion, and hard work.

Can ruling and opposition political parties play a role here? They can facilitate their agenda of strengthening the economy and reducing unemployment by motivating SMEs to sustain and grow.

Micro-judgment from eight socio-behavioral clusters

As per continuous social research, irrespective of income and social class, the 21st century is witnessing eight socio-behavioral clusters (see Figure 2.2). The behavior traits comprise individuals who are low key, value seekers, sober, flamboyant, novelty seekers, critical, techy, and gizmo lovers. This is a change from 20th century's socioeconomic classes and 19th century's colonial agrarian classes. The power of micro-judgment influenced by every individual's behavior is what makes or breaks a brand today. That is why all products are specifically positioned in the market to appeal to selected socio-behavioral clusters.

Just as social inclusion is important for a brand, political parties need passion to enter the social cauldron. They have to understand and care for their political base. Furthermore, micro-segmentation of Zappers to fine-tune their political future may be required, the way brands are micro-segmented for penetration and consumption. Or will caste politics continue to rule?

Figure 2.2 Eight Socio-behavioral Clusters

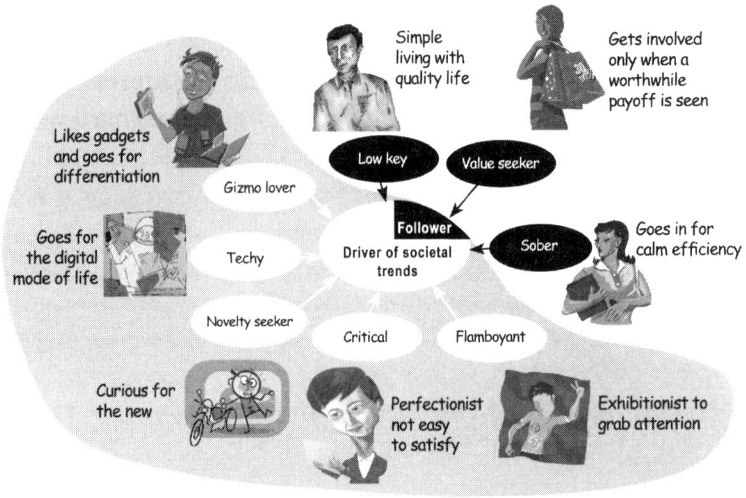

Likes gadgets and goes for differentiation — Gizmo lover

Simple living with quality life — Low key

Gets involved only when a worthwhile payoff is seen — Value seeker

Goes for the digital mode of life — Techy

Follower — Driver of societal trends — Sober — Goes in for calm efficiency

Novelty seeker

Curious for the new

Critical — Perfectionist not easy to satisfy

Flamboyant — Exhibitionist to grab attention

Source: Author's original illustration.

Crunching the distance from rural to metro

Every Indian marketer's nightmare is reaching rural areas. In the marketer's mind it is equivalent to long distances, bad infrastructure, and non-commutable. But these physical barriers have been crunched by virtual media, and are scheduled to shrink more. What is happening in metros, urban, and small cities is almost transparent to people in the rural areas through mobile electronic media and cyber communication.

Rural people will not remain silent for long. They have understood that they constitute the larger vote bank, yet development happens in metros or urban areas only. How soon can politicians bring prosperity to 600,000 small villages, each with a population of 1,200–6,000 people? If they cannot, for lack of livelihood opportunities, these people will be compelled to continue moving to big cities, and grow 21st-century slums at an alarming rate.

Voters exercise their democratic right, and elect representatives to govern. Politicians have to broaden their shoulders now. The masses, no longer spectators, expect their leaders to facilitate for them a better livelihood and lifestyle. From the lowly paid to billionaires, everyone wants to enjoy the fruits of our free economy.

POLITICS OF ROOTLESSNESS

In the free economy of today's digital-technology era, it is possible to connect on a global platform from the lowly paid to billionaires alike, but does our political structure embrace that?

All mixed up

India's constitution has been downloaded from those of eight countries, the UK, US, Ireland, France, Canada, Australia, Malaysia, Japan, and the Weimar Constitution, as well as the UN's Universal Declaration of Human Rights. Enunciating liberal democracy principles from Western legal traditions, the structure of our political functioning is a hotchpotch, with no roots in India's diverse way of life.

Indian media is focused on politics and politicians; democracy is a buzzword in this unique, multicultural society. Different Western societies have embraced democracy in their countries after distilling its various implications.

Up to 1947 democracy was not grounded in Indian soil, so its fundamentals are not rooted here.

As we know it, democracy originated in ancient Greece. Philosopher Plato said democracy was "rule by the governed" as opposed to monarchical "rule by an individual" or oligarchy "ruled by a small elite class." Vaishali, in what is now Bihar, was among the world's first governments practicing democratic ways similar to those in ancient Greece. Scattered evidence shows that democratic institutions in India's independent *sanghas* and *gana*s, "republics", existed in the sixth century BC up to the fourth century AD, but no pure historical source from that period exists.

Since our independence, Indian politicians have been comfortable in the amorphous political structure largely fashioned by the British Crown. Many leading freedom fighters such as Mahatma Gandhi, Jawaharlal Nehru, B.R. Ambedkar, Chittaranjan Das, Subhas Chandra Bose, Womesh Chandra Bonnerjee, and Pakistan's Muhammad Ali Jinnah and Liaquat Ali Khan studied or lived in England. Others such as Rajendra Prasad, Maulana Abul Kalam Azad, Khan Abdul Ghaffar Khan, Muzaffar Ahmed, M.N. Roy, and Bipin Chandra Pal came from wealthy families. So how far they understood the plight of the poor is open to question.

Different faces of an ideology

History shows that even if a foreign ideology is followed, countries adapt it to become relevant to their own political systems. The US has a free capitalist economy, but others in the Group of Eight (G8) countries have their socio-politico-economies clearly rooted in their own values and histories.

Let us take Karl Marx's communist ideology. Different nations have adopted it differently, translating it dictatorially at times. But the key point is that communism was made relevant to the societies in which it was adopted.

Russia

Bolshevik Vladimir Lenin's form of communism was to lead workers in Russia's October Revolution of 1917. Following decades of turmoil, Mikhail Gorbachev introduced glasnost (openness) and perestroika (restructuring), and by 1991, the Soviet Union had dissolved.

China

Maoism is the Marxist–Leninist trend of communism where Mao Zedong declared a Cultural Revolution in China in 1969 to purge "liberal bourgeois" elements. Without changing its communist ideology, China has today become a world power both economically and politically.

Cuba

Fidel Castro, along with "Che" Guevara, overthrew Cuba's dictator Batista in 1959 through guerrilla communist tactics. His government nationalized property and businesses owned by upper-class Cubans, including the plantations of Fidel Castro's family.

France

The world's first revolution against the monarchy occurred in France in 1789. The left and right wings in politics derives from seating arrangements in the Assemblée Nationale (French National Assembly) when the more radical Jacobin deputies sat on benches on the left-hand side. In 1905, the various Marxist parties merged. In 1934, thousands of French workers went on strike against unpaid holidays. This prompted the labor minister Jean-Baptiste Lebas to provide, in 1936, for the first time in the world, two weeks' paid vacation each year for workers. He also introduced the 40-hour workweek instead of the 47 hours then prescribed by the convention of the International Labour Organization.

UK

Since the 1920s UK has had two principal political parties, the Conservative Party and the Labour Party, the latter inspired by communism. In spite of Churchill's heroism in World War II, Labour got a landslide victory in 1945. Labour's revulsion of Hitler's dictatorial ways, and solidarity toward the anti-imperialist struggle in India speeded up Britain's immediate exit from its several colonies around the world. Therefore the change in British politics was of great relevance to, and instrumental to India's independence.

Democracy preparations

A high-level professional school for political leaders is what India lacks. It would have given leaders knowledge on how best to govern the country as per India's political roots.

In France, Charles de Gaulle created the École Nationale d'Administration (ÉNA) after World War II. Having a system based on academic proficiency and competitive examinations made recruitment to top positions more transparent. It was without suspicion of political or personal preference. ÉNA alumni enter politics without risk, while others hold technical, civil service, and global industry positions. French presidents from ÉNA were Valéry Giscard d'Estaing, Jacques Chirac, and François Hollande, while government heads were Laurent Fabius, Michel Rocard, Édouard Balladur, Alain Juppé, Lionel Jospin, and Dominique de Villepin.

Leading parties in India have generally not understood that winning majority votes means they now run a democratic government for everybody. So chief ministers and prime ministers have to stand isolated from their political parties during their tenure in office. The government has an opposition in the legislature, but in a democracy, the population, irrespective of political parties, has to be governed equally.

Anyone talking about politics in India is dubbed to be in some political party. It is difficult to be an independent, high-caliber *politologue* (political commentator) who can scientifically analyze and identify unbiased points for the nation.

What is the root cause of this situation? India's politics is a medley of Western notions that does not match the people's aspirations. Aside from voting, what is the social welfare benefit that our democratic process offers our people?

DUMPS OF OVER-CONSUMPTION

In a democracy, people need to reap social benefits; but does the world also not need wise political leadership to save not just individual countries but the planet?

Incredible inventions

Today's catastrophic environmental situation has come about because of the inability to control the dangerous side effects of overconsumption. Incredible inventions have emanated from sophisticated Western societies in the last 200 years. Most things we use in daily living and business, except for wholesale commodities and cottage-industry items, are from their invention. But these very inventions have simultaneously facilitated the catastrophic situation of our environment.

Automation

The automation concept probably came from the guilty conscience of how to end slavery. The official declaration to abolish slavery was made by the US in 1865, France in 1842, and the UK in 1833. In 1600, William Gilbert first invented electricity, while Thomas Alva Edison the practical light bulb in 1879. Light was the most significant invention toward automation. It eased the end of bonded labor, but helped the beginning of environment deterioration.

Carbon emission

Carbon dioxide (CO_2) emission from burning coal, gas, and oil to generate electricity or run our cars has caused global warming, the gases enveloping the earth like a blanket, capturing solar heat that would otherwise be radiated into space. Atmospheric CO_2 levels rose 36 percent in the last 250 years, half of which did so only from the last decades of the 20th century. During the past 50 years, atmospheric CO_2 has increased by 22 percent.

With just 5 percent of the world's population, the US consumes a quarter of the world's oil. North America's buildings release 2,200 megatons of CO_2 annually, and the US transportation sector emitted almost 1,700 megatons of CO_2 in the year 2000.

Chlorofluorocarbons (CFCs)

In addition, the invention of spray cans and refrigerants that release CFCs has created that hole in the earth's stratosphere. CFCs remain in the atmosphere for over a century, increase ozone depletion, and expose us to ultraviolet rays that lead to biological consequences such as skin cancer, cataracts, damage to plants, and reduction in the ocean's plankton populations.

Al Gore sensitized the world about the West being the biggest culprit in global environment disasters. For exposing these American scandals he was awarded the Nobel Peace Prize. In fact, using technology is the new method to dominate the world.

Nuclear energy

Look at the kind of horse racing going on to establish superior might with the world's biggest pollutant, nuclear tests. The atom bomb may have been required in 1945 to stop World War II; otherwise, we may have become part of Hitler's dictatorial regime. US scientist Dr Robert Oppenheimer was in charge of the detonation of the atom bomb in Japan. He later disclosed his devastated feelings: "I remembered the line from the Bhagavad-Gita, 'Now I am become Death, the destroyer of worlds.' I suppose we all thought that, one way or another."

But was there justification for the 2,000-odd nuclear tests conducted after that? The country count of nuclear tests is: the US—1,054 tests (between July 16, 1945 and September 23, 1992), former USSR—715 (up to 1990), France—210 (up to 1996), UK and China—45 each, India and Pakistan—6 each, and North Korea— 3 tests, the last one in 2013, while Israel has not declared the actual number of tests done. The hydrogen bomb was exploded by the US in 1952 and 1954, UK in 1957, and China in 1967.

Neglect of the green

It is regrettable that green precautions were not promoted by any nation's government from the beginning. Development of alternative fuel or energy could have started from the time electricity was invented. We need not have waited for different United Nations Climate Change conferences because wind and solar energy have always been there. Scientists were aware of the environmental consequences of their inventions.

Globalization has taken such a powerful shape that mass consumption has become inevitable. Undoubtedly, tremendous job and entrepreneurial opportunities are created, but surely the sensitizing of green, green, green could have become the talk of the world a century earlier? Show of political power, mass consumption, and speed beyond human capacity at any cost, all destroy the global environment.

Creating new types of rubbish

Earlier Hollywood would produce version after version of movies that were must-watch, now the computer has taken over this metaphor. All of a sudden a new and faster version is released, and we clamor for it. To keep pace with fast-paced technology, everybody's urge is to upgrade for fear of becoming obsolete. But while doing that, have we calculated the impact of tech dustbins?

Electronic waste or e-scrap consists of obsolete, broken computers, mobile phones, television sets, refrigerators, and electrical or electronic devices used for reuse, resale, salvage, recycling, or disposal. Greenpeace India says that 20–50 million tons of electronic hardware is discarded globally. The US bought electronic goods worth US$125 billion in 2005, and reportedly for every new PC, one was discarded. About 80 percent of US e-waste is exported to India, China, and Pakistan.

According to the NGO Toxics Link, 40,000 tons of used electronic equipment is dumped illegally in India every month. Environmental organizations say Delhi's e-scrapyards employ over 15,000 laborers who are paid less than ₹100 a day to handle 12,000 tons of e-waste a year. Other e-waste scrapyards are in Meerut, Ferozabad, Chennai, Bangalore, and Mumbai.

The processing of e-waste in developing countries causes serious health and pollution problems because it contains contaminants such as lead, mercury, cadmium, beryllium, hazardous chemicals, and brominated flame retardants that gravely damage humans.

Dangerous dumps

Also dumped in India are high-tech scrap, mostly lethal and polluting, from developed countries. The Alang port in Gujarat breaks and recycles approximately half of all ships salvaged around the world. Teams of 150–200 barefoot workers, without protection, dismantle oil tankers, container ships, and other vessels weighing an average 10,000 tons in less than three months, recovering almost everything. In September 2007, India's Supreme Court gave permission for *Blue Lady*, a French-origin, Norwegian-operated ship, full of highly toxic and radioactive substances to be dismantled in Alang. This happened in spite of India having banned the import of ships containing hazardous substances in 1997 in accordance with the Basel Convention.

The Organisation for Economic Co-operation and Development (OECD) commands its member countries to dismantle ships in their originating countries. But a *Christian Science Monitor* report says that organizations falsify the origin of the boats, so that from 2000 to 2008, at least 91 commercial vessels flying the American flag were "re-baptized" with new origins and sent to cheap scrapping facilities in Third World countries. A 2010 European Commission study on global ship demolition estimated that 18 million tons of ships are awaiting disposal, and most of them have set sail for Asia.

West, the biggest polluter

Why was it left to social activists to start the ecology movement? Should it not have hit the conscience of those who have thrown the seeds of environmental contamination, was it not their job to simultaneously handle the ecology? There is no logic of first contaminating, then raising a hue and cry about ecology protection. Sparsely populated developed Western countries, where everything is well structured and highly disciplined, are cleaning up. They are throwing their polluting garbage in developing and poor countries.

In a billion peopled country like India, with great disparities between the poor and rich, living standards are varied, public hygienic conditions are wretched, and sensitivity about the environment is very low. How can we expect the masses to not use plastic bags when the livelihood of rag pickers is to collect them for recycling?

Western societies are now blaming China for pollution. Was it not the West that encouraged China to become the world's cheap manufacturing hub? Does shifting the polluting problem from one country to another solve the long-term global environment issue?

Don't only talk, act

Increasing consumption in everyday life, making everything faster, has resulted in this environment catastrophe. First it was developed countries that consumed more of everything and made underdeveloped countries their dustbin. Now with globalization, developing countries are becoming consuming societies.

The common man on the street continues to hear about green and global warming. Has this hype been created to sensitize people in developed countries, or is it merely a confession to earn admiration for being frank and open?

PLUNDERING BENGAL TO ACHIEVE THE INDUSTRIAL REVOLUTION

Environment pollution stemmed from industrialization, so let us take a look at how the West was industrialized.

Who would have believed that one of India's least industrialized states today, West Bengal, ignited the British Industrial Revolution in the late 18th century? Yes, it is incredible, but it is true. Nobody talks about how Bengal catalyzed this turning point in the West, where industrialization later led to several environmental issues. But for now, let us recount what happened in the 18th century.

Superior Indian manufacture

For millennia India had superior cotton manufacturing processes, with dye technology, mechanical devices, and elaborate division of labor among specialized craftspeople. Indian cotton became so popular among all classes of British women that British silk and wool weavers felt threatened and rioted. So by 1725 Britain banned Indian textiles. But the demand for Indian fabrics continued. This stimulated mechanization of the British textile industry.

No-holds-barred looting

Here is how Bengal fits in. When Mir Jafar, commander in chief to Bengal's Nawab Siraj-ud-daulah, betrayed his boss, the Ruler, the East India Company could defeat the Nawab in the Battle of Plassey in June 1757. This spurred British domination over India. American historian Brooke Adams has recorded that the "Bengal plunder" from the Nawab's treasury was so excessive that it fuelled Industrial Revolution from 1760 onwards and changed the world's lifestyle forever.

The conquerors remitted an estimated £1 billion to Britain. Robert Clive, who led troops against the Nawab, collected £2.5 million for East India Company, and £234,000 for himself. His colleague William Watts grabbed £114,000. To put these figures in perspective, an annual income of £800 was sufficient for luxurious living by British noblemen of those days.

Genesis of British Industrial Revolution

So, history says that the plunder of Bengal after the Battle of Plassey sparked the Industrial Revolution in Britain which rapidly auto-mechanized the British textile industry. The inventions between 1764 and 1785 were the spinning jenny by Hargreaves, the water frame by Arkwright, the spinning mule by Crompton, and the power loom by Cartwright. John Kays had invented the flying shuttle and coal began to replace wood in smelting, while in 1768 James Watt matured the steam engine.

The spoils from Bengal boosted the British economy but its fallout was deindustrialization for India. Once England established industrial capital, it needed markets for selling its products. It was again Bengal, the first Indian region that the British colonized, which was forced to absorb these goods so England could sustain its Industrial Revolution.

The drain of wealth into Britain destroyed India's industries, and impoverishment led to a string of famines. Historian R.C. Dutt writes:

> The people of Bengal had been used to tyranny but had never lived under an oppression so far reaching in its effects, extending to every village market and every manufacturer's loom. They ... had never suffered from a system which touched their trades, their occupations, their lives

so closely. The springs of their industry were stopped; the sources of their wealth dried up.

This domineering British control pushed India hundreds of years behind in economic development.

Looking back at the non-constructive

Those struggling times made our independence movement look like momentary politics. The call was to abandon British-manufactured products, make handloom cloth, and get salt from the sea without industrialization. Did that instigate deindustrialization? Actually, the "fundamentals of India's economy" are very different from those of Southeast Asian countries; there was the public sector and private investors who could somehow muster up a license from the government to set up industries. So the "Raj" changed from British Raj to License Raj. Can this be considered a vision for India or was it just political shock factor of that time?

India today is growing with industrialization fuelled by foreign investment by developed Western countries. This is changing the country's economic perspective for the better. This development is totally opposite to both India's deindustrialization post the British Industrial Revolution in 1760 and tactics of the independence movement before 1947.

Blunders from plunder

Not only did the British plunder Bengal in 1757, they created two blunders we continue to suffer from 258 years later. First, their divide-and-rule policy created fissures between

Hindus and Muslims, which resulted in the partition and persists in pockets throughout India even today.

Second, they divided united Bengal into East Pakistan and West Bengal, aside of course from creating West Pakistan. From 1947 up to 1970, five million people were displaced from East Bengal. West Bengal is yet to recover from the effects of the world's largest displacement event, which continues till today.

My family fell victim to this political chaos and had to abandon land holdings and prosperity in East Bengal (East Pakistan). My father, his widowed mother, and 10 siblings came to squat on a piece of land with other refugees 30 km from Kolkata.

Economists say that West Bengal ranks third among states in the number of small retail shops, some 4.5 million. An estimated 20 million people are directly dependent on these small shops. I can vouch for this. Every time I return to my erstwhile refugee colony, my childhood friends have expanded a section of their house to set up a small store, as they have no other job opportunities.

The most frightening part of my refugee colony child-hood was the arrival of the land-tax man. He would go around tom-tomming a drum, alerting and threatening people to pay land tax on time, or we would be forced to for-feit our houses. Our house with its thatched roof, bamboo wall, and mud floor was small, but at least it was better than the tents other refugees lived in. My grandmother Nalini Bala would console me through this nightmare.

I recently heard from my father that the West Bengal government subsequently regularized the squatters' colony and gave free land rights to refugees where their houses stood. My pleasure in owning this miniscule piece of land is greater than having a vast, coveted farmhouse among the glitterati in California!

Backlash against industrialization

It must have been the same for landless farmers who were given land for free. But nobody taught them the value of industrialization, so these landowners cannot understand why suddenly their land is required for industrial development. People have not been educated about the necessity of balance between agriculture and industry. Without having their buy-in, it is difficult to achieve industrialization, so West Bengal's livelihood continues to be small retail stores.

After 1991's economic liberalization, while India flourished, Bengal languished. With no industry, local people fought each other for power and money, not about how to industrialize the state or educate the masses about industrialization.

Still reeling from the ghost of the British plunder of Bengal in 1757, the unhealthy blunder that continues is the lack of collective spirit for the growth of industry in Bengal today. An evangelist, an ideas person, and an implementer, who can preach to the masses about the value of bringing a balance between agriculture and industry are needed. Such a balance will change Bengal's economy beyond any political manifestation.

TORJA THEATRICS IN TODAY'S POLITICS

Politicians may feel they are resolving the country's woes, but how does the public view them? TV news channels are swaying the airwaves with political plunders and blunders. Let me introduce Bengali Torja theatrics as an apt analogous perspective.

About Torja

Politicians are highly coherent in re-enacting the Torja tradition sans the Torja decorum in contemporary times.

Torja theater is a centuries-old Bengali entertainment program of refutation. Two performing artistes, making eye contact, with participating disciples behind them, engage in a verbal offensive against each other using song. They use social innuendoes and receive apt, scathing replies. When a fitting point is made, an appreciative audience throws money at, or garlands, the Torja singer. This continues non-stop until one fails to reply and the other is crowned Torja champion.

Tactics to melt your opponent

Bhola Moira (*moira* means a sweet maker in Bengali) had become a highly reputed Torja singer when the East India Company set up operations in Calcutta. He would travel throughout Bengal, performing before patron kings, noblemen, and zamindars. A fan of his, Anthony "Firingi", of Portuguese and Indian descent, was in love with Bengali culture, especially Torja songs. He requested Bhola for Torja training, but Bhola dismissed him saying a foreigner could not master this traditional Bengali art.

Anthony however was determined. Diving into Indian religious practice and music training, he began participating in the performance circuit. In time he became so good he defeated all opponents. When the day arrived to challenge Bhola Moira, the audience was full of anticipation: how could an outsider dare to confront the irrefutable Bhola?

Bhola Moira began by chastising his opponent. He declared in song that the outsider had come to perform only to eat the sumptuous food on this auspicious occasion. Anthony's reply brought stunned silence: "May you live long Bhola! Who can have talent as great as yours to challenge you in Torja song?"

Singing with complete adulation, Anthony took the winner's garland and put it over Bhola's head. Bhola Moira melted, totally. He declared that Anthony was no longer his *firingi* rival, that he should henceforth be known as Anthony Kobial, the poet who mastered Torja songs. Among current politicians in Bengal, irrespective of gender, it is up to you to imagine who could be an appropriate Bhola Moira and who an Anthony Kobial.

Disfiguring the electronic media code

It is news when some chaos in the city is broadcast, but chaos inside the studio defies electronic media etiquette. As a viewer of political debates on news channels, you do not understand anything, you only hear the cacophony of two, three, or four people talking simultaneously. The anchor's capacity to control the debate appears minimal.

A democratic practice in Western countries is equal time on TV and radio for all political parties three weeks prior to elections. Doordarshan does that too, but how many watch it? There is no balance in Indian TV channels that are unabashedly aligned to their favorite political parties. Cyber media may not have entered election rulebooks yet, possibly because it is not involuntary viewing, people choose to go there.

Television is a Western invention with its code of conduct centered on soft skills. Culturally every country can be different in the way they conduct public discussions, but when adopting the technicalities of a Western mass-communication medium, you have to respect its viewer code process to be effective. Even in Torja where the game is criticism, the opponent has to listen.

Liberalization of the electronic media does not mean liberty to adopt cacophonic Indian fish-market behavior on public audio-visual channels. In fact, viewers feel so ashamed of such fighting that they heave a sigh of relief when the program pauses for advertisements. Is such bedlam intentionally created to get higher TRPs?

In Torja, winners were garlanded, in today's tele-Torja, does the TV channel purposely encourage heated political high jinks so that the TRP *lakshmi bhandar* (analogy of money collection box) can rake in the cash? When anchors sometimes invite the audience to phone in with questions, if the tenor of the question does not toe a particular political line the TV channel is leaning toward, the question will be mired into oblivion.

Today's politicians often talk in loud and angry tones in public meetings and on TV. What could their purpose be? People do not register a message when anger is at its base, with the purpose not visible. Only dictators like Hitler or Mussolini got away with angry expressions. Their fiery speeches made citizens into aggressive Dobermans who were commanded to kill dissenters without questioning, purportedly to build the nation's power base.

Intellectual disorder

Normally a writer, singer, poet, performing artist, scientist, or philosopher should leave it open for the public to admire and recognize his/her domain excellence and intellectual substance. But on TV channels, aside from political party representatives, there are certain people dubbed "intellectuals" who come to air their views.

Intellectuals seen on television create their brand value perhaps for future political ambitions. Consumers in villages always say that when they see a brand advertised on TV, they think its credibility is very high because it was seen on TV. So the route for intellectuals is to get branded with trustworthiness by appearing on TV.

Some intellectuals seem unabashed in their pursuit of political patronage. A painter, for example, may have certain political leanings, but his/her viewers can harbor any opposing ideology. They need not see the paintings from a political angle. Picasso was a known communist, but everyone, irrespective of their political affiliations, loved his paintings. Capitalists in particular raised the value of Picasso's paintings and made him world famous.

When intellectuals directly manifest affiliation to a political party in a public debate, they immediately abuse their intellectual stature to become party spokespersons indulging in Torja theatrics.

Victimized by Torja politics

The absence of a politologue is another big gap in India. Such an independent political scientist can analyze without bias toward any party. The deficiency of an independent political judge who brings maturity to political discourse is a dilemma throughout the country.

India's young generation finds its future foggy and uncertain. How long they will be victims of Bengali Torja politics?

CHINA IS THREATENING, INDIA IS COMFORTING

The Western mind feels completely threatened by China; Westerners imagine China as the terror that will eat them up. Their current understanding is that the 50-starred American flag may not rule the world any more; the future drivers of the planet are the billion-peopled countries of China and India. Never mind if poverty still afflicts India in a big way.

Controlled billions

A French friend in Paris remarked that Chinatown used to be in the 13th district earlier, but now you can see a Chinese bank in the heart of Paris. A taxi driver in Amsterdam confided his fear about China, a state ruled by a single party. He said their extremely disciplined billions could be driven to do anything at the whim of their government.

China is associated with possessing money power through government reserves, and to being a highly polluting environment. China is perceived as manufacturing counterfeit products, having low-cost, high industrial productivity, and being the biggest consuming society in the world. A business associate of mine from Italy, on his return from China, said he had heard of Chairman Mao's strict regime but discovered skyscrapers in Shanghai like any other Western city. China, with its languages and cultural differences, is a total mystery to the West.

More comfortable with India

But the West has some hope that India will be China's challenger. They are comfortable with India because of its democracy and hospitality, and prefer India at the forefront as the better alternative. India inspires them. The question is whether India can take leadership of the world with its open democracy, communication skills, and multicultural society.

Those who have experienced India say we do not like challenges. But it was not always so. Let me recall how, after the passing of the Government of India Act, 1833, Macaulay was appointed as the first law member of the governor general's council to change things. He came to India in 1834 and found that it would be very difficult to control this highly civilized independent country if he did not demoralize the masses.

Macaulay created Anglicized Indian followers

In his Minute on Indian Education, February 1835, Macaulay said:

> It is impossible for us, with our limited means, to attempt to educate the body of the people. We must at present do our best to form a class who may be interpreters between us and the millions whom we govern; a class of persons, Indian in blood and colour, but English in taste, in opinions, in morals, and in intellect. To that class we may leave it to refine the vernacular dialects of the country, to enrich those dialects with terms of science borrowed from the Western nomenclature, and to render them by degrees fit vehicles for conveying knowledge to the great mass of the population.

So Macaulay was instrumental in creating the foundations of bilingual, colonial India. He convinced the governor general to adopt English as the medium of instruction in higher education, from the sixth year of schooling onwards, rather than Sanskrit or Arabic in the institutions that the East India Company then supported. He allegedly destroyed *gurukul*s (schools) and tortured the teachers. His final years in India were devoted to the creation of a penal code, as the leading member of the law commission. We could say that he was really a visionary, who broke the morale of Indians so that the British could control India with just a few people.

Indian mentality should change

Can we in India now change ourselves after 180 years so that we can take on the world? Challenge means not losing a ready opportunity. I believe we have everything to give a new direction to the world.

What are the challenges? Take Indian companies for example. Why do we confine ourselves to boundaries that do not exist? If a retail store selling products for the home is called Home Town why are other competing retail stores called Home Life, Home Stop, or @home, among others? Look at shops abroad, called Habitat, Ikea, Conran, and so on; they are all different while being in the same ready-to-fit furniture market. Their approach, brand, products, and retail experience all have different characters.

Go local

Global growth starts with the capacity to manage business with local expertise in any country in the world. Indian business houses can achieve global sustainability if they can achieve high localization in foreign countries through adopting local customs and hiring local people. Whatever the political resistance in Europe to Arcelor Mittal, even today it is stirring up passions among ordinary citizens, like taxi drivers who say you have to be Indian to work there.

Forty years ago the Europeans hated the Americans, and considered them vampires. In one way they admired the US, as it fully supported the Allies to win World War II. At the same time, American businesses colonizing Europe, from toothpaste to sanitary napkins, was unbearable. Europeans always liked to colonize, but could not bear to be colonized. Since then, American companies have worked hard toward local customization of their businesses and brands. Brilliant examples are IBM and P&G. These companies among others are considered global, not American, companies with high local expertise and customization.

Outsourcing, cost arbitrage, and offshore development may be devaluing India's image and can be scary for the Western masses, but not at the corporate level. We definitely cannot do away with these drivers that have created essential businesses and contributed to our economy. But they should be used in a tactical way rather than being promoted as "low-cost India" at the core.

Low-cost but aspirational

A simple example is the way Swatch managed its image despite being a low-cost watch. Swatch, the globally renowned highly aspirational watch brand costs only US$30. Yet its reputation is not that it is a low-cost watch; rather, Swatch is known to be a latent fashion statement. We have to be very careful that India's image does not permanently become "low-cost outsourcing."

The extreme-right parties of the politicized Western countries, which are growing, should not use "low-cost outsourcing" as a strong weapon to create antagonism against India. If high resentment grows among the Western masses, that their jobs are being hijacked by India, it could jeopardize our global image. We should not forget that Hitler's Nazi politics started from this background of instigating people against Jewish people who had money power and they were then exterminated.

So India in general does not scare the developed countries like China does. It is in the hands of India and its business community to drive business globally while being sensitive to being local in every country they operate in. Do not ask the world to behave like Indians. Let us take the opportunity to drive different people in the world through their own culture. Let us be flexible yet highly disciplined and with the mentality of taking on challenges, to reinforce that India inspires.

ENACT DEMOCRACY BUT MONOPOLIZE IT

Indian politics is full of family legacy that is handed down from generation to generation, like the succession rights of royal families. Even Bollywood is the same, sustaining largely through family sutra and kinship. But is this aspirational or is it considered monopoly? It certainly would not be encouraged in the other nation with a billion people, China.

Bollywood knows how to monopolize

The families of the Kapoors, Bachchans, Khans, Dutts, Khannas, Dharmendra, Roshans, Oberois, Tagore, Sens, among others, have sustained the film industry where talent is supposed to be self-expressed creativity, not an inheritance. Exceptions are possible, but in India, film-family fraternity is the benchmark. However, when individual craftsmanship, which is not hidden, as in music and sports, tries to ride on heritage, it gets exposed, like the inadequate performances by the sons of singer Kishore Kumar and cricketer Sunil Gavaskar.

Bollywood's monopolistic blockades break the morale of newcomers. The country cannot be devoid of creative people. The very stars that are famous today undoubtedly debuted with hard work. But fame has turned them into Gods. The entire paraphernalia of films, from producer, director, cameraman, set designer, sound engineer to extras, and the media, are the ruling stars' worshipping subjects.

So it is extremely easy for indulged star progeny to become movie stars. This obliges Bollywood to produce, decade after decade, similar types of stories, dances, action, suspense, makeup, and music to prop up star children with nobody questioning their ability. When the expression of art becomes monopolistic politics, it is no longer art; it turns into the formula of a system.

Transformation to Marilyn

Consider how differently Marilyn Monroe, the star, was born. Like so many others, a black-haired woman named Norma Jeane was working in an aviation blades factory. A man once took her picture, sent it to *Yank* magazine where it got published. Encouraged by that she applied to the Blue Model agency, but they wanted golden haired girls. She promptly bleached her hair and went on to become a famous model; then changed her name and became a famous film star.

Just look at this perspective: when black hair became blond, it made all the difference, intertwining Marilyn's identity with blond hair for all time to come. It shows that the silver screen is a big manipulator.

Can commoners make it?

The Indian media gets sucked into popularizing star families by reporting candid intra-family relationships. For example, different members of the star's family will talk about the mother's tenderness, the father's ingenuity, human qualities of the son, or appreciate the daughter-in-law. As a "commoner" your dream of becoming a great actor one day will forever remain suppressed as you compete with star children of doubtful acting caliber, ill-gotten publicity gains, no box-office hits, but the advantage of family heritage that Bollywood kowtows to.

Manufacturing and service industries in India use this kind of legacy to establish their brand. They may not have found any better industrial platform of quality. The Bachchan father and son have supposedly brought "stature and youthfulness" in advertising a car together. Cricket star Pataudi advertised royal paints and passed on the mantle to his son, second-generation actor, Saif Ali Khan. Don't establishing brands with such references reek of force fitting?

In 2007, the US produced only 453 films as opposed to 1,164 films produced in India. The *Hollywood Reporter* conducted the StarPower 2002 survey on Hollywood's most bankable stars, and ranked 1,000 top-selling actors on their bankability. On the other hand, *Indian Cinema News* reported in 2008 that in spite of India producing the highest number of films in the world annually, "the dependence of the entire filmdom on half-a-dozen saleable stars and even lesser number of production houses is bad economics.

Yash Raj Films and Karan Johar's Dharma Productions share this set of saleable actors."

Other production houses are dubbed mavericks, close-knit family affairs, corporate moneybags, or working in silos. Bollywood dampens the spirit of newcomers, so hope-fuls without film-family connections use shock therapy, as Mallika Sherawat did, to grab attention and successfully release her creativity.

Monopoly in politics

In the same vein, monopolistic legacy is the backbone of our nation's political system. I may not agree with Mahatma Gandhi's politics. But that he did not dominate politics through his family members, in spite of having such mass adulation countrywide, is certainly highly admirable. The biggest voter list in India comprises the underprivileged people where illiteracy is very high.

The British Raj made the *babu* (administrator) culture so effective that poor Indians always did, and still do, con-sider rich people as their *babujis*. As respect for the rich is entrenched in India, left movements like the Bolshevik or Chinese revolution could not grow here. Most of India's feudal lords and landowners went into politics after inde-pendence, and are growing like banyan trees.

Strong family power and respect for heritage allow political families to retain their controlling foothold, genera-tion after generation, even if, by origin, they are not Indian. At the same time, if an Indian in the same family has a dif-fering opinion, that member can be totally cornered. Even after the death of a politician, or if a politician is discredited because of corruption, overnight, a son or wife can become the replacement candidate. This certainly is hardcore monopoly of politics in the name of democracy. More disgraceful are the sycophants surrounding that power. They feed the legacy that only that leader can be supreme.

Much public adherence is required to maintain this monopoly of politicians over generations. Does it mean that our country lacks political intellectuals, that we only have a set of legacy families who can dominate as politicians? The 2014 parliamentary election has broken that hegemony to prove that the time for non-dynastic politicians has come. Let us hope that democratic process trickles down to politics at every level of governance.

Such family continuity is not comparable in business as economic power is technical by nature. A first-generation businessman puts in all his effort and risks his own money, to grow his business. So it is quite normal that he bequeaths it to his family. His inheritors do not necessarily run the company; they can own it and appoint professionals to run it. Here they are not playing with public fame or money.

In the liberalized economy, with many avenues opening up and extracurricular activities in and outside schools, let us hope the monopoly of stars and politicians will decisively break, sooner than later.

STUMPED BY SEX

Having watched dynastic politics and power-grabbing in India and Bollywood, let me scrutinize events relating to my adoptive country, France. Having lived there since 1973, I have become a French citizen.

So when the shocking news broke, of Frenchman Dominique Strauss-Kahn possibly having to spend 74 years and 3 months in jail in the US, I was all ears. Was this a

Hollywood movie? A shrieking can of worms was let loose. This hot plot was a blend of sex, money, politics, reputation, women, crime, and outrage. Did the chief of the International Monetary Fund sexually assault a hotel chambermaid in New York May 14, 2011? For that, was he slapped with seven charges, all of which he denied?

Hullaballoo that even changed women's uniform

The upshot of this case even changed the dress code of New York's Sofitel Hotel chambermaids from skirts to trousers. Supposedly the mechanism of taking off trousers makes women less vulnerable to unwanted sexual advances. How did they find Strauss-Kahn, one of the world's most powerful decision-makers, to arrest him? He was the guy who disbursed billions of dollars of international funds, decided on bailout packages for countries in extreme recessionary crises.

When Strauss-Kahn called his hotel to enquire if he left behind his mobile phone, the police heard, and got into action. They rushed to the aircraft about to leave for Paris, entered the first-class cabin and got kudos from a section of society for "retrieving a criminal from his escape bid." Paraded handcuffed before TV cameras in court, Strauss-Kahn was packed off to maximum-security prison Rikers Island where diehard criminals serve tough sentences. He was put on suicide watch.

Hubbub let loose

Simultaneously, pandemonium had broken out internationally. The press ran amok, detailing every move, speculating

reasons, consequences, dissecting and bisecting Strauss-Kahn's character, and unearthing his alleged romps with prostitutes from different countries. Women's groups found much to add in the cause for justice to rape victims.

France was in utter shock, and severely criticized the US judicial system. Strauss-Kahn was tipped to contest and win the 2012 presidential election as the Socialist Party candidate. The French could not believe that on a woman's complaint, and sans any proof, American police are empowered to take the ferocious action of relegating a responsible, high-profile public official to solitary confinement, destroying his reputation, snatching away his job, even destabilizing another country's election process.

There was even gambling on whether Strauss-Kahn's French political opponents orchestrated this. Tabloid website *Le Post* said the first person to tweet the arrest, even before the arrest, was Jonathan Pinet, an activist in the French right-wing UMP party then in power. Pinet said he got the news from his friend who works at the hotel. *Le Post* said the first person to re-tweet Pinet was Arnaud Dassier, who had previously been implicated in revealing anti–Strauss-Kahn material. And the first website to mention the news, before the *New York Post* broke the story, was *24heuresactu*, a right-wing blog.

To Strauss-Kahn's defense

"I don't believe for a single second the accusations of sexual assault by my husband," said the ex-IMF chief's third wife then, Anne Sinclair, who is more famous than this second husband she married in 1991. The couple has been divorced since in March 2013. I was an avid fan of her brilliant TV show called *7/7* in the 1980s. Her 500+ interviews included those with Presidents François Mitterrand, Mikhail Gorbachev, and Bill Clinton, and stars Yves Montand and Madonna. A wealthy heiress, her grandfather Paul Rosenberg was the art dealer of Picasso, Braque, and Matisse, she rushed to New York, bringing "brains, beauty & cash to save her man," reported the website Whatsonsanya.

She hired the best lawyers, put up US$6 million in bail and spent US$50,000 a month to rent a New York apartment to live in house arrest with her husband. He had to wear a non-removable electronic security tag on his ankle. She also paid US$200,000 a month for round-the-clock armed guards as per mandatory rules to prevent his escape. From the beginning Strauss-Kahn had stated it was consensual sex, that he had seduced the chambermaid. Women have criticized her tolerance, but Anne Sinclair was determined to prove that her husband was not a rapist.

Tables turned

Then suddenly the tables turned. In a stunning court hearing on July 1, 2011, Strauss-Kahn was freed from house arrest. His security tag was removed, bail money returned. What happened?

Prosecutors admit to "serious credibility issues" with his 32-year-old Guinean-immigrant accuser. The *Daily Mail* in the UK reported:

> Two official sources said the unnamed woman, within a day of her encounter with Strauss-Kahn, spoke telephonically to an imprisoned alleged drug dealer who is accused of possessing 400lb of marijuana. In the recorded conversation she reportedly discussed possible benefits of pursuing charges against Strauss-Kahn.

One paper even said she was a sex worker. It appears the maid's bank account over the past two years had cash deposits of over $62,000, and her five phones ran up hundreds of dollars bills every month, although she admitted to possessing one phone only.

Prosecutors said that the alleged victim had falsified her 2004 application for asylum in the US. She said she lied that Guinean soldiers gang-raped her, and tortured her husband who died in jail. She also admitted to tax fraud, and lied about "a variety of additional topics concerning her history, background, present circumstances and personal relationships."

She then changed her original police statement that

she fled to an area of the main hallway of the hotel's 28th floor, waited until she observed the defendant leave suite 2806 and the 28th floor by entering an elevator. Now she says that after the alleged incident she proceeded to clean a nearby room, then returned to suite 2806, began to clean that suite before she reported the incident to her supervisor.

She allegedly owned up to falsely claiming a friend's child as her own to get a higher tax refund.

Silver-screen style

Is this Hollywood film-like episode of display of American bigness sounding like a Bollywood entertainment fantasy? In the frightening movie *Jaws*, the shark at sea was only a robot shot in a big pond at Universal Studios, a background screen created the skyline. But this was real life.

SEX-THEATRICS OF POLITICAL LEADERS

Sexual harassment was probably unknown when monarchs reigned with all-pervading command. Emperors, kings, feudal lords womanized to their libido-fill. The spectator-public scarcely raised a murmur, the sought-after girls enjoyed luxuries denied to commoners.

Democracy infringes on sex lives of leaders

Then along came the 1789 French Revolution, which eventually led to 20th-century democracy. Political color changed in fits and starts, kingdoms became democracies, and most countries won rule by the people, of the people, for the people. Political leaders who have since sprung up are human too. Power fostered their foibles, just like yesteryear's rulers.

So should it surprise us when the heads of power-hungry politicians became bloated with new-found authority? Their primitive instincts, the unconscious sexual energy of Freudian fame, storm out of their id?

French experience

France has historically been secretive about the private lives of politicians. Until the non-fiction potboiler *Sexus Politicus* (2006) by Christophe Deloire and Christophe Dubois declared that a successful politician is also a seductive politician in France. The book revealed that President Félix Faure (1895–1899) died in the bed of his mistress.

Tellingly, Edgar Faure, prime minister in the 1950s made "President of the Council" said, "When I was a minister, some women resisted me. Once I became president, not even one." Deloire and Dubois quote an unsubstantiated story in Guy Birenbaum's 2003 book, *Nos delits d'inities* (Our Insider Trading), about President Jacques Chirac fathering a child with a Japanese mistress, and enquire whether President Valéry Giscard d'Estaing really had as many mistresses as the Paris salons claimed.

It seems even political disgrace is not new in France. President Valéry Giscard d'Estaing in 1975 declared President Jean-Bédel Bokassa of the Central African Republic his "friend and family member." France supported him with financial and military backing as he declared himself emperor in 1977. When his empire fell in 1979, Bokassa went into exile and wrote his memoirs. He claimed he had shared women with Giscard d'Estaing, and gifted him diamonds worth a quarter of a million dollars in 1973 when he was the finance minister. Giscard lost his 1981 re-election bid when the scandal broke.

French broadmindedness was illustrated when President François Mitterrand bore a daughter out of wedlock, and both mistress and illegitimate child were invited by Mrs Mitterrand to attend her husband's public funeral. France also accepted Ségolène Royal as a Presidential candidate (2007) in spite of her not being married to her children's father, François Hollande. Then Hollande was accepted as the President, even when he fathered four children without marrying their mother, had a live-in relationship with a twice-divorced woman on entering Élysée Palace, the official Presidential residence, has since broken off with her and started an affair with another woman.

Roland Dumas, Mitterrand's foreign minister, was convicted and sent to six months in prison, along with his mistress, Christine Deviers-Joncour, who was sentenced to 18 months, in a 2001 sleaze scandal. He allegedly pulled strings to appoint a new president of the state-owned company Elf Oil. In return his mistress Christine got an Elf job, unlimited credit on her credit card, an apartment worth US$1.7 million, and £6.4 million from Elf in four years. The *Independent* said Dumas and Christine, 25 years younger to him, "became very public lovers, although both had other affairs." When released from prison Christine defiantly wrote a tell-all bestseller calling it and herself *Whore of the Republic*.

The high-pitched sex saga of "hot rabbit" Dominique Strauss-Kahn, ex-IMF chief, occupied tremendous media space. The French said, on TV, that a rapist and seducer are not the same, seducing is a human right. Call-girl suppliers and journalists are tumbling out stories on Strauss-Kahn's uncontrolled sexual imprudence. Strauss-Kahn on his part has alleged that for political gain, agents loyal to Sarkozy had had a hand in politicizing a sex scandal in May 2011 that cost him his job and political future, as per extracts from Edward Epstein's ebook, *Three Days in May—Sex, Surveillance, and DSK* released to British daily the *Guardian*.

American exploits

Then California erupted with another sex scandal. Former governor Arnold Schwarzenegger confessed that his housekeeper of 20 years had borne him an illegitimate child. His wife, President Kennedy's niece, pressed the divorce button. *Los Angeles Times* reported his several sexual misdemeanors, alleging that six women complained that he groped them on movie sets and studio offices for three decades without their consent. Others said he grabbed their breasts, touched buttocks, and talked dirty; former child actress Gigi Goyette was paid US$20,000 silence money in 2005.

On the website Hubpages.com, Nolan Thomas writes on "Sexual Affairs by US Presidents":

> John F. Kennedy chased women like a man possessed. His numerous sexual encounters are ... affairs with White House workers, gangsters' girlfriends, staff members, reporters, movie stars ... Angie Dickinson, Kim Novak, Marilyn Monroe.

He allegedly used the Secret Service to cover his tracks so wife Jackie would find no "evidence."

Thomas cites a string of sexual indiscretions, long-term liaisons and one-time encounters, when Bill Clinton was the governor of Arkansas.

> In the White House, his promiscuousness didn't stop. Monica Lewinsky, a good looking 21-year-old intern ... had a dress with Clinton's sperm stain on it.... Clinton adamantly denied sexual activity with Lewinsky, later rebutting his story and admitting that it did happen.

Italy's macho tentacles

The *Guardian* alleged that Silvio Berlusconi, media tycoon and former three times Prime Minister of Italy, from 1994 to 1995, 2001 to 2006, and 2008 to 2011, was taught the bunga bunga dance by Libya's Muammar al-Gaddafi. A bunga bunga party can have erotic pole dancing, and in this case it was an underwater orgy with 20 nude young women encircling their nude host Berlusconi in his swimming pool, the prize being prostitution for the host. Prosecutors in Milan charged three showgirls with procuring 33 young women for Berlusconi's bunga bunga sex sessions.

Among several criminal allegations against him, on April 6, 2011, the 1936-born TV magnate-turned-conservative politician was put on trial. The accusation was that he had paid an underage prostitute and abused his official position to cover up the offence.

Even communist regimes have their share of sex

Sexual exploits under communism are not too different. Robert Service, professor at London University, wrote *Lenin: A Biography*, where he said that Vladimir Lenin, exiled to Siberia, married his comrade Nadya Krupskaya in 1898. He went to France 1910, and met beautiful French-born revolutionary Inessa Armand, an advocate of free love. He wanted both Inessa and Nadya, who had become like his personal secretary and household organizer.

When Lenin moved into the Kremlin in Moscow in 1918, he convinced both to be with him. All three had separate bedrooms. Nadya and Inessa felt no hostility for each other, and worked together in the party school.

In *The Private Life of Chairman Mao*, his doctor Li Zhisui revealed Mao's liking for "naked wrestling with young women from People's Liberation Army, his preference for enormous feather beds filled with giggling busty lasses … mainly daughters of poor peasants for whom sleeping with Chairman was life's greatest experience."

Philip Short's 2001 biography, *Mao: A Life*, confirms Dr Li's account, "Mao bathed in women, filling his bed with up to eight at a time." Mao also prioritized freeing women from foot-binding and Confucian practices that subordinated them to husbands and fathers. Dr Li says, "Mao became an adherent of Taoist sexual practices…. He needed the waters of yin (vaginal secretions) to supplement his declining yang (male essence), the source of his strength, power and longevity." After its publication in 2006, Chinese authorities attacked Random House for producing a book "awash in lies and malice."

Politicians, irrespective of countries, seem to indulge with a vengeance in juicy sex antics. Their frolics crowd up public airwaves, cyberspace, print media, and wagging gossipy tongues. Now you know what could be in store if career ambition drives you headlong into this public personality league of political leaders!

CAMARADE WITH CHEESE

From sex to politics across the world, let me recount interesting tidbits from France's 2012 presidential elections, which I closely followed. In the complex social electioneering drama, two distinct, historical Frenchie factors popped up for attention: camarade and cheese.

Origin of comrade

Camarade, translating to comrade in English, is used by all hues of leftists worldwide, but it originated during the 1789 French Revolution. It means hearty friend or confidant. The sudden astonishing comeback of the French Left Front under Jean-Luc Mélenchon made poll statistics bob up and down for a while with youth support. This erstwhile Socialist Party member and minister in 2000–2002 made fiery extempore speeches to "Take the power," create France's sixth republic and introduce 100 percent taxation of earnings beyond €360,000.

Favorite in France

And cheese? France cannot exist without cheese, the stronger and smellier the better. I went to France with the taste of Indian jalebi in my mouth. It took me a while to get accustomed to the ancient food, cheese, whose origins predate recorded history, ranging around 8000–3000 BC when sheep were first domesticated. My work in Europe is highly associated with French culture so I have had to dive deep into their gastronomy. I actually learnt from my son, who was born and brought up in France, how to appreciate cheese.

Ever since, my tongue has absorbed the taste and logic of French cheese, nothing can now shift that enjoyment and habit. My favorite cheese is one of Emperor Napoleon's favorites too, Époisses, made from raw cow's milk. It definitely stinks. To give you an idea of its repulsive odor, Époisses is banned from public transportation vehicles all over France. Many a foreign visitor in my home in Paris has asked, "Open the window, quick! There's a foul smell…" when I tried inviting them to taste Époisses cheese.

The way French people obsessively identify with different cheese varieties made Charles de Gaulle, national hero after World War II, once ask in exasperation, "How can you govern a country in which there are 246 kinds of cheese?" The political history of my cheesy–camarade adopted country is really spectacular; other societies have picked up its deeper meaning.

World's first revolution

Political balance in governance is not new to a country like France where the world's first revolution took place in 1789. In abolishing the monarchy, they taught us about "Liberty,

Equality, and Fraternity." After World War II General Charles de Gaulle returned as a national hero and established a government of national unity as the only possible solution to ensure national stability. Pierre Mendès France, as president in 1954, brought together radical and center-right politicians for negotiations, ending the Indochina war. In de Gaulle's next term, in 1958, he successfully brought in leftists, which allowed France to find the road to recovery.

François Mitterrand in his first term restored the historical Louvre with a pyramid, built the modern era with the Channel Tunnel, Grande Arche at La Défense, Bastille Opera, and National Library. Co-opting four center-right politicians in the cabinet in his second term, including Michel Jobert and Jean Pierre Soisson, helped quell the people's protest against usage of public funds for the monuments and allowed him to complete them. These monuments have helped make France the world's number one tourist destination.

The ability to balance both right and left, but avoiding the extreme sections, gives a political edge where the mass public gains. Having done that, France today has "best overall healthcare" as declared by the World Health Organization. France also has the most comprehensive social security, and free education in secondary and technical schools for its people.

Monarchy reborn

It is incredible that the French demolished monarchy to form the first republic, then in 1804, voluntarily brought back monarchy by crowning military-man Napoleon Bonaparte as emperor. Undoubtedly Napoleon's political and administrative prowess make him France's favorite emperor. Through the Napoleonic wars he secured a dominant position for France in Europe.

Until the British defeated him in the Battle of Waterloo in 1815, the French greatly enjoyed peace and order that helped raise comfort standards. Provisions became cheap and abundant unlike earlier frequent bouts of hunger, thirst, and lack of light; trade prospered, wages ran high. Napoleon's war campaigns are studied at military academies throughout much of the world.

The Napoleonic code has influenced legal systems in several countries including the Indian Penal Code drafted during the British Raj. Among his legacy still practiced in France is the baccalaureate exam and Legion of Honor awards recognizing hard work and talent. But his unacceptable, abhorrent words were, "Women should not be regarded as equal to men. They are nothing more than machines for producing children."

Working-class democracy

To return to the subject of communism, France was the first to introduce working-class democracy with two-weeks annual paid vacation and the 40-hour workweek.

So French communism, unlike the Soviet, was liberal enough to practice the working-class ideology it preached. French socialists turned the system upside down again by adopting the 35-hour workweek effective from 2000, although I am not sure this was a right direction.

Camarade Mélenchon's impact was significant for rounding up the support of protesters because that reduced the weight of the Extreme Right FN party. In France's 2002 Presidential election, this party became, for the first time, the second party against Jacques Chirac. This shocked and scandalized both France and the world, that the French people were becoming so anti-liberal.

Born in Chicago, May Day reverberates worldwide

To respect workers and woo votes, France's extreme-right National Front holds a rally to honor Joan of Arc on every May Day. This teenage warrior born 600 years ago symbolizes patriotism; she fought to oust the British from France. Actually May 1 commemorates a general strike at Chicago's Haymarket in 1886, which demanded an eight-hour workday, where violence broke out killing dozens of workers and policemen. Subsequently, across the world, socialist and communist trade unions recognize May Day for working-class rights. Except, ironically in the US, where to avoid any revolutionary character, Labor Day is in September.

Marine Le Pen, leader of France's resurgent, mostly anti-Muslim-immigrant FN party, invoked Joan of Arc's memory. She firmly opposed Anglo-Saxon domination of French politics through NATO and the US, which had sent French troops to Afghanistan.

Amour with liberty

Hollande best personifies French liberty. He perforce lost 10 kg for the French electorate, which appreciates aesthetics. He won the Socialist Party primary candidature, fighting his former domestic partner, Ségolène Royal who lost the 2007 Presidential race to Nicolas Sarkozy.

Just imagine, an unmarried couple with four children, both *diplômé Énarques* (graduates from France's most prestigious l'Ecole Nationale d'Administration, i.e., National School of Administration), both from the same party. They fought each other to become the Socialist Party's presidential candidate. Royal won in 2007, Hollande in 2012. He went on to defeat the UMP party.

AMOUR IN POLITICS

When the 2012 French election saga was on, could amour have been far behind?

Wielding the photo-weapon of a handsome hunk with distended biceps, lean abdomen, sleek briefs, the Extreme Right FN party's presidential candidate. Marine Le Pen, bemoaned the collapse of French diplomacy. "Was it an ad for Eminence [male underwear brand], or the real ambassador in Tunisia?" she questioned. She demanded that the sexy-underwear-wearing, 41-year-old French ambassador Boris Boillon resign, "for the honor and dignity of the French and Tunisians."

Playboy girl

Daughter of Jean-Marie Le Pen, who for 35 years tried becoming French president with the "French first, immigrant out" slogan, perhaps Marine is over-sensitive about body exposure. After all, her parents' explosive divorce in 1987 led her mother to take revenge by appearing nude in *Playboy* magazine. Madame Pierrette Le Pen wanted to ridicule her "misogynistic, despot" husband who had humiliated her, using "housemaid" as a reference word. So she posed wearing an all-revealing maid's apron, white cap, black collar, high heels, and nothing more. Her torrid pictures had her performing household chores in sexy submissive servitude.

Woman-loving president

In contrast, France's longest serving president (1981–1995), François Mitterand's reputation was one of *coureur de femme* (womanizer); he loved women. They say his extramarital affairs were numerous. He met Anne Pingeot in a French village 1974 while preparing for his presidential campaign; they parented a daughter, Mazarine. As president he secretly provided his mistress and Mazarine with security at the taxpayer's expense. The French public was unaware of this, as Mitterand prevented the information from leaking out by ordering illegal wiretapping of journalists, among others, as part of his campaign against terrorism.

Mitterand had incredible political shrewdness. He had joined Marshall Philippe Petain's pro-Hitler-Germany government at Vichy (1940–1944), then about-turned in 1943 to join the French resistance. After World War II, Mitterand became a socialist, but such was his political acumen that Conservative Charles de Gaulle appointed him minister.

At the end of Mitterand's two-term presidential tenure (1981–1995), he revealed Mazarine's existence. French society appreciated that he had recognized her, not abandoned her. Even in death in 1996, Mitterand made gossip headlines when his wife, Danielle Mitterand, went against Catholic practice to seat Anne Pingeot and Mazarine with the legitimate family at his funeral.

Amorous bling–bling president

Nicolas Sarkozy and his second wife Cecilia divorced soon after he became president in 2007. "I don't see myself as First Lady," Cecilia had said. "It bores me." Sarkozy did not waste time feeling dejected. At a party he met Carla Bruni, Italian supermodel, singer, and heiress, who had walked out of a live-in relationship with philosophy professor Raphaël Enthoven.

Bruni and Sarkozy became paparazzi fodder world-wide during a whirlwind 80-day romance. Their marriage in February 2008 glamorized the somber Élysée Palace, setting a new benchmark. Sarkozy welcomed celebrity and multi-billionaire visitors, wore expensive suits, stylish sunglasses, and conspicuously large wristwatches, which prompted newspaper *Libération* to baptize him "the Bling-Bling President."

Christie's International chose April 2008, when she accompanied Sarkozy as First Lady to New York, to auction a black-and-white photograph of nude Carla Bruni taken in 1993. It fetched US$91,000, almost 20 times its estimate. Two years later into marriage, rumors started on Twitter about it being shaky, that both Sarkozy and Bruni were supposedly no strangers to infidelity. British tabloid *Sun* quoted her saying she was "easily bored by monogamy." Gossip romantically linked Bruni with musician Benjamin Biolay, and Sarkozy with his ecology minister Chantal Jouanno.

Broken-hearted presidential candidate

Sarkozy's 2007 opponent in the presidential election, darling of public polls, Ségolène Royal, lost, many said, largely because of broken love and scant support from male chauvinistic Socialist Party members. François Hollande was then the party's general secretary. She had discarded Hollande in 2006, after 30 years as partner, when he started an affair with Valérie Trierweiler, a journalist with the celebrity magazine, *Paris Match*. But they hid their broken relationship until after her defeat.

Hollande officially declared Trierweiler "woman of my life" in 2010. Much to her chagrin, Trierweiler's own magazine splashed her on the cover page as Hollande's "trump charm."

Loss of presidential candidature in seven-minute sex scandal

Actually former IMF president, Dominique Strauss-Kahn was considered the Socialist Party's hot presidential candidate. But seven hot minutes in New York's Sofitel Hotel irreversibly changed his stars. According to the hotel's electronic key records, chambermaid Nafissatou Diallo entered Strauss-Kahn's suite at about 12.06 p.m. His BlackBerry phone recorded 12.13 p.m. as the time when he spoke to his daughter Camille.

For what happened in those seven intervening minutes he had seven criminal sexual act charges slapped against him at the New York Supreme Court, although his version is "consensual sex, no rape, no constraint, no aggression, no criminal act." Anne Sinclair in a *coup de foudre* (sudden fiery love) had married him in 1991. She rushed to New York and extricated him from this mess of lifelong imprisonment. Women criticize Anne for supporting her sex-maniac husband, but she is among those rare persons who prove real love is beyond social trauma. Since then they have been divorced.

Largesse of old girlfriend

Rising above the alleged Socialist Party backstab she received during her 2007 election campaign, Ségolène Royal surprised everyone by campaigning for François Hollande. France and tabloid newspapers were waiting to see them kiss on stage, if not on the lips, at least pecking each other's cheeks in the French tradition. But they merely shook hands, maintaining the high standards of their alma mater ÉNA.

Protocol issues prevented unmarried Carla Bruni from accompanying her newest love Sarkozy to India in 2008. After they married she visited India as the French First Lady; the Taj Mahal was for her "like a dream." Since then India has overlooked protocol and invited President Hollande's girlfriend to accompany him to India, which she did twice, the second time immediately after breaking up with Hollande.

Revealing underwear and political amour, France, with Paris dubbed as the world's most romantic city, lives up to her coinage of liberty, equality, and fraternity.

GRABBING AT BELIEFS

Electronic media has made Indian politics more and more entertaining. It is beating Bollywood's typical clichéd story-lines of love, hate, fight, prison, and poor man becomes rich man. Indian politics has more or less the same storylines, except the love-affair bit, making it Poliwood. Wonder why our political journalists are avoiding love-affair diagnostics?

Invoking celestial powers

Actually we have enough titillating stories of politicians invoking celestial powers to get jobs done. Even animals enter the picture. Dethroned chief minister of Karnataka, Yeddyurappa, and chief minister of Tamil Nadu, Jayalalithaa expressed gratitude by donating elephants to temples after their political wishes were fulfilled. When the United Progressive Alliance won a trust vote in 2008 with support from the Samajwadi Party during its first term, a Madhya Pradesh MLA sacrificed 265 goats and buffaloes, equivalent to 265 winning votes, in Guwahati's Kamakhya temple.

Indira Gandhi visited Ma Anandamayi with daughter-in-law Maneka, and Rajiv Gandhi, according to the news agency IPS. Her son, Rajiv, called on holy men when campaigning for re-election in 1989; a sadhu who lived in a tree placed his feet on Rajiv's head, assuring him of success. But that did not work as his party was voted out of power. During the Trinamool Congress' rule in West Bengal, instead of investing, local industrialists held a *yagna* (religious ceremony with fire) for getting business into the state. Did it work? A believer pointed out, "Didn't Hillary Clinton come to Kolkata to promise American economic partnership?" That turned out to be mostly rhetoric.

Divine interpreters like swamis, bhagwans, astrologers, gurus, yogis, palmists, babas, faith healers, *acharya*s, and numerologists intrude and dominate beyond politics into believers' daily lives. Several TV channels dedicated to religious *pravachan*s (lectures) have god-men dancing and singing in uncontrollable religious fervor, their audience of thousands following suit. It reminds you of the effect rock stars in concert have on screeching fans. Some *swamiji*s give 10–30 second predictions to individual disciples on live TV. Devotees kowtow, scraping forward with folded hands, and openly discuss even intimate conjugal problems. They seem oblivious to the millions viewing them on the idiot box, or other disciples jam-packed behind them, awaiting turns for confession or guru's advice.

Social convergence is difficult

Indian politics veers around a few intellectuals in the metros pandering to 20 percent of the population. The remaining 80 percent comprises the country's poor who struggle for a livelihood. They have no time, inclination, or choice to protest against what is meted out to them in the name of democracy. They come into the picture only when some political party herds them into trucks and buses to show "number strength" in processions in the metros.

Politicians are elected largely from votes by the 80 percent of poorer people who follow diverse cultures, languages, food, and religions with multiple deities. There is no single belief system that people subscribe to; their mentality, behavior, way of acting differ radically. In contrast, cultures with one god have a principal belief system. It is easier to get collective focus for a goal there as the overwhelming majority shares the same work ethic and worships in one direction.

As there is no single adherence point in the Hindu way of life with multiple gods, the system can become irrational, with no established point of convergence. In industry, when everyone interprets the quality practices it disrupts the laid-down business process. Just as individuals can fragment quality, can the situation in politics be any different?

Compromise deters the right decision

Members of parliament (MP) get elected from their own states; not everyone has a national political background. When a winning party MP becomes a national minister, partiality to his/her state of origin is obvious and human, as is the voters' expectation. So there is a continuous dilemma in the minister's mind. The dilemma increases when the government is formed by an alliance of several parties: should the minister serve the party, national interests, or his/her constituency? This makes the central government system quite vulnerable, and no national leader can emerge from such compromise.

Like a spring that stores accumulated force at a certain gravity to release and retract its power, perhaps the dynastic political family brands we have in India such as the Nehru–Gandhi brand, have been so stretched that they wear everybody thin. If you continuously stretch the spring, it evens out like a string. Eventually it breaks into pieces. Is this the situation with our different styles of national leaders today? On all issues of governance we seem to witness Bollywood-style histrionics. Or banana-skin slips, where the banana skin is clandestinely put in front of a politician by any of the many vested interests.

Is the Indian President PRO or priest?

The exception is the Indian President who is elected not directly by the population but selected by their representatives to live in luxury's lap in the world's biggest presidential palace. The semantic is President, but the activity performed is like a priest who is required only for officiating at ritual maneuvers to uphold the people's mental satisfaction in a belief system. In other words, it is public relations as India's brand ambassador.

Merit of the presidential system

In a one-party majority presidential system of government, the whole nation directly elects the leader, so there is less chance of a Poliwood drama. A strong personality with a supportive party can make the government stable. An interesting episode on Armistice Day, May 8, in France perhaps illustrates the strength of the president retaining control.

France has voted the socialist François Hollande as President. Outgoing president, Nicolas Sarkozy, for the first time in history, invited his successor to accompany him to the Arc de Triomphe to commemorate the end of World War II. People suddenly warmed to Sarkozy. In his May 6 defeat speech, he admitted that his personal defects made his party lose, and offered total cooperation to the new government. That is democracy and reconciliation, forgetting the past to collaborate for national interest.

Escape the banana skin

In India, after being colonized by a gun-toting monarchical, British political system, we chose our current parliamentary politics. Our democratic process seems to match the diversity of our Hindu-dominated, multiple-god culture. All politicians are perforce wary of banana skins, from voters as well as the opposition. In dodging banana skins, elected politicians barely seem to have the time for keeping electoral promises.

Only when the quality of politics reaches a higher level can there be better governance. Instead of giving us Poliwood stories of corruption, divisive politics, managing caste equations and allies, can we resolve our many economic problems? Elected representatives should work to provide employment, education, and health to the masses.

GOVERNED BY ENTREPRENEURS

I believe if Indian politicians were to acquire an entrepreneur's caliber, the lot of the governed would positively improve.

Professional politicians: An entrepreneur can set a vision for the common good. With domain knowledge and risk taking ability, an entrepreneur administers to make things happen, as the objective is to promote industry growth and create wealth for the people. But not everybody can be an entrepreneur, similarly everybody cannot be a politician.

Just as abolition of illiteracy does not come without specific effort, political standards cannot change unless professional politicians drive politics. A government program on how to make Indian politicians and civil service more entrepreneurial driven would be very useful. If minimum knowledge and skill criteria are established to qualify for public and political office, we won't be worrying whether those with criminal records will be eligible to govern us. The masses will benefit when political leaders become entrepreneur driven.

The real estate boom is an example of how ignorant, unprofessional politicians can be harmful. Suddenly a city corner gets 5000 additional apartments, yet infrastructure surrounding this improves barely 10 percent. Won't these areas become miserable 10–15 years down the line? Governments and bureaucrats are not taking an aerial perspective of what the side effects could be. From Independence onwards, there's been lack of vision or initiative to reform civic areas in hygiene and security. I've seen expensive apartments having large open drains alongside carrying black sewage dirt of the city. The foul smell reaches the 3rd floor, yet occupants with low civic sense don't revolt, nor does the municipality bother to fix the system.

Sorry state of public toilets

Try entering a male public toilet even at the airport. You have to fight people pushing to get in or out. Sometimes a new toilet has a rush of flowing water in the urinal which can even touch your body or mouth! If you stop to use the toilet at a highway dhaba, it's at grave risk of disease infection from insect infested excreta not cleaned for days. When you rush out holding your nose, can you imagine the hygienic condition of those who are serving you drinks and eats? As an income tax paying citizen, aren't you eligible to demand better public facilities?

There's the related issue of uneducated masses misusing any good public initiative like roadside toilets. They destroy the facility not only out of ignorance of the usage system but from total lack of civic sense to respectfully protect public property. In the last 10 years Indian salaries have risen considerably. It's evident from the new technology possessions the social climbers have amassed, but on visiting their homes for research I've found their toilet condition has barely changed. Irrespective of earning, unless people understand "better hygiene, better mind" to be the real dimension of life, things will not change.

Twenty years ago I came on a cultural mission from France with 12 journalists. Landing at 4 o'clock in the morning in Mumbai, on the way to the hotel we watched people sitting on their haunches at the roadside. The same scene was repeated driving in from Kolkata airport. The French scribes appreciatively remarked on the religious devotion of Indians in early morning prayers. Little did they know these poor slum dwellers had no access to toilets.

Heighten civic sense

Individual poverty should not affect individual and collective hygiene and civic sense. If we don't strategically and instantly take care, within 10 years our country will become the breeding ground for disease and the world's garbage dump. There's immoderate growth of the consuming habit, but I don't see the government or political parties take any action on this unhygienic, polluting subject our billion+ people have to put up with every day.

Disease spreading phenomenon like prostitution can easily get legalized to become a hygienic profession with mandatory medical verification for sex workers. Their customers can be trained to demand disease free service. Is it not a crime that red light areas have no easy access to condoms? Why should protection of sex workers become the sole responsibility of NGOs or Melinda & Bill Gates Foundation? The overall prevention of disease has to be enforced as part of the agenda of political parties and the government.

If entrepreneur politicians prioritize public health, they can drive hygiene and civic sense as a disciplined, project with a task force that has clear responsibility. The public will never demand such a scheme; the government has to take the initiative to prevent disease and provide cleanliness to society. I hope India will embrace a high quality political persons to change our country's infrastructure, remove poverty while providing education, job and living comfort.

TWO LAUREATES ON APARTHEID ROAD

I move over to South Africa now where political rumblings under white apartheid rule involved basic denial of liberty, physical torture, and humiliation.

"Being black is our only crime," innocently sang the South Africans, struggling against it all. The revolution to dismantle such racial isolation was driven by swaying to beats, music, and impromptu songs. "Speeches or lectures in meetings are too laborious and intellectual," said one of the black political heroes, "people connect better when you drive a simple message with the natural African rhythm of life."

In their daily life during the apartheid days, blacks were continuously uprooted from homes to segregated areas, and given passes that prohibited entry to most places. Protesters were gunned down indiscriminately and en masse, their dead bodies strewn untended. That was the time when blacks would stealthily pick up murdered bodies from mass killings to bury them as per Christian rituals.

It is very painful to go through old documentation of that time. White missionaries had entered their land, converted, and baptized unsuspecting natives into Christianity. Yet these religious fundamentals disappeared disrespectfully into thin air with the white man's craving for dominance. After attaining freedom, the black community fished out the bones of known people and intellectuals who were tortured, and gave them fitting reburials. Aside from total breakdown of human dignity, abject poverty drove black people astray toward crime, yet the demoralized homeless would sing and hum together, "Ancestors, tell us why black is our mistake that white people hate us so."

Madiba's struggle to free his country

Their hero of heroes is known as Madiba, his Xhosa clan name. Even from the ferocious, highest-security, solitary-imprisonment torture cell of Robben Island he could inspire the South African youth to mutiny against their white oppressors. From 1976 to 1986, adolescent students and college-goers revolted, braving gunfire. Poets and singers who inspired the uprising were exiled. Desmond Tutu, the first black South African Anglican Archbishop of Cape Town rose to global fame as an unequivocal opponent of apartheid.

When the world was sensitized to the persecution and inhumanity practiced by South Africa's white government against the blacks, economic sanctions were imposed on it. In 1985, the US and UK stopped investments in South Africa, and the Rand currency plunged more than 35 percent, pressurizing the government toward reforms. What finally resulted was Madiba's freedom after 27 years in 1990 and South Africa's liberation in 1994.

Madiba initially started opposing apartheid with Gandhi's theory of nonviolence. But after a certain time, he understood this was not going to work. He fled the country, became trained in guerilla warfare, and returned to advocate fighting with firearms. Students became violent, retaliated against the governing regime's violent attack with counterattacks.

Madiba understood his enemy so strategically that when he was imprisoned, he ignored a "foolproof" escape opportunity a fellow prisoner had planned. Sure enough, that turned out to be a government ploy to kill him; if he had tried to break out, his death would be blamed on the crocodiles and sharks in the waters encircling the island. He knew his country needed him, so he had to take every precaution to keep himself alive.

Madiba inspires action

When their beloved Madiba was released at age 72, the black masses were ecstatic and of course pelted out victory celebrations in song, dance, and rhythm under the African sky. Madiba bore a peaceful temperament, grudged no anger toward the white regime, but he too danced in his now-famous typical swaying style.

His powerful leadership had inspired several black African intellectuals, musicians, and singers to create world propaganda against South Africa's white dictators. From 1960 to 1990 musicians like Miriam Makeba, Hugh Masakela, and others not only sent a message to the world about the tyrannical rule through song, they also influenced world music with African beats and rhythm.

Soweto, the liberation hub

What is most remarkable about the erstwhile apartheid colony, Soweto, which was forcibly created by the whites to segregate the blacks is that it produced two Nobel laureates.

And both lived on the same street, the only street in the world that houses the homes of two Nobel laureates. Madiba won the Nobel Peace prize in 1993 and Archbishop Desmond Tutu in 1984. When in Soweto, we saw white people cycling around freely, our guide Japh said that this signaled that this is not a trouble-prone area, unlike downtown Johannesburg, an anti-aparthied epicenter.

But socially, the black–white divide continues in South Africa. Is it hypocrisy on the part of so-called sophisticated Western societies that they chose to give the most admired Nobel Peace Prize to anti-apartheid workers just to assuage their own guilt feelings? Or to keep the blacks in check, and non-hostile in future? In India we have gone through colonization, but the visible experience revealed to every visitor to South Africa compares more or less to Auschwitz-Birkenau's mass murdering museums where innocent Jews were brutally killed by Hitler.

Madiba, the all-rounder

Madiba was a superb intellectual, strategist, fighter, influencer, and leader in the body and mind of every black African. He was the recipient of about 250 awards worldwide; international rock concerts, songs, and films were inspired by his struggle for social justice. His statue adorns several public places in the world. As you enter Johannesburg's Sandton Square you are suddenly dwarfed by a 6-m Madiba, not on a pedestal, but allowing you to reach his ankles.

My curiosity was aroused in Johannesburg airport when I saw large Madiba photographs inside a garment boutique chain. Called Presidential, this store was selling colorful, African-origin batik-printed shirts that was Madiba's trademark dressing style. I have seen San Francisco's Alcatraz prison sell prisoner outfits, but what an extraordinary tribute this was to the freedom fighter imprisoned for 27 years, who emerged to liberate his country and become its first democratically elected president from 1994 to 1999. I find it outstanding that people can experience his iconic image by wearing a Presidential shirt.

I leave the identity of Madiba for you to discover. When you search you will find that every trouble can be diminished when we as human beings have the tenacity and self-confidence to overcome woes.

It's time to go globetrotting now, continuing further from my African sojourn.

3

GLOBETROTTER

Having left India for France in 1973 when I was 19, I got used to look-ing at everything the jalebi way. That means you will find me ferreting out the twists of life in every country I have been to for my work, and relishing the sweetness people there weave into their lives. The corru-gated slices of the social jalebi are fascinating because no two cultures are the same, nor people similar, just like every jalebi is different.

The globetrotting mini-tale-slices in this chapter chew on the worldview of feelings that people and places stir up in us, whether or not we are in business. How do people approach things in different countries, how differently do they behave when coping with uncom-mon situations, doesn't this also impact business management? For example, would you believe that Japan, with a gross domestic product (GDP) of US$5 trillion, has slums? Most Japanese are shocked to hear this. So they mentally deny that thousands of old men of over 60 years scrounge dustbins in Osaka's Nishinari ward.

Take another instance in the jungles of Africa: did civet "poop" inspire the inventors of email, Facebook, or matrimony websites? A male civet marks territory; the interested female emails him by leaving him her poop trail in the jungle. Animal interactions find cognizance in human communication. A slice of contemporary trend I found globally is the way Apple has crept into society. Whether you are chauffeured around in a Bentley carrying a Louis Vuitton bag, or are traveling in a three-wheeler with a bag you picked up at Delhi's old Chandni Chowk bazaar, both of you possess an Apple iPod. It is an invention that appeals across hierarchies of class and across continents.

The jalebi, of course, is even more democratic than the Apple iPod. The jalebi is affordable for every income group, it charms every class and age group, it is available and consumed in every culture across the length and breadth of India. While trotting the globe, I have found the jalebi in pockets where Indian and Arab communities dominate. And everywhere, the jalebi's connotation is of making naughty loops to purposely link a subject. Leaf through this chapter and discover the corrugated slices of the social jalebi as it traverses the world.

UNDER THE AFRICAN SKY

From California came my sister-in-law's invitation for a family get-together under the African sky. My in-laws' family, composed of multiple nationalities, Indian, American, Canadian, French, was getting ready to celebrate the 20th anniversary of her wedding amidst nature and animal beauty. Before the safari trip my wife would regularly turn on to Discovery TV channel. I found my eyes riveted to lions and crocodiles killing their prey. Was she mentally preparing me on how we would soon be gobbled up by all kinds of animals?

British branding

So there we were in Livingstone, a Britisher's name in Zambia. Just like our mountain Everest is etched with an

Englishman's name. That is supreme branding by British colonial explorers who then bequeathed their discoveries to the international community. In so doing, they maintained five aspects:

1. Missionary zeal to convert people to Christianity.
2. Discovery of unique natural phenomena.
3. Looting colonized societies.
4. Creating the black–white people divide.
5. Making the colonized speak English.

Scottish missionary David Livingstone discovered the world's highest waterfall called Mosi-oa-Tunya, literally meaning Smoke that Thunders, and renamed it in honor of Queen Victoria. Nobody knows how many Zambian natives had seen the falls before him. But Livingstone marked his discovery, and the town got his name.

On the banks of the Zambezi river bordering Zambia and Zimbabwe, people told us that dangerous crocodiles and hippopotamuses inhabit the calm 3,540-km waters. If you fall in there, the crocodiles will not take more than seven minutes to put you in their stomach. Then suddenly the river's beauty changed dramatically, tumbling headlong down 108 m to become the gushing, misty Victoria Falls.

Victoria is followed by Iguazu Falls between Brazil and Argentina, the world's second highest at 82 m, and the third highest is Niagara Falls, 51 m at the US–Canada boundary. In terms of worldwide fame it is Niagara's majesty we have always heard of, perhaps because it is part of the developed West. But when we compare, the widest falls are Iguazu at 2700 m, followed by Victoria at 1708 m, with Niagara again occupying the third position being 1203 m wide.

The C-town landscape

Driving from the airport, Livingstone did not seem too different from an Indian C town. Except, there were fewer people, and tourist information in English indicated tourism to be the most important income. The good part of British colonization is that it paved the way for livelihood of local natives. The few hotels and hired cars in Livingstone proved they were living off tourists.

Election billboards had smiling mug shots of the president; others of his opponent called for corruption clean up. It was still not clear to me that we had reached Africa, as I was coming from the public outcry against scams in India too. An insurance company hoarding displayed a big electric bulb, pointing out that you could die of electric shock, so it is better to insure! This signaled to me that we might be in Africa.

Going forward, a man on a bicycle was overloaded with plastic cans. It appeared we were back in India again. But why was he nervously waiting by the roadside? Our guide Simon clarified that he had stopped for fear of crossing the elephant pathway. We gasped as we suddenly spotted several huge wild tuskers and baby elephants ahead. They were frolicking on both sides of the road, enjoying an afternoon's picnic stroll. Simon halted for our obvious camera clicks, but warned us not to get off the vehicle. What I learnt is that if you are at their level, that is, ground level, wild animals can attack. But as they do not recognize machines or read them as prey, you are safe when inside a vehicle.

Behind the elephants we heard the thunderous rumble of Victoria. The African jungles parted as if in an unending chasm. We were awestruck as the sunlight created unimaginable colors, reflections, and illuminations in the mighty waterfalls. But when you looked down, you felt the vertigo.

No change in local living style

While our family members went to minutely check Victoria from the Zimbabwe side, my wife and I decided to visit Simon's village. Without understanding the social aspects of African life, this trip would have been incomplete for me.

Simon's village folk lived exactly like they had always done. The small round mud huts with low roofs had a single door and no window, because through windows animals can attack at night. Villagers perforce went far for water and firewood. We met a 17-year-old girl holding a baby. Simon told us she was raped by a married man. For this abuse the tribe's headman obliged him to pay regularly for the child's upkeep.

This small village was empty of adults, they were away working in another village. A few children with goats and chickens for company, greeted us. In such native surroundings you see a different kind of life from the beauty of the jungle, river, and animals that tourists get to know. You can ask whether it is poverty or culture that makes people live like this, without being eaten up by capitalism or digital-world devils.

The open markets of Livingstone were gypsy-like with fruits, vegetables, dry fish, furniture, secondhand apparel, and the occasional tourist handicraft-ware all hanging under temporary thatched shelters. By 7 p.m. everything shuts down. This is like the weekly *haat* (bazaar) on the outskirts of Indian villages, but here it is the main city market. So it is easy to gauge that investors of different hues were yet to come to Livingstone.

Here too, voters are fed up of corruption

Simon's biggest crib was against the then-president Rupiah Banda whose election slogan was "A President for all Zambians." His party had been ruling for 20 years. Michael Sata, a former train-station sweeper nicknamed "King Cobra" for his rough-spoken ways, was his electoral opponent. He had served in the ministry of Kenneth Kaunda, liberated Zambia's first president. Aside from anti-corruption, Sata is against Chinese investment. China is Zambia's biggest foreign investor, with US$2 billion invested in copper, cobalt, nickel, and coal mines here.

The day we left Africa we heard "King Cobra" had won. Even under the African sky, anti-corruption has become the contagious winning strategy.

FOREST FACEBOOK

Continuing the family reunion of our four siblings and spouses in Africa, we reached Kapani safari camp outside Mfuwe, north-east Zambia. Here I learnt of a certain ecological balance from the animal–jungle habitat we were immersed in.

Don't disturb them, they won't disturb you

It was nighttime; a guard escorted us to our cottage in the middle of the jungle. He waited to take us for dinner by the river deck. Shining his torchlight he casually showed us what looked like a big cow within 15 m of our lodge. In reality it was a wild hippopotamus that had wandered into the camp and was grazing grass. I almost collapsed! Would we become the hippo's dinner? The guard assured us that hippos are vegetarian; if we do not disturb them, they would never attack. That was tough to believe. My mind's eye recalled the Discovery channel where we had watched, in the safety of home in India, animals enjoying each other as food. Was there much point in traveling to the southern hemisphere only to be eaten by animals?

Our guide Lawrence mentioned that on average, two fishermen die in the crocodile-and-hippo-infested Luangwa river every year. He said that white tourist guides with little practical knowledge or feel for the jungle come with books to guide others. He narrated this ghastly tale of fatal bravado.

A few years ago an American tourist group had a highly professional swimmer who wanted to cross this dangerous river. He had out-swum man-eating sharks and other predators in different parts of the world's waters, so what was a slow-moving crocodile in comparison? Everyone in the forest camp forbade him, but the adventurer had to prove his point. During the hot mid-afternoon siesta, he slipped out alone. Of course a croc chewed him up in the river.

In the ensuing chaos, a local forest guard traced the American's footprints. Unfortunately, he too could not wriggle out of the crocodile's big jaws. This gruesome drama was happening just below a bridge from where another guard shot the culprit crocodile. Inside the crocodile's stomach they found dismembered body pieces of both men. The American's hand was intact and still wearing his watch. This is all his family received as testimony of his demise.

Digitalizing jungle learning

I was conversing with Andrew, another extremely knowledgeable local guide, about the jungle's heart being so divergently different from the digital world we had left behind. Andrew pointed to a pile of animal dung and asked, "Is it so different really? Look at the 'poop' of the civet. Perhaps the inventors of email, Facebook and dating or matrimony websites were inspired by it." As I stared at him incredulously, he explained the animal kingdom's communication methods.

Every male civet marks his territory by leaving his droppings in several places in the forest. Every day he opens his Facebook account by visiting his marked places to check who has responded to his activities. It seems animals can find out from every poop heap which animal the feces belongs to, the age, sex, and health condition of that animal, and at what preparatory stage of mating the female is in. If the female civet visiting the male civet's poop site is interested in dating him, she leaves her email address by doing her own job next to his. Then at regular intervals she leaves her poop trail so that her chosen mate can find her in this vast jungle.

In a day, if about five female civets have left messages indicating their interest, the male civet examines them all, then makes his life plan. Of the five, one may be about to ovulate in two months, another in two days, a third may be much older than him, the fourth much younger but has some illness, and the fifth about his age but with no indication of when the mating time will come. If he wants a family immediately, he will choose the second girl, if he wants to play around and be fancy-free he will choose the fifth one. So, who said human beings are superior inventors to animals?

Invigorating Chitalele

When Lawrence heard about my fascination for the Chitalele dance, he was so enthused that an Indian knew his culture that he immediately organized nearby village folk to perform. It was marvelous. Under acacia and "sausage" trees, a dry riverbed as backdrop on that wintry afternoon, no microphones, no speakers, just six voices were singing with gospel harmony. Their astonishing voices had multiple chords synchronized with African percussion accompaniment. If you did not see this with your own eyes you would think the dancing was to prerecorded playback songs.

The fabulous Chitalele involves call-and-response songs, coordinated handclapping, and energetic legwork. They danced to local song stories of elephants destroying crops, the tweets of myriad birds, interspersed with some humor using impromptu paper props of binoculars and cameras to caricature how white people go into the forest to watch animals and birds.

Interpreting animal talk

In the far distance behind the dancing we could see an elephant family bathing in the wet spots of the dry riverbed, a hippopotamus foraging for food, a male deer whistling. Lawrence had explained that when the deer whistles thrice, he is communicating his presence to females during mating time. If he whistles continuously, it means there is danger, a predator is nearby, so everybody, just run!

In the forest the next day, Lawrence suddenly stopped the safari jeep. He showed us the pug marks of a crocodile that had crossed that way the night before. The crocodile would have felt very hot and was going toward water. In between the feet marks we could decipher the tail's inscription. It seems the crocodile progresses slowly as he has to drag his very heavy tail, so he needs to rest every five minutes.

I marveled at the language of the jungle, so different from our metro, urban, or rural civilization. Here you can feel that you are in a world apart. What is the balance or reconciliation between the two ecosystems, nature's technology and digital technology?

MATTERS OF SKIN

Before reaching Johannesburg from Zambia, I had asked friends about the city's must-see sights and sounds. Surprisingly, all I got were scary warnings. We could be mobbed at anytime, the hotel should arrange airport transfers, and even driving a rented car was not safe. This immediately raised my curiosity about South Africa's inner picture that had not changed even after liberation from official apartheid racial-segregation laws since 1994.

Skin color decides

The bitter black-and-white-skin divide still matters. In most workplaces I observed African natives doing menial work, while their bosses were white. A week before we met Japh, our native South African guide, a young white boy had deliberately smashed his car's rear windscreen. Why? Because he could not overtake him as the traffic light turned red. The white boy's mother was driving the car, but she did not interfere. The boy toted a gun.

Instead of getting into a fight, Japh went into the police station. However, without witnesses the police hesitated. The government of this "rainbow" nation represents 40 million black native Africans, 4 million coloreds, 1 million Asians, and 5 million whites. Yet since historical times, the money has largely been with white people. They drive the economy even today, so the blacks tread warily.

Downtown Johannesburg looks very disturbed. You do not see white people on the street, daytime or night. The whites were mugged and robbed here during the black uprising, so they fled. Now indigenous Africans and Indians man the shops. If you are unfamiliar with the neighborhood's unexpressed feelings, you are advised to stay away.

Only the financial section did not move out, these large downtown buildings housing banks have white employees. But white tourists are not encouraged to be here. In fact, even when we wanted to see a jazz show downtown, our hotel in Sandton was on the lookout for the right taxi to take us, wait for us, and deposit us back after midnight.

Shameful actions even in the 20th century

The torture and indignity apartheid inflicted on the blacks, making them homeless, herding them into makeshift black-only colonies like Soweto (South West Territory) created about 50 km from Johannesburg, cannot be forgotten so easily. But today all areas are technically open to everyone. Soweto had boasted of 23 native African millionaires at the turn of the century. However that number has dwindled in Soweto as wealthy blacks are moving to costly, sophisticated places earlier reserved for whites.

The Dutch and English together monopolize the mining rights for diamond, gold and minerals that South Africa is rich in. Their exclusive mine owners club is so exclusive that even women are barred, although of late they have condescended to allow women through a side door! White living areas are up-market, resembling places like Monte Carlo. Native Africans, poor and in lower stations in life, are generally intimidated about navigating such places. So the continuous racial and rich–poor clash has made a foreigner's movement in South Africa uneasy and frightening.

Humankind being overshadowed by skin issues

We crossed beautiful farms en route to the anthropological site from the Stone Age, named Cradle of Humankind. In these limestone caves near Gauteng, over 500 hominid fossils from 3.5 million years ago were discovered, including the first human fossil nicknamed Mrs Ples, dating 2.3 million years. In this land we visibly realize how human beings have evolved to conquer nature and rule the world.

"This countryside environment we are passing has gone through many changes in recent times," explained Japh. Earlier white farm owners used to build homes for their farmhands, provide for this captive labor force generation after generation. But now the owners have hired white managers to run the farms. These managers have asked native laborers to vacate those homes. Their fear is that they will be accused of keeping farm workers as bonded slaves, and of snatching away labor rights and liberties. So a large number of blacks have become homeless.

During Nelson Mandela's presidency he began a housing scheme for the homeless. From the highway we saw these rows of basic council houses. If people can prove that they earn wages below a certain level and are homeless, they are allotted a house free of cost.

Why did the rich white farm owners leave their land? Japh's perspective is that they fled to coastal towns Cape Town and Durban so that if, by chance, the sleeping volcano of native anger erupts, they can quickly take boats to escape the country. "This burst will surely come, we cannot say if it will be in 5, 15 or even 100 years," Japh said. "White people will have to exit one day just like they did from all our neighbouring African countries."

No racial discrimination in the arts

From Uncle Tom's days to apartheid, racial tensions have choked societies in North America and Africa. So the black community in both continents has inculcated a warrior mentality against the whites, a mentality that erupts as soon as the occasion arises. But when it comes to the arts, white society has gleefully borrowed from African culture, thus enriching the arts and themselves. During his famous African period (1907–1909), Pablo Picasso painted in a style strongly influenced by African sculpture.

The seminal black influence on rock-and-roll king Elvis Presley was Sister Rosetta Tharpe's black gospel music. African rhythm and sounds, first brought to the US by African slaves, led to the creation of blues and jazz. It can be established that African music is at the root of a very significant portion of all recent popular or vernacular music in the West, including genres like heavy metal, punk rock, and pop music.

Musicians like Paul Simon, Paul McCartney, and Mick Jagger have contributed to lessening the skin matter, but it has never been resolved. It seems to be like the solar system that cannot be displaced. There have been great integration initiatives from white Americans, but their mind space is somehow blocked, the two colors cannot make the same cup of tea. The black and white races of the world continue to carry this shame to this day.

OPULENCE HAS A SHADOW

From Africa to Japan, the world's second largest economy. Iconic images come to mind, cherry blossoms and high technology, Mount Fuji and dazzling neon lights.

Unbelievable, but unfortunately true

But slums in this country of a GDP of US$5 trillion? Can such a cocktail exist? Nobody would believe it, not even people in Japan. Yet if you walk down Kamagasaki in Osaka, you cannot escape the desolate old faces and stink of urine in this affluent commercial capital of Japan.

Dilapidated, small lanes of Osaka's Nishinari ward are home to thousands of homeless men of 60+ years. I actually saw them scrounging large waste bins for food (see Figure 3.1).

Figure 3.1   Japanese Slum Dweller Scrounging for Food or Cigarette Butts in Garbage Piles

Source: Author.

A scraggly, grey-haired man found a disposable plastic container and licked stale gravy off it. Another was vigorously shaking a Coke can into his upturned mouth in the hope of a leftover drop. Two others in soiled clothes fought over a cigarette butt on the pavement that was long enough to give a couple of puffs.

As you get off the train station, you will find Sun Plaza hotel where you have to take off your shoes, and wear the slippers they provide you at the door to walk the few feet to its reception. I could only gauge that it is to prevent the mud on the feet of the grimy men in the neighborhood from dirtying their premises.

Who are these slum dwellers?

Japan, the most technologically advanced producer of cars, electronics, machine tools, ships, steel, chemicals, textiles, and processed foods, has the majority of its economy based on the service sector. These old men came to Kamagasaki either by choice or compulsion to populate the construction-service sector. These casual laborers, if lucky, get into trucks that come at dawn to pick up whatever number of them is required at some house-building site. All of them have some sad, personal story, either of failed marriages, being outcast by the family over property tussles, financial ruin, or ill health.

Kamagasaki's tuberculosis infection rate is said to be three in every 100 residents, about 40 times the national average. Extreme poverty afflictions here, where two die every day, include hepatitis C, high blood pressure, alcoholism, depression, and drug addition.

The difference in this slum, they say, is that 95 percent are educated, and you do not see women and children here.

These aged elders are too proud to return to their families in a penniless condition.

I saw veterans with thick, unclean glasses reading torn newspapers during the daytime. Japan's culture of discipline is ingrained in people on the breadline too. By about 3 p.m., they grab roadside space in advance (see Figure 3.2) by lining up their bedding or rucksack at the edge of a large public building's open ground floor. This is a prime begging spot. Office-going commuters getting off the train will pass by here to go home, and are likely to give alms to the destitute.

Kamagasaki actually has several paid public lockers in which the shelter-less can keep whatever little belongings they have (see Figure 3.3). Catering to them are vending machines too, and flea markets that suddenly appear, selling secondhand clothes and cheap toiletries and cigarettes.

Figure 3.2   Grabbing Prime Begging Spots in Advance at Kamagasaki, Osaka

Source: Author.

Figure 3.3 Public Lockers in Kamagasaki Slum Area in Osaka, Japan

Source: Author.

Global slum situation

Figure 3.4 The Homeless Poor Sleeping on the Street in Japan

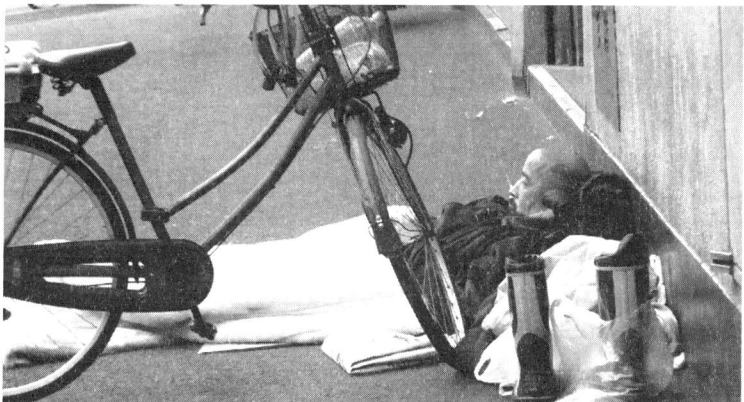

Source: Author.

I had heard of Tokyo's high-tech slums, and was shocked to actually see them. As per UN-HABITAT, a slum is a run-down city area with squalor and substandard housing, lacking in tenure security. Parts of Tokyo have housing that is cramped; about 400,000 people use public bathhouses as they have no toilets at home, and modern buildings coexist with older urban landscape in slum-like suburbs of Chiba, Saitama, and Ibaraki. I have even witnessed the homeless sleeping on the street in prime areas like under the Yurakucho station on the Yamanote line near the impressive Tokyo International Forum (see Figure 3.4).

Our planet's human population is 6.5 billion, with the number of slum dwellers shooting up to be two billion by 2030. In Mumbai alone the slum growth rate is larger than urban growth rate. Currently, 55 percent of Mumbai's population lives in slums, which cover only 6 percent of its land. Is it not time we took stock of this alarming situation? Although not all slum dwellers are poor, the UN has warned that unplanned, unsanitary settlements threaten political stability and trigger an explosion of social problems.

LEGALIZING THE DEVIL'S WORK

In Switzerland next. "Do you really want to die today?" asked the nurse, a small glass of deadly barbiturates in her hand. On July 29, 2010, her 74th birthday, Michèle Causse was lying in bed dressed in a white suit, complete with a rose on her jacket buttonhole. In the backdrop of classical music, she replied with a cool head, not a trace of hesitation or regret in her voice, "Yes, it is my wish to die."

Rituals of dying

My hair stands on end every time this incredible preparation for death flashes through my mind. I call this murder, killing someone even though they are asking for death. Do you think it is mercy killing? Just see how it happened with Causse, who went from France to die in Zurich. A French radical lesbian theorist and author, Causse's criticism of heterosexuality is well known, "As long as a woman wishes to please a man, she is inauthentic.... She does not have the integrity, the un-corruptibility that comes with not wishing to please."

Accompanied by her girlfriend, Causse enjoyed a boat ride at a Zurich lake, sat on a park bench, chatting, laughing, drinking coffee. Looking elegant in Dior dark glasses, Causse then entered a home where a white-haired woman greeted her like she was welcoming a friend home. In reality this was Erika Luley, a nurse from Dignitas, an assisted-suicide organization in Switzerland. Suffering from a non-lethal but incurable and extremely painful bone disease, Causse was here because she decided she had "the liberty to die."

A video recording of her last minutes showed her voluntarily coming to bed, while Nurse Luley prepared the poisonous potion. The way the little glass exchanged hands, it appeared as if Causse was accepting a stimulating shot of cognac. Perhaps to obliterate pity and help Erika do her job, Causse asked, "Are you again going to remind me this will be my last drink? Of course, I know it." Erika Luley smiled, warmly kissed Michele on both cheeks, Michele reciprocated. "How long will it take?" Michele queried with no anxiety on her face. "Two to five minutes. It will make you sleep, but I'll give you some chocolate to sweeten your mouth." Swallowing the fatal drink Michele chortled, "I want another chocolate, this is bitter." She then chatted with her girlfriend, the official witness to Michele's suicide act, hugged her goodbye, the nurse too, and closed her eyes.

About 30 minutes later Luley took Causse's pulse to ascertain her death, called Ludwig Minelli, the Swiss lawyer who founded Dignitas in 1998, and informed the police. As has happened for the over 800 suicide cases that Dignitas had assisted, the police, prosecutor, and coroner opened an investigation that concluded with a dismissal.

Should mercy killing be allowed?

In early March 2011, the controversial subject of euthanasia made headlines when India's Law Commission decided to recommend that the government allow its passive form. This jogged my memory back to when I had first read about it.

In my initial career in Paris I had sought and got advice from the famous Russian artist, Maitre Arte. To him I owe the big idea of reading a few classics all at the same time, but focusing on an economic viewpoint, to develop a wider perspective of the world in different areas. I used to rush to FNAC at Rue de Rennes and to WH Smith, and I will never forget their kindness in allowing me to pore over books for hours in their bookshops.

I simultaneously read Karl Marx, Vladimir Lenin, Sigmund Freud, Mao Zedong, Adolf Hitler, Victor Hugo, Bhagavad Gita, Koran, and Bible. My biggest learning about life and business came from these nonstop readings. While doing so, I was shocked to find the devil's workshop of euthanasia was crafted as early as 1924 in *Mein Kampf*:

> He who is bodily and mentally not sound and deserving may not perpetuate this misfortune in the bodies of his children. The völkische [people's] state has to perform the most gigantic rearing-task here. One day, however, it will appear as a deed greater than the most victorious wars of our present bourgeois era.

In 1939, the German parents of a severely deformed child wrote to Adolf Hitler, seeking his permission for their child to be put to death. Hitler approved, obsessed as he was with "racial purity." He then used this as precedent to establish euthanasia, his euphemistic term for systematic killing of the mentally and physically disabled in a clandestine Nazi murder program called Action T4. In Hitler's words, such people were "unworthy of life." The Nuremberg trials after World War II found evidence that up to October 1941, about 275,000 people were killed under T4.

Paying to die with dignity

The Greek word euthanasia, which means painless, happy death, raises questions today of the morality of killing. Is a pain-suffering person's consent valid, and what are the duties of doctors? Euthanasia is a pressing issue because advanced medical technology such as dialysis, intravenous feeding, and respirators can sustain and extend life unpredictably for years. Active euthanasia means assisting in the direct act of ending life, while passive euthanasia is discontinuing life-sustaining medical treatment for the terminally ill. But can helping people die be a profession? With the motto, "To live with dignity, to die with dignity," Dignitas charges patients €4,000 for preparation and suicide assistance, or €7,000 for funerals, medical costs, and official fees.

Switzerland's mountains and lakes conjure up everyone's dream vacation. At the same time Switzerland also maintains a kind of hypocrisy. It is the only country in the world that allows foreigners to come to commit suicide or to launder their ill-gotten money. Somehow staying profitably afloat by being neutral during the two World Wars, Switzerland became a haven for refugees, revolutionaries, and spies from the Allied and Axis powers alike. Everyone banked with the Swiss, including the six million Jews that Hitler exterminated in the Holocaust.

Personally, I believe in the importance of human breath. Nobody can give life at will, human beings have human value. You may or may not agree, but I do not believe any person has the right to cold-bloodedly take the life of another, whether in mercy killing or death sentence. Let us hope India does not take a decision in favor of euthanasia. That is because, aside from moral, religious, or human rights issues, there is likelihood of it being misused.

PRISON THAT'S IRRESISTIBLE FOR TOURISTS

Like euthanasia that some people connect to, the dark side of life can also attract sizable numbers, hence Dark Tourism.

Prison glorified

Alcatraz, the dreaded high-security federal penitentiary for 104 years in California, USA, fits the Dark Tourism bill. This former military prison also demonstrates the ultimate success of marketing action, that even the "Devil's Island" of despair can be transformed into a most sought-after tourist location.

Walking down San Francisco wharf is very enjoyable. There is the famous organic food farmers' market, restaurants offering fresh seafood, curio stores, and you can see sea lions up close, sliding and growling with different gestures. The misty distance has small islands and a mysterious big ship-like rock, Alcatraz, which has inspired apparel outlets. Prison fashion of black-and-white horizontal-striped trendy garments for men, women, and children are show-cased here.

The crowds on Pier 33 alert you to the rush for Alcatraz, a mile and a quarter away, used over time as a fort, a lighthouse, and a prison. It' is now a part of the Golden Gate National Park that preserves its buildings, protects its birds and other wild life, and interprets its history. Visitors can go for a cell-house tour to Alcatraz island.

Origin of Devil's Island

The US Army first established a fort in Alcatraz in 1853 to protect the Golden Gate from Confederate raiders. It became a military prison from 1859 to 1933. As it was not for maximum security, several escape attempts were successful. Ingenious get-away methods included commandeering boats, using disguise and forged documents, drifting away on logs, smearing grease on the body to protect against the cold seawater and swimming away. But attempts by stealing a butter vat from the bakery or a bread-kneading trough to paddle away in were unsuccessful.

Escape magnified

When in 1934 the federal government took over Alcatraz, they made it escape-proof to correct dangerous criminals. But 14 escape bids have proved that daring crooks have extreme intelligence, breakaway ideation, and will go to any length for freedom. In fact these attempts have stimulated hundreds of novels and Hollywood films such as *The Rock, Escape from Alcatraz, Birdman of Alcatraz,* and *Murder in the First.*

You can imagine the frightening plight of the staff, wardens, correctional officers, and security guards, who only got standard government training, when they had to manage these most dangerous, notorious, and recalcitrant inmates. Somehow they too lived with the 250 prisoners they had to rein in. It required 90 officers to cover the eight-hour shift. Some of the correctional officers lived on the island with their families but many lived in San Francisco.

To discourage escape attempts they even used psychological tactics like revealing to prisoners that dangerous sharks abound, the frigid water was too cold at 58 degrees Fahrenheit, and the strong current, 6–8 mph, would wash away swimmers. But that still did not stop 36 men from trying to flee to freedom.

The first attempt was very desperate—the prisoner climbed a fence and was shot down. So other inmates realized that real escapes would take real planning. The 10th escape attempt was called the Battle of Alcatraz. For three days, six inmates overpowered the guards, captured weapons, and took over the cell house, but they could not get the keys to the exterior door. The battle ended with five dead, two guards and three prisoners, and two convicts were later executed. By the 13th escape bid much more sophistication was used. Dummy heads were made with soap and human hair, left on the bed to fool the guards while three convicts climbed to the roof along a ventilator shaft, entered the water with flotation devices made from raincoats, and were never seen again.

Living in high-security prison

On a day-to-day basis Alcatraz was different from other prisons and more expensive. Each inmate had his own cell with a bed, toilet, basin, stool, and table. Their clothing and bedding were frequently exchanged and laundered; meals were good and plentiful because officials realized that adequate food was conducive to good behavior. After 1950s, the well-lit cells were individually equipped with radio headsets that prison officials monitored and edited. From portholes inside, inmates could see San Francisco, and hear sounds of New Year celebrations, which probably inspired their dreams to run away.

"Hellcatraz" for some prisoners, life here was highly regimented, hard, with limited privileges. Pitch-dark solitary confinement for the most disobedient public enemies was meant to be for a maximum of 19 days, but rumor has it that it was more. In fact prisoner Henri Young, part of the fourth escape bid with three others that sawed through window bars, scrambled to the water's edge but were captured, made Alcatraz infamous when a 26-year-old rookie lawyer called James Martin MacInnis fought his case in court. After his escape bid, Young was allegedly confined to the underground "dungeon" for a long term. After his return, one day, he killed a fellow prisoner in the dining hall. His lawyer argued that this murder was not Young's own doing but a consequence of the impact of inhuman conditions at Alcatraz.

In a landmark judgment, a 12-member jury gave this verdict:

We find Henri Young guilty of involuntary manslaughter for murder of a fellow prisoner. It is our additional finding that conditions as concerns treatment of prisoners at Alcatraz are unbelievably brutal and inhuman and it is our respectful hope and our earnest petition that a proper and speedy investigation of Alcatraz be made so that justice and humanity be served.

Young did not get the death sentence but was returned to Alcatraz. This case created very negative public opinion for the prison system.

Preserving the memory of Alcatraz

By the 1960s, US Attorney General Robert F. Kennedy ordered Alcatraz be re-evaluated. Among other problems like escape bids becoming too powerful, Alcatraz was too expensive to run, needed heavy maintenance expenditure, and a national campaign to rehabilitate inmates was gathering momentum. The prison was closed on March 21, 1963. Since then, fanfare has built around Alcatraz, the museum. Tourist memorabilia include steel replicas of prisoner cups, prison keys, and Alcatraz-branded chocolates being sold at high prices.

In travel parlance, dark tourism refers to visits to Holocaust sites, Nazi gas chambers, and other disturbing places to see what the world does not want repeated. I have seen France's Bastille, the Tower of London, and Port Blair's Cellular Jail, but it is only in Alcatraz that such trumpet blasting seems to happen, so consistently and so successfully, to make a negative image positive, and make tremendous commercial profit from it.

CAN CRIME BE A CULTURAL HAPPENING?

Crime is rife across the world, but only in the US does it seem magnified as a tourist attraction like Alcatraz or an extension of sociocultural life. Would you say danger lurks at every corner in the US, which is why the gun is a necessity? It is a country where everybody is allowed to have a gun.

Crime, an evergreen story

Of course Americans are scared of crime too, but they seem to lap it up as entertainment. Like mythological stories that every child listens to, American crime stories about gangsters and the Mafia, bank robbers and serial killers, drug cartels and bootleggers, gun-toting cowboys, and any number of tales of criminals have become the subject of films, comic books, and TV shows. They cover Great Depression and prohibition times to famous prisons like Alcatraz created to punish the most dangerous of criminals.

Literally millions of American tourists and other foreign tourists have visited Alcatraz island's prison museum. Here you learn that disobeying society's law gets you in prison, but disobeying prison laws takes you to Alcatraz. This maximum-security federal penitentiary, jail to 1,576 crooks for 29 years, overlooks San Francisco Bay where, in contrast, opulent American lifestyle is visible. I have never seen any museum so crowded that you do not get a ticket on the spot. You have to do advance bookings.

Even as you queue up to buy advance tickets or board the boat you can see crooks being hero-worshipped. They are on large billboards with their quotes. "It looks like Alcatraz got me licked," inmate 85, Al Capone, among the most dreaded criminals, had said. George "machine gun" Kelly, Alcatraz inmate number 117 recorded, "These 5 words seem to be written in fire on the wall of my cell: Nothing can be worth this!"

Just imagine, Americans like Bill Gates or Steve Jobs who have contributed so much to changing mental processes across the globe and dictating how we do business, communicate, or entertain ourselves, still do not have a museum on their lives where the public can get inspired, but famous crooks do. Alcatraz houses memoirs of these dangerous antisocial men.

Banner stories abound of escape bids by 36 prisoners caught in the crossfire of bullets and strong undersea undercurrents. You can join an audio tour of former inmates, correctional officers, and residents as they reminisce about their thundering-storm life in Alcatraz during the time it was open. The thrill you experience is like visiting Disneyland or Universal Studios.

CAN CRIME BE A CULTURAL PHENOMENON?

American society has evolved from the killer instinct, from fights and battles that united 50 states. Of course its pioneering and inventive spirit that changed the world cannot be questioned. A multitude of crimes are committed here not for money or drugs, but because the criminal was psychologically or socially unbalanced, depressed, or just plain bored, lonely, angry, or wanted to kill.

From real crime in high-security American prisons, writers write books that are translated into spectacular Hollywood blockbuster films, or programs that get spectacular TV TRPs. Let me portray three live examples where FBI professionals have displayed deep sensitivity and the art of making prisoners talk for reality TV shows with face-to-face emotional conversations.

Case one

Thirty-four-year-old Joe Rifkin told the FBI he was a serial killer. He had brutally strangled 17 prostitutes and dumped their body parts all over the New York metropolitan area. "There were nights I'd be with two girls and then a third girl, and she would be the one I would kill," he recalled. His murders went unnoticed for four years until 1993 when he left the 17th girl's corpse in his family's garage for three summer days. The decomposed smell gave him away to the New York police when he went to dispose of the body.

Rifkin very calmly recalled details of each of his murders. In his bedroom they discovered scores of items he had collected from his victims. He said he would use these items to remind him of the crime and relive that sexual pleasure. Rifkin is serving 203 years in jail now.

Case two

Ron Luff followed Jeffrey Lundgren's fanatic religious cult without hesitation in Kirtland, Ohio. Lundgren used guilt to manipulate his 20 followers to eternal damnation mandated by God if they did not follow his every word. He would test their devotion by holding Bible classes from morning to 2 a.m., and making them fast while he ate lavish dinners in front of them. "The whole Ethiopian famine was personally attributed to my failure," said Luff. "I remember tears coming out of my eyes and thinking Oh my God, it's my fault people are dead. I felt these things and they were real to me."

Lundgren convinced Luff that Christ's second coming would only be possible through human sacrifice. To "quench the fire of God" he chose to murder his followers, the Avery family. He made Luff dig a huge hole in the farm barn. Luff first brought the adults, tied their hands, mouths, and eyes with duct tape while Lundgren shot them. The same routine was followed for their three small children, and they were all buried. Months later, Luff realized, "I began to doubt whether I could continue because God had gotten too ugly to follow anymore." He gave himself up to the police, which led to Jeffrey Lundgren's end too.

Case three

In 1994, Reginald McFadden, just out of prison two months earlier for two previous murders, gave his broken-down Cadillac for repair. Shocked to hear the high cost of repair, he loitered around the Long Island railroad station. "There was rage, full rage in me. I decided to go ahead and go back into my hell. I got to a platform and there was Margaret Kierer," he recounted about 78-year-old Kierer who became his third victim.

McFadden attacked her, bound, and dragged her to the backyard, brutally raped her, and stabbed her to death. "I'm not remorseful. I'm not sorry. I don't fear death. I have learned to hate white people. You mark your own fate," he said.

From Hollywood films to TV reality shows, crime stories make a huge amount of money in the US. If you are a story-writer for Americans, cater to their thirst for crime as entertainment. Get a subject embedded with a crime by taking advantage of real facts of the many different types of crimes recorded in America.

CIRCUS AND CRIME AT TIMES SQUARE

Here is a subject for a Broadway show in New York.

Act one

Street entertainment

Overflowing with digital billboards and neon lights, New York's Times Square at night looks like Las Vegas, the vibrant gambling city in the US. An amphitheater-type seating gallery has been built under the famous Coca Cola advertisement landmark where people sit only to watch other people, illumination, billboards, and street entertainment events.

Naked cowboy

In the 12-degree Celsius cold, a very handsome, muscular playboy wearing just a v-shaped underwear and cowboy hat is creating showbiz, singing with a guitar. With "naked cowboy" written on his backside, he has got women of all age groups joyfully flocking to him. He reaches out to the women, and creates an erotic pose for a souvenir photograph they carry back home. Holding a woman chest to chest, he takes off his hat and puts it in front of her face, as though he is pushing a strong kiss through her bent body. Another much loved photographic pose is bottom-to-bottom. He takes the woman's hand, places it on his exaggerated sitting-in-the-air "naked cowboy" backside, takes his own hand and puts it on her backside even as he pouts a kiss at her.

Sometimes he does a tango dance putting his leg in an erotic gesture between the woman's legs. The woman's companion clicks the picture while she happily gives him some money that he puts inside his guitar as though it were a piggy bank. In return he gives her a postcard to remember him by; in actual fact it is his business card. Police presence is high here, even mounted police on horseback, but they have a very public-friendly attitude, and everybody is in a hearty mood, having a rollicking time.

Presidential condoms?

Suddenly a beautiful woman passes by, manifesting a picture of President Barack Obama in a billboard hanging on her neck. She has a tray of condoms at the bottom of Obama's smiling face. She's proudly selling "Obama condoms." Men and women crisscross her, open up their purses, and buy Obama condoms with no qualms, complexity, or fuss. You may argue that this shows genuine liberty in the hands of American people, that anyone can brand even an intimate product like condoms with the president's face and openly sell it on the street. Perhaps it could mean the president is passing on a friendly message on AIDS prevention. That really is breakthrough action.

We can never imagine that any politician in India would allow his/ her name to be associated with AIDS; in fact, AIDS is a subject we fear continuously and try to hide its existence.

Feel like stars

Suddenly in another corner, a highly decorated pink collapsible van, almost like a festival float, drives in slowly. Poster girls made up dramatically give live demonstrations of a color cosmetic brand. Women walking on the street suddenly get up and sit on gaudy chairs outside the flashy pink van to experience what it feels like to be made up and look like Hollywood stars being watched by adoring crowds.

In such ostentatious surroundings there is unexpectedly the irony of homeless people carrying their worn-out luggage in trolley bags. They ask people for money and sleep on the road. Beggars are commonplace in India, but in Times Square it is shocking to see beggars.

Act two

Cordoned off

As my colleague and I were walking down Broadway through Times Square, I was telling her about how the advent of terrorism has made European countries like France change even their street dustbin systems. They now use huge, transparent, plastic bags as dustbins on the streets so everything discarded inside is very visible from the outside. But the US still uses hard, opaque plastic dustbins on the street. We reached the Juniors restaurant on West 45th Street, had a quick bite, and stepped out at 7 p.m.

Suddenly the police had cordoned off the Times Square area with a yellow ribbon to stop passersby. I always carry my video camera in hand to collect social aspects when I travel so I was covering this incident even as it unfolded. It appeared fun at the initial stage and went on to become dramatic.

Act three

Act of terror?

We were made to walk back toward Eighth Avenue. Many cameramen started to shoot the scene. The police first used a yellow ribbon then pushed us back a little more. The original spot cordoned by the yellow ribbon now had a red ribbon. We smelt danger. Suddenly fire brigades were bracketing the road. Ambulances started to make their appearance.

Manhattan's Broadway, the theater district, was about to swing into action at 8 p.m. A few young actors and actresses were seen trying to negotiate entry to the barricaded streets as they had to rush for their theater performance. Theater musicians with their huge cellos and violins did not know what to do. An actress was pushed aside by a burly fireman, and she fell down on the road.

A rumor ran through at lightning speed amongst this public that a building on Times Square was on fire. Some of the public speculated that terrorists had struck while others ran for cover. The cynical ones suspected that the police were running through a dummy test to keep themselves busy instead of enjoying the fun activities of the street. Electronic shops on Broadway were vociferous in voicing their gripes. Here finally it was a bright sunny day and they expected to make some money. As it is the Icelandic volcano had erupted around that time and depleted their business on account of low tourist arrivals, and now this loss. They proactively offered 80 percent discount but there were no takers. People were scared, irritated, concerned, and angry, and even having some fun with this heavy police action. Every now and then they would try to defy the cops by pushing at the red ribbon, and the police would retaliate with warning words and gestures.

But my colleague and I were completely blocked on Eighth Avenue for nearly three hours. In a corner of 45th Street and Eighth Avenue, I spotted a woman police officer. She whispered to me that they were expecting some heavy explosion somewhere in Times Square. I called my sister-in-law in San Francisco and my wife in India to ask them to find out from CNN what exactly was happening. At 10 p.m. we were allowed to walk in the periphery of the heavily populated Times Square area, now totally vacant and eerie.

Conclusion

On returning to my hotel I got the news from CNN at 2 a.m. on May 2, 2010 that it was no more a hallucination of my Broadway show, it was a reality show. I was dining on 45th Street, even as the action happened between 44th and 45th Streets. A robot was directed to conduct investigations and defuse any bomb in the suspected car, which had smoke spewing from it. This was a real Broadway show in the heart of Times Square with officers from the New York police department as actors. The curiosity of the masses was high. Everybody wanted to watch the show from the sidelines, and it certainly was a hit in real life.

Only in America can you see things in such a spectacular way. In world-famous Times Square where the New York Times originated, unique things can happen, from entertainment to catastrophe. We were enjoying the different acts, and saw the face of the policemen change from indulging people's fun to controlling them toward safety without causing panic so as to ensure that Times Square would never become a deserted place in future. It was commendable that they controlled the vast crowds with skilful and sensitive police work.

A recent American TV program I saw had an administrative authority requesting citizens to help by immediately reporting any suspicious moves they saw. It is not always possible for a central source to detect acts of terrorism. It is a good suggestion that we too can take up in India to save our people's lives.

STEVE'S APPLE IN BIG APPLE

I am still in New York, walking up 72nd Street and Central Park West.

Dakota fame

In New York's Manhattan, I have always been impressed by the Dakota, built in 1884 where the figure of a Dakota Indian keeps watch. Its high gables, deep roofs, profusion of dormers, terracotta panels, niches, and balconies give it a German Renaissance character, yet it is influenced by French architectural trends. Rich and famous artists have lived here including composer Leonard Bernstein, actors Lauren Bacall, Judy Garland, Boris Karloff, Robert Ryan, singer Roberta Flack, playwright William Inge, and dancer Rudolf Nureyev, among others.

But best known as being the home of Beatle John Lennon from 1973, Dakota is also the location of Lennon's murder by Mark David Chapman on December 8, 1980. Yoko Ono laid out the Strawberry Fields memorial in her husband's memory in Central Park directly across here. It is now a public pilgrimage place with "Imagine" written in a beautiful round floor mural. Lennon used to frequent here with his second son Sean, and his fans now come, often with guitars, to place flowers for him and sing his songs.

Extending along Central Park South is the landmark 20-story luxury Plaza Hotel. It overlooks Fifth Avenue, and was built by the same architectural firm of Henry Janeway

Hardenbergh who designed the Dakota. It cost US$12.5 million to construct at the turn of the century, Donald Trump paid US$407.5 million in 1988, and Manhattan developer, El Ad Properties spent US$675 million to buy it in 2004. This hotel has been the setting for several films including *Barefoot in the Park*, *Scent of a Woman*, *Home Alone 2*, and *Eloise at the Plaza*.

The bitten apple

Apart from stories of these two century-old buildings full of artistic and entertainment memorabilia, nothing had attracted me to this high-rise concrete jungle. But now a new philosophical landmark has emerged at the corner of Fifth Avenue and 59th Street. It is Steve Jobs' imaginative idea of a bitten Apple that has become a magnet for visitors of all age groups.

When mainframe manufacturer IBM had been ruling the computing roost (from 1936), the colorful, mysterious Apple computer suddenly appeared in 1976 to invite consumers to bite into individual small computers. The name Apple was discomfiting as it subliminally conjured up the Catholic religion's forbidden fruit that Adam and Eve had bit into to discover prohibited pleasure in the Garden of Eden. Apple reflected scientific discovery too as Newton had sat under an apple tree and proved the theory of gravitation. The Beatles had called their record company Apple, and New York is known as the Big Apple.

All these other apple associations may have become history in front of this new Apple store with a glass cube housing a cylindrical glass elevator and a spiral glass staircase that leads to the underground store.

Attracting all layers of society

Just as the Louvre Museum in Paris has a huge glass pyramid to highlight its ancient treasures, so does this historical part of New York. A glass cubicle rouses your curiosity from a distance when you spot the bitten Apple. Drawn closer you discover an incredible techie bunker full of Apple electronics under the road. Every moment it is open this huge basement store stays incredibly busy from eight-year-olds to 80-year-olds demanding the attention of sales assistants in blue T-shirts. They seem to be from all classes of society. A very *bon chic bon genre* (BCBG, the French conventional style of dressing) woman sporting a Louis Vuitton bag was being trained on the iPad at the demo table. Young students were selecting their iPods and techie geeks were trying out different computers and accessories.

You become quite crazy in this fabulously designed shop where every item looks precious. In a totally commoditized market of electronics and computers, Apple is exposing tech art here, and people are enjoying the high-tech experience. The difference between exiting the Louvre's glass pyramid and emerging from the glass structure of the Apple store is that instead of just buying a souvenir in the Paris museum, you come out of the Fifth Avenue Apple store carrying a happening product from a 21st-century museum.

Cultural phenomenon

Steve Jobs undoubtedly imagined that a 21st-century-category product invention has to be introduced by creating a cultural phenomenon. He did this through a store that allows all kinds of consumers, from the rich to the poor, to experience tomorrow. A few years earlier he surprised everyone by taking over Manhattan's Soho post office to open an Apple retailing store that looked like an art gallery, and had a large glass staircase where no joint could be seen. Soho is New York's sophisticated art district with plenty of art galleries, although many of the smaller ones have since moved uptown to Chelsea, as the area is getting too expensive.

Coming out from the basement Apple store I wanted to contemplate with a cup of tea. What better place than the renovated Plaza Hotel. A young Indian waiter there mentioned that recession had hit this landmark hotel, so they had worked out a new strategy of transforming 800 rooms into residential condominiums, and leaving just 200 rooms for hotel occupancy. These private apartments have been sold for as much as US$50 million each.

From red to flying colors

Steve Jobs was highly criticized a few years ago when Apple plummeted into the red. But he believed that Apple is more universal than a technology product. With the iPod, he sprang back, the bottom line reflecting this upswing, re-establishing the Apple way of ideation for an entire generation across the world.

Then, by introducing the iPad, he had young people queue up in all continents, and sold millions of pieces in the first week itself. This just goes to show that a man's creativity can change the world. You can debate whether he was a genius who was ahead of his time or he just had good luck, but you cannot ignore how differently he acted in the commoditized category.

Set amidst fountains in an open sitting place overlooking the historic Plaza in the world's most advanced city, Apple has conjured up totally new reflective by plonking itself in a well-established, open space.

I can imagine Fifth Avenue having its name changed to Apple Avenue one day. This could have been Jobs' secret dream. His sustaining high-value business is not only about making shareholders happy with money, it is also about enriching different generations to experience technology and muse differently by owning or touching an Apple from Steve's ideation tree.

POWER TO THE FINGERS

And then this world's all-time hero succumbed to disease on October 5, 2011. I stopped in my tracks. Without paying homage to the greatest contemporary inventor who continuously created discomfort to change the world, how could I proceed with anything else?

Steve Jobs broke our old habits

He empowered our fingers so we experience things differently, whether in corporations or in society. His discontinuity with mediocrity is the ultimate example of creating discomfort.

Apple has acquired many nuances. "Apple of my eye" is what we want to be for our loved ones. Aside from assigning values and imagination to apples, we find lots in the market coming from different countries. When organic, we pay a higher price for their supposedly being more natural than others, when generic, the apples get sprayed with pesticides or can be genetically transformed. But Mr Jobs' Apple is obsessively focused. It has proved his purity as an inventor, designer, disruptor, entrepreneur, and lover of humanity.

I have just narrated in the earlier mini-tale slice about how knowledgeable salespersons were inducting both scruffy-looking below-teens and a sophisticated woman to Apple products in his Fifth Avenue store. I was curious to see what car Ms Sophisticated left in, and sure enough it was a Rolls Royce. Her expensive bag and car give her show-off value, but a US$50 iPod Shuffle in the pocket of a basic-income person and a billionaire is invaluable for the joy it brings to both.

With his products, Steve Jobs had the ingenuity to create real socialism between the rich and poor, which both hunger for. Yes! Fifth Avenue should become Apple Avenue, the apple of Jobs.

"Reduce Effort, Increase Comfort"

The Western inventive character and discipline prioritize on how to go against nature, to have control over nature. From my industrial product design experience in the West, I have learnt about increasing the functionality of an engineering product to reduce human effort. A few years ago I created my engineering design framework to be "Reduce Effort, Increase Comfort." If you look at the evolution of human society's aspiration to live better, you will find that functional improvement has been prioritized in every day-to-day life product.

The ultimate reference of my "Reduce Effort, Increase Comfort" is the inventive power of Jobs Apple. Steve Jobs unlocked the apple from being forbidden to becoming officially permissible. You may or may not believe in Adam and Eve's Garden of Eden, in religion or God, but you have no choice but to believe that Jobs Apple is the universal religion of human rights. Jobs was extremely conscious about connecting his inventions to everybody, both for their entertainment and livelihood.

Research for differentiation

Across all continents, the CEO's function is defined as the engineering of finance, human capital, and PR. But Jobs Apple has proved that the CEO's job is different, others should manage a corporation's transactional jobs. Jobs first broke the practice of ivory tower R&D where doctorate intellectuals have no connect to end-users. So I can say he transformed R&D terminology to "research for differentiation." The common man has to perceive extra benefit in the products.

Jobs established that the ideal CEO should have unbelievable thirst to intercept human need and desire beyond anybody else. So first, he should be sensitive to human society's hidden desires; second, know the performance of his product or service in any competitive environment; and third, create a simple story to sell the product or service to the masses.

Unfortunately, most CEOs are primarily fixated on positive quarterly results, and not aligned to these three elements. Jobs Apple also proved that the digital world does not need rocket science invention, just an instant leapfrog in vision. The vision has to be very practical to fill the consumer's desire gap. It must inspire whole teams to work in an unconventional way to break the mold. The CEO should empower himself with the ability to take risks, to create the hunger for self-discomfort. Only such action can catapult a loss-making company as Apple was in 1997 when Jobs rejoined it, to becoming the world's most valuable company in 2011. In terms of global market capitalization Apple has since touched the number one and two spots.

Non-forbidden apple

Twentieth-century history has multiple examples of invention driven by struggle, especially from the effect of the two World Wars and how to get rid of Adolf Hitler's devilry. Now when its democracy that largely reigns, the prevailing jargon is to take and deploy the opportunity. But how? You cannot deploy opportunity in a merry-go-round that is merely turning. You need to create discomfort to bring discontinuity to the monotonous, boring aspect of business. So Jobs delivered a new, non-forbidden apple to the world. As a CEO or wannabe CEO, you can eat the Jobs Apple, and empower yourself to proceed in that alternative way that will connect to the masses. That discomfort will make you thrive.

Total fingertip control

Steve Jobs not only contributed to creating an all-new digital delivery, he connected people emotionally to their digital devices. He fulfilled their unstated desire of having total fingertip control. Just lightly maneuvering our fingers on the screen of a device is allowing us ingenious freedom to drive a new type of pictorial language in the digital world.

Steve Jobs' last eight years, when he fought his fatal pancreatic cancer, were the most critical for Apple and him. While everyone speculated about the timing of his death,

Jobs did not hesitate to deliver his best creative work. What mental power and courage! The digital-technology movement will surely unearth something new in future, but Jobs Apple will always remain the summit of creating a difference for the masses to enjoy.

MARKETING THE NEW YEAR

What is considered the best marketing job to date, that it even surpasses Steve Jobs' Apple products? To Christianity's credit, their globalization of New Year is the clear winner (see Figure 3.5).

Figure 3.5   St Sylvester

Source: Illustration modified by the author.

Marking the Christian New Year

Different religions and cultures have different year endings, but when it comes to December 31, it's a date representing a unified, one-world global culture to ring in the New Year. The world's longest-running, unique, uninterrupted, sustainable government is vested in the Pope of the Roman Catholic Church, of whom the first was St Peter, who was born in 1 BC and died in AD 67. Today's businesses, politics, kingdoms, and governments have a huge lesson to learn from the incomparable Holy See, modern-day Vatican. It has survived undisrupted, in spite of rivalries, splits, and complicated politics, as a sovereign entity for over 2,000 years.

Sitting in India or non-Christian countries, people accept the Gregorian year numbering system as the predominant international standard. This New Year celebration is actually of Hebrew origin to mark December 31 as the last day. Pope Gregory XIII calculated, froze, introduced, and imposed a calendar named after him, signed by a papal decree on February 24, 1582, which has now become the global norm. The previous Julian calendar assumed the time between vernal equinoxes to be 365.25 days, when in fact it is about 11 minutes less, resulting in the equinox not being on a firm date.

Since the equinox was tied to the celebration of Easter, the Roman Catholic Church considered this steady movement to be undesirable. Hence the Gregorian calendar, which continued the previous year numbering system of Anno Domini that counts years from the traditional incarnation of Jesus, spread throughout Europe during the Middle Ages.

French and German-speaking countries celebrate New Year's Eve as St Sylvester's Feast. Pope Sylvester I died in AD 335; it is a coincidence that his feast is celebrated on December 31, the day of his burial in the Priscilla Catacomb.

We can therefore say that December 31 as the end of the year has been imposed by Christianity (Gregorian calendar). A century sounds very long, but since the Judeo Christian diktat, there have been only as many new years as the year date we write.

Religious celebrations that did not spread

Of course the Muslim's first day of Muharram or Chinese Yuan Tan and Japanese Oshogatsu, among others, are unique new years, but nobody could make it as universal as Christianity's dominating power did. The Hindu way of life has several calendars and consequently new-year dates based on harvests, language, culture, or regions such as Maharashtra's Gudi Padwa, Karnataka's Ugadi, Punjab's Baisakhi, Assam's Bihu, Bengal's Poila Boishak, or even the Parsi Nav Roz in March/April, and of course Diwali for all in October/November.

Through different eras of handmade goods to mechanical, electronic, and digital technology, festivities surrounding December 31 and January 1 are intensifying. Western Christians and converts in their colonies used to have local merriment, but with subtle autocracy, Christian doctrines have unified all societies, so people erroneously consider December 31 as devoid of religion. So happily everyone welcomes January 1 in their very own celebration.

Vatican reigns regardless of scandals

Taking this forward, no other religion has a living god-like summit as the Pope. Notwithstanding scandals of homosexual prostitution rings, pedophilia among priests, Pope

Benedict XVI being a Nazi conscript, prohibition of condoms, and denying women liberty for abortion, the 'Holy City' Vatican remains recognized by international law for centrally governing the Catholic Church.

Pope Benedict XVI who resigned in 2013, was called Joseph Ratzinger; he joined the Hitler Youth in 1941. Drafted into the military, he was an anti-aircraft unit member protecting BMW's aircraft-engine factory that used slave labor from the Dachau concentration camp. When transferred to Hungary, he set up tank traps and watched as Jews were rounded up for transport to death camps. Eventually he deserted and became a prisoner of war. He said he had never participated in combat or fired a shot.

When I asked my friend Bernard Offen, the 80+year-old survivor of Nazi death camps, whose 51 family members were gassed to death among six million murdered Jews, whether there were any good Nazis, he said, "They were all cruel." Hitler's dream was 1,000 years of Nazi power. Ratzinger said he had resisted Hitler then; however, dissenters were then punished, he was never punished. His past was questioned because he was the head of Christendom.

After satisfying papal politics, he became Pope Benedict XVI, and in 2007 went to pray in Poland's Auschwitz concentration camp. This most horrific place was where Nazis publicly tortured, court martialed, and gunned down Jews and dissenters, and purged prisoners in gas chambers. Nobody can believe such brutality could have been committed from reading about it in faraway lands.

The brainwashed

Spreading afar its influence, Christianity's December 31 celebration has delightfully gripped India's newfound liberalized economy. Cabaret dancers are invited from places like Brazil, Russia, Philippines, and Las Vegas to show their beautiful legs and writhe other parts of the body. Five-star hotels encourage the "vanishing-glass trick" where people compete for grand prizes on how quickly liquor-filled glasses can "vanish." Western disc jockeys surprise with huge collections, not forgetting to play *bhangra* amid techno and hip-hop to localize their entertainment.

While living in homogenous Europe enjoying December 31 celebrations, it never occurred to me to ponder over St Sylvester's Day. But experiencing New Year's Eve among a billion people whose culture, language, and religions are so varied, I must confess to being part of this brainwash too.

FANTASY, FICTION, OR REAL?

Let us globetrot to enter Latin Europe now. In a small village on the foothills of the Pyrénées was born the second son of a strict, bourgeois notary.

Traumatic childhood

At the age of five, his parents took him to his brother's grave, saying he was nothing more than his brother's reincarnation. He felt traumatized and outdone. When he fell sick in childhood, he was packed off to stay with a family on the Mediterranean coast, where he discovered modern painting, and on the sly, practiced how to boost his ego. His Catholic mother enrolled him at Christian Brother's school.

A painting by Jean-Francois Millet hanging on the school wall became his obsession. It had a woman's head bowed, and a man holding his hat in front of his body. The boy's Freudian interpretation was that the man was seducing her by hiding his sexuality. This inspiration was a constant theme in his artistic career later, and became his icon.

Recalcitrant at school

In an art college in Madrid he befriended two other equally egotistic, eccentric, outside-the-box ideators, one of whom metamorphosed into a famous filmmaker and the other an influential poet and dramatist. The notary's son was expelled from this school because he insulted his professors. He said they were incompetent to examine him; that he knew more about art and artists than they did.

The expulsion devastated his father, whose summer home he returned to. But he continued to draw huge public attention with his mastery over painting skills, flamboyant dressing style, long hair, and unusually pointed moustache. He realized and implemented deep-dream imagery on canvas.

Finding his love

One day a few Parisian friends came visiting, among whom was a French poet and his Russian wife. Our protagonist and this woman, 11 years his elder, fell in love at first sight. Immersed in his magnetic power, she decided to stay back, impelling her husband to return to Paris alone.

For the audacity against Catholicism of taking another man's wife, his father asked him to leave home. Totally flustered, he sought purity by shaving off his hair to become bald. But realizing his unique talent, his lady love took control of things. She became his business manager, aside from being his muse and inspiration, and went about the task of milking his immeasurable talent for commercial gain.

Living on the shores of the azure Mediterranean waters with no steady income was difficult. So she encouraged a move to Paris, hobnobbed with nobility and the rich, and rented a sophisticated place for his painting studio so nobody would know that they were penniless.

Creating the unforgettable

One evening, the protagonist did not want to accompany her to a dinner because he did not know how to finish a painting. He had started it with a stark, wide, expanding landscape, and a leafless olive tree. He was staring at the painting while eating Camembert cheese that melted, creating a stretched chewing gum effect. For him time was like that, not rigid or deterministic. So he hung soft, limp, melting pocket watches on the olive-tree branches and called it *The Persistence of Memory*.

When she returned that night, her eyes stayed riveted on the canvas, "Nobody can ever forget this painting," she said. "It is much beyond its time."

She confided in a few prosperous art lovers that the artist was a genius. To sustain the limpidness of his creativity so he could avoid becoming commercial, she told them she had a plan. Twelve chosen wealthy patrons would help unleash his imagination by financially supporting the lifestyle he chose to live. In return, they would each get a painting from him every year. The chosen patrons were convinced; the couple managed a luxurious living style even as the artist was exceptional and totally weird.

Outrageous exchange

The artist's father was outraged when he read of his son's exhibition in Paris of a painting called *Sacred Heart of Jesus Christ* which had a provocative inscription, "Sometimes, I spit for fun on my mother's portrait." He demanded his son recant publicly, but the son refused. Instead, in response, he handed his father a condom containing his own sperm, saying, "Take that. I owe you nothing anymore!"

The artist had bizarre and unreal ways. He believed in painting transparently, without censorship of morality and conscience, and ignored doyennes who criticized him for depicting a man with excreta in his pants on a canvas. In fact, his fellow eccentric intellectuals at their 42 Rue Fontaine, Paris headquarters put him on trial and expelled him from their society.

"I am too intelligent to be a good painter," he said. "Painters are stupid. Really talented creative artists like Raphael and Mozart died very early. I prefer to live longer and be a bad painter."

Americans loved him

Before World War II began, he did not, unlike his other artistic compatriots, condemn Hitler. He refused to do so by saying he was apolitical. He went off to the US, where his paintings caused a sensation, and Americans lapped up his eccentricities and strange antics.

When the wealthy feted him, he showed up wearing a glass case on his chest, which contained a brassiere. He also took part in Hollywood and was sought after by advertisers to endorse different products like chocolates. He was extremely particular about his creations. When a retail design that he had done was changed during implementation, he smashed the window of the shop.

The roaring success of several art exhibitions in the US and Europe made him stand apart from most other artists who never became famous in their own lifetimes. At a lecture in London he wore a deep-sea diving suit and helmet. He had arrived carrying a billiard cue and leading a pair of Russian wolfhounds, and had to have the helmet unscrewed as he gasped for breath. He commented, "I just wanted to show that I was 'plunging deeply' into the human mind."

What does this story sound like? Is it fiction, fantasy, or real? Tell me!

SURREAL DISRUPTION

"The man belongs to a mad house," was the response I got to my "Fantasy fiction, or real?" mini-tale slice.

> He may be eccentric, but misbehaving with his father was bizarre. So is the American public for giving him iconoclastic position in society for the crazy things he did to attract attention. I don't know what to think, pure fantasy or fiction, but instinct tells me it's real. 'Genius' is mostly flawed they say.

Yes, you have correctly guessed the protagonist to be surrealist artist Salvador Dalí.

Birth of surrealism

What does it all prove? That after 80 years, an artist who had lived 6,800 km away from us, could still make an impact with surrealism. This disruptive mental activity, phantasma-gorical way of life, experiential expressions and paintings together created an osmosis, a metaphor for a genre that influenced every walk of life thereafter.

"I am Surrealism," Salvador Dalí had declared, allowing surreal philosophy, that is, absence of all control exercised by reason or morality, to possess him completely.

From 1900 to 1945, the impact of economic recession, turmoil of two World Wars, and Hitler, left the Western world shattered. But the paintings of those disastrous times were so imaginative that they portrayed another world of ideation. Fortunately society's drivers, Dalí among others, were there beyond the distraught social life, to help even the business world do things differently.

The generic is taking over

Today's worldwide turmoil is about digital language and glo-balization. Digitalization is making the world totally generic, snatching away individual identities, while globalization is breaking society's multicultural flavor. Since its inception in 1887 until 1929, the mechanical hand-machine gramo-phone with the same functionality had diverse aesthetics and designs that are identifiable as being American, Italian, French, Swedish, English, or German.

In the electric gramophone age, from 1930 to 1983, there were a variety of expressions like the record changer, two-in-ones, among others. But the last 30 years of digita-lization have made the physical element of music playing instruments look similar, either in a metal or plastic box. Several small companies had to close shop; only those with economic muscle can now dominate the world. Of course, the positive aspect is that music became available to the masses at low cost. But we have lost the art of differentiation. Surrealism is required here.

The digital can be surreal

Actually, digital functionality is itself surreal. Nobody would have believed, 40 years ago, that a mobile phone could connect you in the remotest forest or desert of the world where with your computer you even have your office for a few hours. The problem is that this generic, surrealistic digital technology sits inside devices like automobiles and electronics, white and brown goods that have negligible differences in identity, making people interact with these devices they do not relate to culturally.

In the late 1970s, Hollywood was becoming boring with historical films like *Cleopatra*, *Ben Hur*, and *Ten Commandments*, or depicting American social life as in *The Graduate* or going on a *Roman Holiday*. After Hitchcock's mysteries, John Wayne's westerns, and Clint Eastwood's spaghetti westerns, the film industry seriously turned to science fiction. Surrealistic paintings were a niche category in 1930s, but the power of surrealism is so strong that huge money was made by science-fiction films like *Star Wars* that were highly inspired by paintings with surrealist figures, atmosphere, and styles. The masses gobbled up these surrealistic images in box-office grossers like *ET* and *Terminator* among other science-fiction films.

The surrealist movement of the 1920–1930s was a great departure for science and business too. The shape of the first nuclear device resembles *Elephant Celebes*, a 1921 painting by surrealist Max Ernst. Most art manifestations, from religious to realistic paintings, expressionism, impressionism, and cubism, have been left out as high-value museum pieces.

But surrealism created disruption in the world by combining ideation with application in mass appeal. Museums sell reproductions of an artist's painting as souvenirs. But Salvador Dalí designed products so people could experience Dalí and surrealism. He reproduced his 1931 painting *The Persistence of Memory* depicting time in an undulated watch, as a real watch of asymmetric design. No watch brand can imitate that, as they are all symmetric. To sell fragrance, everybody knows the nose comes into play. Dalí designed a nose-like bottle that is still among the most famous perfumes today.

Spread of surrealism

In the 1980s, French haute couture designer Jean Paul Gaultier broke all codes of French fashion tradition and protocol through his irreverent style. He put his perfume bottle, shaped as a woman's bust, in a pet-food tin, a totally surrealistic notion. This was unimaginable when classic designers like Dior, Channel, and YSL were ruling French fashion. Gaultier's avant-garde designs sustain with phenomenal commercial success.

Strategy planning and business vision are inevitably determined by benchmarking or best practices, that is, only looking at what other industries have done. You may never know their mental process, and having spent millions of dollars, effort, and time you may find yourself back in square one. This may be lack of surrealistic thinking, which can be the catalyst of future business success.

Surreal act of turning CEOs into painters

I must confess of a surreal action I have taken too. Check it out on www.painterceo.com. I would arrive by appointment at the office of CEOs, pulling in a suitcase full of paints, brushes, a drawing canvas, and a palette. When I began arranging everything on the CEO's desk, he would ask, "Do I have to paint?"

I have made so many CEOs paint by explaining to them that there is no real difference between the management palette and color palette. I would say, "You are a successful CEO because you carry a high value management palette in your mind. There's no shareholder, promoter, employee, or competitor scrutiny on this. You have total liberty of expression."

CEOs engaging in painting may have made history unfold. They have all acknowledged that they were totally engrossed while painting, the proof of which is that each and every painting is outside the box. This shows that CEOs require a divergent atmosphere in the world of business where they can contemplate in an unlimited way to create differentiation that can bring high net worth to their organizations.

The prime objective of my initiative of making CEOs into painters was to prove that in this uniform, digital world, tangible difference in a product or service will bring business success. That is why I will continue the journey of finding CEO painters.

HEADLONG INTO THE UNKNOWN

CEOs who have painted for me have often asked about my own artistic journey. So let me oblige by penning my start as a struggling artist.

Diving headlong into the new

From experiencing Kalipodo Dey's miraculous ointment in Kolkata's crowded suburban train, I landed in the Paris metro in 1973. Rushing in, I stepped on a passenger's toe, very apologetically looked at her and said, "*Merci.*" When she frowned, I suddenly realized my blunder; I was supposed to say, "*Pardon,*" the other French word I had learnt. In complete embarrassment I longed for the station, abruptly got off to escape her, and continued my journey on the next train.

To fulfill my artist's dream, I had convinced my mother to buy me Air India's ₹2,700 youth-fare Delhi–Paris–Delhi ticket. In those days, the Indian government allowed US$8, and US$200 called FTS, for traveling abroad. I could only afford US$8. To collect the foreign exchange I had to take my passport to the Reserve Bank of India. Being unsure how to handle things, I asked a Kolkatan classmate to accompany me. Our art college had two types of students, villagers like me, always very shy and scared of making mistakes, and the savvy Kolkatan who knew everything.

My classmate insisted on taking Kolkata's only automatic elevator installed at the Reserve Bank, but I refused. I had been observing small-town people like me bravely trying to get on, hesitating, failing, and timidly taking the staircase; I did not want to become the public laughing stock too. But little did I know then that on disembarking in Paris, direct from my refugee colony outside Kolkata, I would face a similar problem.

This time it was a flat, automated moving "road' inside the airport terminal. With a thumping heart I would awkwardly advance my leg toward it, and retreat immediately in fright. Several Air India air hostesses passed me by without paying any attention. I did not speak any French, only tattered English. Suddenly a French woman appeared, held my hand, and taught me how to walk on a road that moves relentlessly.

Will to stop struggling

Underprivileged people do not have much scope or choice in life, so they struggle to take whatever is easily available. For 95 percent of such people, it is very difficult to take a visionary step to create a new scope. Being part of this situation, an art student with no promising future, I had to take the big risk to venture out of struggling times. I left for Paris with US$8 in my pocket, courage in my heart, an ambition to be an artist, and earn to improve my family's living condition.

I did not know a soul in Paris, but had heard of a Bengali scientist called Dr C.K. Pyne who did not know me at all. After negotiating the airport's moving road, I arrived directly at Dr Pyne's laboratory on a cold November day. I will never forget his incredible generosity. He heard my story and gave me shelter without questioning who I was; it turned out he was an art lover too. Had he been on holiday that day, I do not know where I would have been today.

Learning about life while living with Dr Pyne

Living in Dr Pyne's 13th-district apartment in Rue Champs de l'Alouette, I went out the next day for toothpaste. Dr Pyne even gave me F300 to live on, saying I could repay him when I started earning. At the supermarket I gestured teeth cleaning and was shown Colgate. But I wanted to buy something different, for I had seen enough of Colgate in India.

So I gestured the cleaning action more vigorously with my hands and people directed me to another shelf in the store. I returned with a large-sized toothpaste tube and kept it in the toilet.

After dinner I opened the packet and found the tube integrated with a brush that was round, sponge-type. When I squeezed, the paste came onto this, and I put it in my mouth to clean up. I kept brushing and brushing, but there was no lather, the color was brown, and I was getting a waxy feel in my mouth. I felt shy to talk to Dr Pyne about this strange toothpaste but mentioned how very different toiletries are in France. "I've seen your purchase in the toilet, I hope you haven't put that into your mouth," he said. When I asked why, he said I had bought shoe polish.

Every day I would go helter-skelter looking for a job, and still could not speak French. In December 1973 I met a man in Alliance Française who promised me a job if I went to him the next day at 3 p.m. From Dr Pyne's house my appointment was about 8 km away, in Pigalle, north Paris. When I reached Pigalle to get my job, I entered a house in a small lane; everything looked quite bizarre, a large room was separated into cubicles with flowing curtains. I wondered if I had come to the right place, and peeped inside the cubicles. Cubicle after cubicle, all I found were nude couples making love. It was a brothel!

I was petrified and did not know what to do. I quickly made an exit and stood by the staircase. An old lady came and explained that I should be in front at the lane, from 3 p.m. to 4 a.m. My work would be to bring people from the road to the room, and I would get F25 per day, that was ₹37 then! With the only objective of making money, I was not considering the brothel or the job being offered. I could start right away, she told me, or come tomorrow. I said I would come the next day.

I told Dr Pyne I had got a job without explaining more; he did not probe either. The next afternoon, a freezing winter day, I boarded the metro, dozed a bit, and traveled a few stations. A sudden jerk from the metro changing tracks sent shivers down my spine and I hastily got off midway. The uneasy discomfort I had been feeling told me this was not the purpose of my coming to Paris. At that time I did not even know there was a professional called a pimp!

I walked home and did not return to Pigalle. I decided this opportunity was not right for me. This is the first episode of my life's livelihood journey, from Kalipodo Dey's dramatic sales pitch in Kolkata's local train to my mental trauma over a pimp's job in the Paris metro.

CRACKING OPEN CURIOSITY

From my struggling-artist stage, I did manage to break free into the world of creative, strategic business. I entered the intellectual blah-blah period working for global companies. Let us travel to three countries, where I unlearnt blah-blah to attain the reality of social insight.

Bangladesh

Researching the classic Reckitt and Colman product Robin Blue in Bangladesh, we conceptually prepared consumer-interaction stimuli that had something called rebirth or rejuvenation of clothes that the product enabled. We ran the research in Dhaka, Chittagong, and a few provinces. Four days passed, I was amazed that consumers were silent on this particular subject, nothing interesting was emerging.

Then one of the women respondents took me aside and advised me to stop talking about rebirth. Muslims consider it an insult to their religion, she said. Simultaneously, the consumer-recruiting agent got information that some people, hearing about rebirth discussions, were considering action against us for anti-religious marketing. I was shocked and seriously wounded mentally. I apologized, saying it was out of the question that we would disturb religious sentiments, and packed up.

After spending time to understand their social milieu and how to connect the brand without touching religion, I returned with the concept of "purity." The connect was immediate and very high. Purity, a crucial factor in Islamic thought, linked people to quality, efficacy, and the emotive factor. Purity connected to Indians as well from hygienic and religious angles. Instead of the product making clothes only white, it also made the clothes pure, an added benefit.

Japan

Twenty years ago, the Japanese largely drank their traditional sake, but would covet sophisticated Western alcohol. The crisis for Western brands was imitation of Taiwan and China, so authenticity for differentiation was important. Remy Martin, the French liquor company, appointed me to expand a category called Armagnac in Japan before its global penetration. The brand name was Cles des Ducs, meaning Key of the Duke. I carried all kinds of French sophistication as stimuli to bounce off consumers in Japan.

After three weeks in Tokyo, Osaka, Hiroshima, and other cities, nothing exceptional was coming out. I wanted to connect culturally so requested Remy Martin personnel in Japan to arrange visits to Japanese homes, a difficult task, but they somehow managed it. In unstructured discussions, it turned out that Key of the Duke was the handicap. A key in Japanese culture represents a closed mindset and life, particularly for the pleasure of alcohol. They understand cognac as being from Napolean's period, but Armagnac? The greenish-brown bottle had no glamour; it merely hid the expensive golden alcohol. Was this fake cognac? I understood that this brand cannot work here.

Returning to Paris I shared with the client the deficiencies in the brand's name, bottle color, and authenticity. How can I ask the client to change such an old authentic brand? However, the client allowed me to dive deep into these three subjects. My historical research proved that Armagnac was the oldest brandy in France, dating back to 1411 in the Middle Ages, whereas cognac was officially born in the 17th century. It clarified that a Amagnac's genesis was in France and monks gave this agricultural alcohol to poor people for therapeutic purposes.

We first addressed the look, making the bottle transparent and giving it a hammered texture to represent a Middle-Ages temple. The brand's typography treatment followed those times. Spending time in liquor cellars, I thought to leave the cellar door open in the packaging design to connote that the Duke was inviting people, rather than closing the cellar door with his Key.

When I returned to Japan with this story, consumers started to talk from day one. This is the way Remy Martin relaunched the brand in Japan and was able to take it global. Here again, preconceived blah-blah had failed to connect to consumers.

Argentina

Appointed by Argentina's Bagley biscuit company, we presumed health and hygiene to be of paramount importance in a developing Latin American country. We accordingly prepared for interactions with people at large there. Day after day we did research after research; people looked at us, but showed total disinterest. So to integrate myself strongly into Argentina's cultural life, I went to see Buenos Aires' famous tango dance.

I have always thought the elegant tango to be joyful, but discussions with local people in the theater revealed that it originated in lower-class districts from former slave peoples in melancholic situations, and spread to working-class slums. The audience, mostly aged over 45 years, said life's nostalgic aspect is very significant in Argentine society. Later interactions with younger people corroborated that through their country's political turmoil, they would rather remember stories of good times heard from older generations.

A Bagley salesman observed my curiosity about nostalgia, and spoke of his father, a former Bagley employee. I immediately sought an invitation to their home. Spending time with the 80-year-old, I discovered that 150 years ago Melville Bagley came from Boston, established this company, and created a drink, jam, and *criollita*s, which is a cracker-type biscuit for poor people. Criollitas have since become almost staple food, transcending generation after generation in Argentine life. This uncommon factor had escaped us; the brand had lost the essence of its origin. We revisited memories, calling Bagley the "Link of Generations"; and putting Mr Bagley's 150-year-old signature as the brand identity connected to everybody.

So reminiscences were more admirable than my pre-conceived hygiene and health blah-blah, which Argentines found boring, as they were actually more advanced than developed countries in these respects.

Connecting your brand to people

In the course of my business journey, I had to unlearn many things I had picked up in my initial consulting career. From prepared corporate intellectual blah-blah on market hypothesis, how to interact with and direct consumers, or create the trend, I had to radically reverse preset ideas. I discovered from my experience that the more I interacted with people, initially with an exploratory mind, acting stupid, the more I gained valuable insights. Common people across the world are so genuine; they open their mind and discuss a variety of things. I have translated these practical primary insights from people into business success for my global clients.

So I understood, "Marketing is story telling of a selling proposition which has differentiation as an extra benefit." This story cannot be created in the boardroom nor be pre-determined. It has to capture the real essence of human society. My learning from the field is that no matter what business education you have from renowned universities or gray-haired experience you possess from running mega-companies, it is practical social reality that will give you the insight you need to connect your brand to people.

FOOTBALL CAMARADERIE

While implementing the global project in Argentina in 1994, I was thrilled to find my football genes awakening.

Football in the slums

Much to the chagrin of my client, Elizabeth, I would wander into unauthorized "dangerous" Buenos Aires slums to experience life and social trends. I found that companies like Pepsi and Coca-Cola had sponsored good football grounds to encourage slum children to become heroes. Indeed from a tall block of buildings with a high crime rate comes Manchester City striker Carlos Tevez who had played street football in these "no-go" areas as a child, and became part of the Argentinean team.

At that time, as I watched young boys practice football, others quarreling, one even had a gun, I remember musing how terrific these sophisticated sports arrangements were. This crumbling slum had murky streets where even emergency services often refused to enter. In our poor village in Bengal we could never think of such sports facilities or of anybody from our village becoming a world-famous football player. Yet even football champion Maradona, Argentinean team's coach, was raised in a poor family living in a Buenos Aires shantytown. When he was 10 years old, he was spotted by a talent scout.

After quitting the slums Elizabeth and I went to a coffee shop of a national football club. A gang of boisterous people was gesticulating wildly about an imminent major local football match in the city starring Boca Juniors and River Plate. I absolutely wanted to join their table talk.

Being a sophisticated French woman, Elizabeth was getting angry but I explained that the food company they had acquired had its roots here, so its transformation required us to gather cultural aspects of Argentina where football was highly relevant. This kind of social phenomenon would bring us the right insight for this acquired company's future plans.

Instant connect through football

I walked across to those guys and introduced myself as a Bengali Indian living in Paris. You cannot believe how, the moment they heard Kolkata, they spontaneously hugged me. It seems a few in this group of football journalists had gone to "Mother Teresa's city" with the Argentinean team in 1984 for the Nehru Cup. They marveled at how Kolkatans are so enthusiastic about football. In their happiness over meeting a fellow football lover from across the globe they offered me a ticket to the famous match that day.

I will never forget this immediate attachment that football can create anywhere in the world. I have experienced two World Cups on the field in France and Spain, and during other European football matches, and found the excitement that emanates here to be incomparable to any other bonding experience.

The first time I had watched the World Cup on TV, wide-eyed, was in 1974, a few months after arriving as a greenhorn in Paris. That match was in Germany. I had only experienced the transistor radio earlier, the spectacular voices of commentators Ajay Da, Kamal Da, and Pushpen Da. They were so good that without being in any football stadium we could visualize a match with Kolkata teams like East Bengal, Mohan Bagan, and Mohammedan Sporting, among others.

Being Bengali football freaks, even without electronic media, we felt very close to the World Cup in those days. Brazil was almost a part of the Bengal team where Pelé, at 17 years and 239 days, won the World Cup for his country in 1958. I was barely eight then yet I recall a wounded Pelé could not finish the tournament in 1962. In 1966 brutal fouling on Pelé by Bulgarian and Portuguese defenders obliged him to continue with a limping leg, as substitutes were not allowed at that time.

The greatest footballer of all time, Pelé played in four World Cup tournaments, thrice bringing home the Cup for Brazil, including in 1970. Argentina's Diego Maradona is as big a world football icon, sharing the FIFA Player of the Century award with Pelé. Maradona made his full international debut at the age of 16 and played in four World Cups too, from 1982 to 1994.

The thrill of TV viewing

I am sure today's young generation can never understand the exhilaration of sitting in front of a black-and-white TV set, watching our sports idols enact their magic. I was mesmerized the first time I watched a game on TV. That was in Cité Universitaire, in Paris' 14th district, where a Greek house director, Mr Yourgoulis allowed me hostel accommodation because I was a student in École Nationale Supérieure des Beaux-Arts even while earning my livelihood as a sweeper. I would grab a chair in the small TV room (that doubled as a table-tennis lounge) an hour before the match. I could not speak French then, so had to gauge everything, including the incredible moves of Beckenbaur and Muller. I became adept at peppering my fervor using Greek swear words like *malacca* and *putanis*, while watching along with other Greek students.

The word *ralenti* often occurred. I asked the only other Indian student who had made me understand that he spoke very good French what it meant. He said ralenti is another discipline like penalty. I believed him. But by 1978 I had learnt French and discovered while watching the 1978 World Cup that ralenti means slow motion in French.

Merit brings immediate fame

Fortunately, there is something beyond elite intellectual global awards like the Nobel Prize. Excellence in sports can also create international heroes with huge fan following. Actually nobody knows how you get a Nobel Prize; the youngest Laureate, Lawrence Bragg, was 25 when together with his father he received the Physics Nobel in 1915. But it is quite incredible how in sports teenagers like Pelé and Maradona could acquire world fame, having proved their genius to the masses, and continued to perform.

Look at the poverty Pelé, the greatest icon, grew up with in São Paulo. He could not afford a football, and usually played with a grapefruit or a sock stuffed with newspaper and tied with a string. He would earn extra money working in tea shops as a servant until he was discovered and taught by his coach. When he scored his 1,000th goal he dedicated it to the poor children of Brazil. These famous players are a great inspiration and powerful motivator for underprivileged youth.

In India, sports is always shortchanged; we push everyone toward school or college education. But everybody in society cannot be, or does not need to be, a graduate, basic school education is enough to become a globally renowned sportsman. Here, where slums are prevalent in every city, sports can be a great medium to encourage disadvantaged people to acquire prowess instead of abandoning them in ghettoes where crime generally grows unabated.

SELF-CONFIDENCE IS THE KEY

Unlike slum dwellers who can play football but barely get any formal education, people who are literate generally rise

in life by moving up the institutional ladder. Or a handful dare to scale a steep mountain with a mere rope. Of this planet's almost seven billion people, perhaps just 1 percent takes this risk of dangerously ascending life using a rope.

The institutional ladder

The institutional ladder starts from below the poverty line. You climb a certain hierarchy step by step, armed with education, years of experience, and the right contacts. But only specific expertise, self-confidence, and persuasive ability can place you atop the pyramid. Exceptional people like Bill Gates can break the mold or skip steps.

My ambitious corporate friends, in the different companies that I have worked with in the West and India, have asked me how to break conformity in their lives, leapfrog professional conundrums to land on their dream profession. Beyond my professional assignment with these companies, I always execute an unarticulated responsibility of creating passion among my large circle of manager friends. People daydream of entrepreneurship, but hesitate to leave comfortable jobs. Job security kills the human spirit of challenge.

Self-confidence is the only asset you need to advance

Let me narrate a real-life experience. A client friend in Paris, after important meetings, would suddenly not be seen for two–three months. I became despondent when I came to know that he was undergoing therapy for stomach cancer. This top-class managing director, immensely knowledgeable, an expert in full control in a global corporate environment, is a beautiful human being who maintains relationships with graciousness. He would always call me "Crazy Creative." At our next project development meeting, I wanted to wish him a speedy recovery without mentioning his problem. I went to Brentano's, a Parisian literary fixture since 1895, which unfortunately closed doors in 2009, and picked up books on the sociological and romantic aspects of living.

After quite a while he called me to reveal that the books I chose became his best mental curative medicine. That overwhelmed me. I knew he was an avid reader but without knowing his taste I had selected for him in my creative way. The best part is 20 years on, he is in perfect health, mind, family, and profession. He had the courage to quit the job, start an enterprise, which he is running successfully. His remarkable self-confidence continues unabated.

Being entrepreneurial is a state of mind, not about self-employment. When you intrinsically have strong control over yourself, you will drive it, whether you work as an employee or start your own business. Your entrepreneurial grit can make your boss your subordinate. Years of experience do not count in today's fast-moving digital world, only specialized expertise matters.

Don't take your high post, big room, bigger staff, and comforting corporate facilities as your achievement. When your intelligence, self-confidence, curiosity, and innovative, productive ability are under your grip, you have everything to rise, succeed, and fatten your wallet. That is your shelter in the institutional ladder's open sky; you know you can go anywhere.

The alpinist has self-determination

Mountaineering is uncertain, creative escalation emanating from a huge self-urge. Unconventional creative people are society's deviants tugging at this alpinist's rope. They choose to escape the institutional ladder in spite of societal pressure to conform. They perforce develop a bulldozer mentality to climb creatively while continuously producing emotion on high ground as writers, musicians, painters, philosophers, or actors.

The creative person's mountaineering mindset is at odds with institutional climbers. Frustration can diminish their creativity. If during creative execution you think your output will make you wealthy, you will suffer.

Never take the successful period of a creative alpinist as your benchmark. Nobody knows the struggle that the person underwent in formative years. Pursuing the creative rope track from early years, your first priority is your artistic pursuit, not money, car, family, home, or holidays. Avoiding the comfort of possessions and family support, your devotion to master your creative talent will automatically bring you wealth when you are true to your creative power.

Art legend Pablo Picasso was a communist who knew that only rich non-communists could buy his paintings. One of his marriages was with Olga Khokhlova, a ballerina who introduced him to the Parisian high-society life where his art sales boomed. Later he left her. Van Gogh's alpinism was the opposite. A true genius, he sold only one painting for just F400 a few days before he committed suicide from frustration at the age of 37.

Several 20–25-year-olds today watch famous entertainers on TV and the Internet, fall in love with them, and want to take the creative route. They never analyze the entertainer's trajectory, how after struggling against odds and competition he/she reached the top. Indian parents can be unrealistic too. They try achieving what they missed out on in life by pressurizing children with extracurricular activities, the affluent may even buy a piano. But when the child becomes motivated to become a musician, the parents shatter his morale by reversing gear to make him a doctor or engineer.

Develop expertise in your chosen domain

For me, both the institutional or alpinist climb culminates in self-confidence. No parent or god-man can transmit this totally self-driven attitude. Domain expertise is the main source of confidence; arrogance and complacency comprise defense of a deficiency. Boxing world champion Cassius Clay (Mohammad Ali)'s early practice demanded a 5 km run but he would run 15 km. When his coach reprimanded him, he announced that the extra 10 km was for becoming the greatest boxer on earth. He was just a teenager then; his self-confidence allowed no one to interfere with his personal challenge.

Creative people come from both poor and rich families. The clear difference could be that author Charles Dickens started with an empty stomach without shelter, whereas Victor Hugo's childhood was reasonably comfortable. But both had to climb the mountaineering rope to be recognized as being authentically creative.

Society's system can always disturb you to lose your confidence; you need powerful inner gumption to fight and build it. When success is yours, people will drum it out of you, but lack of confidence can make you a fossil, irrespective of the genius that is inside you.

DOWNLOADING MEMORIES

Having lived in a refugee colony, I had nothing to lose when recklessly and filled with confidence, I set out to leave my home and country in 1973. Since then my long-standing agenda had been to one day take my parents to their lost home in East Bengal, now Bangladesh. It finally fructified in December 2011 when my father was 85 and mother 80 years old.

Home misplaced

Forced to live in a refugee colony, my parents have never been able to digest their families' sudden, compulsory deportation to West Bengal in 1947 after the partition. I have traveled through every continent since 1973, but this visit to Dhaka and Comilla is taking up unending GB space as I download memories. Someday I may have to narrate this to my grandchildren who are currently growing up in London and will want to know about their roots on this side of the world.

The glorious past of our family told in a dreamy way by my grandmother, Nalini Bala, was like a Hollywood story for me. I loved listening to her during my childhood when we lived a castaway joint-family existence in a dark and penniless situation in our refugee-colony home outside Kolkata. When the wind howled outside, and monsoon water leaked in drops from the thatched roof flooding our floor, my grandmother used to recall stories of bygone days to distract me.

After I immigrated to France, and would return to meet my grandmother, even at the ripe age of 95, she never stopped talking about her luxurious homeland on the other side of Bengal. This Dhaka trip, December 2011, made all her words ring true.

Mother's home mislaid

But let me first take you to my mother's ancestral home in Batisha, in Comilla district. On November 29, 2011 the Bangladeshi parliament passed a landmark bill that would enable the return of property seized from the country's Hindu minority. Called the Vested Properties Return (Amendment) Act, 2011, this dealt with "*orpito*" property, meaning vested land that had been occupied by people without family heritage or without paying for it. What this signified is that those who had lost their land from 1947 onwards stood a chance of getting back their property if they possessed authentic documents to prove their legitimate ownership.

We were not aware of this new law being passed, nor were we visiting her father's village to reclaim anything. It was just nostalgia tugging us there.

Our Bangladeshi contact from Comilla was careful to meet us 50 km from my mother's heritage home. He greeted us warmly but appeared a little edgy. The area was a little troubled he said, being on the border with Tripura, India. He took my father aside and asked whether my mother could remove her red bindi, which is clearly a sign of a Hindu. I was shocked initially but adjusted my disquiet to be in tune with the country's culture. Driving on we could see verdant paddy fields, crossed the Border Security Force guarding the borderline, which is just a wire fence that disintegrates into no-fence after some distance.

Turning off the highway on our right, we reached Bodhiya Bazaar. The kindhearted Bangladeshi gentleman told us that we should say we had come from Dhaka. I could sense a hostile feeling building up in my parents; my mother asked why she should lie when she had no bad intention. We explained what our contact had said.

The Jamaat-e-Islami, a far-right, anti-Bangladesh-liberation party, which collaborated with Pakistan during the 1971 war of independence and later joined the current Opposition Bangladesh Nationalist Party was politically strong here, and against the new property law. Our contact caught different people to trace my mother's *puber bodhiya bari* (eastern house of Bodhya class) where her family had lived. He conversed with people on the road while we followed in the car. Everyone kept questioning him about why we were here. He would frequently turn to warn us not to forget to say that we live in Dhaka and not India.

The brutal consequence of staying back

An 85-year-old man waddled up to the small group that was trying to find out what we were doing in that area. When he heard about tracing my mother's house, he grinned toothlessly and asked, "You know my friend, Sengupta, who shifted to Dhaka after his father was murdered in the fifties?" Gesticulating with his hands, he indicated that my granduncle's head was chopped off under a big tree in his own huge orchard where he was resting at noon. He quickened his pace and excitedly went ahead with our contact on foot to show the house.

At the turn were several large ponds on both sides of a narrow lane leading to the house. My friend did not allow me to take the camera saying it could be risky. My mother was dejected; she could not control her emotion that the large main house had been torn down. She sadly remembered all the different places after being away for 60 years.

The present occupant of this property recognized my mother's family and hospitably invited us to tea. Meanwhile our contact nervously urged us to leave at the earliest, as more people were becoming alerted that unexpected visitors were in the village. It was an emotional moment for both my mother and the present occupant, yet I had to be rude to get out of the situation. I have never seen my mother so distraught, but I pulled her away. Fortunately, we left the place quickly.

The next day we heard about the chaos our trip had instigated. It appears a large gang of politically inclined people had come armed with sticks to chase us away. There was great suspicion, especially as we were visiting within a week of the new law being passed. In general too when an outsider visits with a local person as guide, villagers think the guide is the middleman, with the original owner in the background.

It was very difficult to make people understand that ours was an innocent visit down memory lane.

REMINISCING ON RED STEPS

"*Shani kheer* (milk dessert) turned upside down will never fall, it's like a thick plate," is an incredulous childhood image that is etched in my mind. My doting grandmother Nalini Bala had relived her erstwhile luxurious life in Burma and East Bengal for me, who doted on her too. She would brainwash me with myriad little stories of that fantastic time before becoming an impoverished refugee in India. Arriving next to my father's ancestral village in Bikrampur, we found evidence that my grandmother's stories were not the figment of her imagination, but absolutely accurate.

The route was etched in my father's mind for 63 years

Untangling our car from the perennial traffic jams in Dhaka, we drove with bated-breath anticipation to Madhyapara in Bikrampur, just 35 km away. This was my father's nostalgic trip to retrace our original home. In the backdrop of my father's wistful recollections expressed in peaks and troughs of emotion, we discovered that the Buri Ganga bridge had deprived us of a steamer ride from Dhaka Sadarghat that he used to enjoy. His running commentary said we would cross Kirangunj over two Dhaleswari rivers, and enter Munshiganj district to Siraj Dikhan police station.

The region, famous for early Buddhist scholarships, is the oldest capital of Bengal since the Vedic period. We would read about Buddhist scholar Atish Dipankar from the Pala empire, scientist Jagdish Bose, freedom fighter Chittaranjan Das, and Benoy, Badal, Dinesh (after whom Kolkata's Dalhousie Square was renamed as BBD Bagh), who gave up their lives while revolting against colonial rule. My grandmother would say that they had all originated from Bikrampur, but I never believed her. When their courageous tales were endorsed here, you can imagine how Nalini Bala was accompanying me to our lost home.

Our Bangladeshi navigator stopped at a local sweetshop, more than a 100 years old. A hard, yellowish, milk sweet, about six inches in diameter laid out on a banana leaf totally displaced me, my grandmother's voice reverberating in my body and mind. So this unique shani kheer, available only in Siraj Dikhan, en route to our village, was real! The owner of the heritage sweetshop even recalled tales of the revered Raisaheb Ruhini Sengupta, my great-grandfather.

My grandfather is still a legend here

Going forward, our contact hailed a 95-year-old Hindu religious man in one of those extremely colorful rickshaws that dot both the urban and rural Bangladeshi landscape. Everybody knew that he survived on fruits and knew everyone here from way back when. Visiting after 63 years, my father started recounting long-lost experiences. The sprightly, wrinkled swamiji, his forehead vertically divided by a one-by-three-inch thick vermillion streak up to his surprisingly natural black hair, corroborated each recall just as enthusiastically, and they would hug each other like long lost friends. I had never witnessed my father express such bonhomie.

The swamiji embellished my father's childhood tidbits with detailed information on Ruhini Sengupta. He also mentioned that Bikrampur's Durga festivities comprised 80 *pandal*s before partition, while now only two pujas are celebrated.

The road to the village was extraordinary. Arched trees on both sides touched one another to filter in patches of early winter sunlight to welcome our disoriented homecoming. I recognized the "*shanko*" my grandmother had described, the single bamboo walkway with bamboo railings that connect houses separated from the road by water bodies. People would balance tightrope-like, walking with perfect grace, even with large bundles on their head, on shankos that were up to 100 m high.

Veering into a small brick road alongside paddy and potato fields interspersed with water hyacinths, my heart skipped a beat as this signboard appeared: "Madhyapara Union Parishad." Our navigator escorted us to the local village chairman, Mohammad Azim, to make us acceptable here.

The chairman was waiting with several old people. He honored my father, making him sit on his tall chairman's chair.

Myth-like stories were emerging of Raisaheb Ruhini Sengupta's prosperity, power, and fame. My father would start a topic, "My grandfather used to walk…" and old Karim Mia would excitedly continue, "and if turbulent oxen are fighting there, they'd stop, and respectfully step aside to let him pass."

This reunion in the chairman's bureau reminded me of Mafia recognition methods, where two unknown Mafia men on a predetermined meeting are each given a torn currency note. If their two pieces converge exactly, the men know they have correctly found each other, and can proceed unhindered. The spontaneity of my father's memoirs was as incredible as the response from the increasing number of white-bearded, hennaed men overcrowding the room. I was just an open-mouthed listener matching their conversation to my grandmother's stories.

Just steps to the pond and women's bathroom remained

On extreme brotherhood terms we walked the next 2 km to our lost ancestral home, Subal Dham. Amid lush greenery and mustard fields, several questioning people kept joining our party. My father's eyes moistened as he saw his 400-m-by-100-m *dighi* or fishpond. He was shocked that his large red mansion was demolished, sprouting in its place small houses with tin roofs. All that remained of his homeland gone adrift were a set of red British-style steps that jutted into the pond, and a concrete bathroom for women at the back.

A current inhabitant of our property, Mohammad Mofiz, recounted the heritage property of Raisaheb Ruhini Sengupta, which amounted to 400 acres. He said, "The 360 degree horizon you see would have belonged to your family." I was utterly shocked. After the Sengupta family was forced to flee during turbulent times, the government had appropriated the property, cut them into bits and pieces for many to occupy. Mofiz also knew that this was only the country house of Raisaheb, that his principal home and property were in Rangoon, Burma.

My great-grandfather was initially a worker in the public works department during the British Raj. The British rulers rewarded him with the title of Raisaheb for his excellent performance as the principal engineer in constructing the Burma–China border road. He maintained a high establishment in Burma, and my grandfather was the eldest son of his 10 children. My grandfather became a successful advocate in Insein, Rangoon, before he suddenly died, leaving his family with his father.

As my father narrated his childhood memories, sitting atop the red steps, occupants of our erstwhile property crowded in to hear him. I am grateful to Chairman Azim for smoothening our visit. Some people were scared that we had come to repossess our 400 acres. We had to reestablish that ours was an emotional nostalgic journey to discover our vanished legacy, and not to reclaim our 400 acres that had been branded as "enemy property" and auctioned off after the partition.

TANTRUMMING FOR ARMANITOLA

Unforgettable memories are all we returned with from Madhyapara village outside Dhaka. For my father, this was a

nostalgic return after 63 years to our ancestral home that he had abandoned during the partition riots.

"Enemy property" being recovered?

Hospitable occupants at our lost home invited my parents to spend more time here, but unknown to us, a hostile undercurrent was gathering momentum. They were afraid we were coming to repossess our 400-acre mislaid property, especially as the Bangladesh parliament had recently passed an amendment to ease "enemy property" recovery. We later heard they were livid with the man who first identified my great-grandfather. They mistakenly thought we had bribed him to help us reclaim our land.

Father's memory lane

My father's childhood memory determined the places we would visit. He recalled the Padma river ferry junction from where they would travel to different places like Faridpur, Madaripur, and Barisal. I later understood his main intention was to re-experience the Padma river *ilish* (*hilsa*) fish, the benchmark of all hilsa according to East Bengalis, although West Bengalis may not agree. A Bengali is identified by his love of hilsa fish. Eating Padma ilish at the ferry ghat is a tradition, even public buses advertise "ILISH" in large letters across buses to entice people to this fresh hilsa destination.

This reminded me of how everyone rushes to eat fresh oysters on the spot at San Francisco wharf as the fishermen haul them in. Unfortunately, I had to brutally stop my parents enjoying the freshly caught hilsa displayed in rows, cut into slices, marinated in turmeric, invitingly ready to fry, for hygiene was doubtful here, with swarms of flies partaking of the fish first, the oil was used and reused and the frying pan was totally black.

Psychological connect

Back in Dhaka, my father was enjoying a green mango drink in a modern café. He asked for one more, but without ice. The café waiter flatly refused, saying the formula called for ice. Surprised, we explained once again, but he was adamant. Then he came near me, switched to a very local Dhakai Bengali accent, and confessed that without ice, the tall glass would look vacant, as it is the ice that gives it the big-sized impression. My father gave a mischievous laugh at the boy's honesty, and happily accepted the iced drink.

In fact, I noticed my father was continuously embracing the people of Bangladesh, as though they were a part of his family. This was clearly a psychological connect; I have not witnessed it in him in West Bengal.

Nor have I ever seen my father making a tantrum to go to any place. But Armanitola in Dhaka he absolutely had to visit. He perfectly recalled his last journey here as a 10-year-old after his father's death, from Rangoon to Kolkata by boat, then to Gualnanda by train, by ferry to Sadarghat in Dhaka to stay with relatives in Banshibazar and Armanitola. Then from Sadarghat, they would reach Madhyapara by steamer, where you can now so easily go by road.

Enjoying Dhaka's traffic jam session

But the traffic jam in Dhaka city is unimaginable; traveling a kilometer takes an hour. Our dead-slow car ride to Armanitola was to find a field where he used to play with his relatives living there.

When moving tortoise-like, you have to toggle the gears in your mind to enjoy the jam session street festivity to avoid boredom. Were Dhaka's auto-rickshaws obsessed with safety? They have a metal mesh, as in police vans that carry convicts. Suddenly a three-wheeler auto-rickshaw sidled up to the side, a birdcage door opened, passengers began emerging. My eyes were riveted there, I counted one, two, three … a total of eight people were traveling in that auto-rickshaw, and they all reached their destination. With nothing to do, I was calculating the high efficiency of these three-wheeler transport cages with the luxury of the Pajero, Land Cruiser, BMW, and others that were stagnating along with us in the massive traffic squeeze.

The Armenia connect

My father was utterly disappointed when we arrived at Armanitola. We could not find the playground, nor his relative's house. I suddenly awoke to the name Armanitola. Does it have anything to do with Armenia? Armenians had come to India much before the British to trade mostly in silk, muslin, and jute. There is an Armenian church in Kolkata and other cities. My on-the-spot Google search confirmed that Dhaka has an Armenian church built in 1781. After Madhyapara, this beautiful heritage church is now etched in my mind.

The kaleidoscope of my Armenian connections in Paris appeared before my mind's eye, they are all highly rooted to their homeland. Even Patrice Civanian, who had worked in my company, is from Armenia but born in France. His parents had told me that Armenians came to India as early as 327 BC, with Alexander the Great.

That evening I met an Armenian gentleman who had come to pay homage to his ancestors at Armanitola church. He knew little about Bangladesh; the tourist guide informed him he could experience golf and rickshaw at the same time. He said he wanted to take home a beautiful decorative pedal rickshaw displayed at our hotel. He thought it was to draw tourists, and had no idea that the livelihood of poor people in Bangladesh depended on rickshaws.

The unfathomable loss

It is time to say au revoir to my erstwhile native land where I experienced five of my life's most memorable days. On the 30-minute flight back to India, it felt like we were distancing ourselves, with thousands of kilometers in between. This feeling was reminiscent of the romantic, heartbreaking Hollywood movie *Roman Holiday*, starring Gregory Peck and Audrey Hepburn. After a short but intense relationship the couple knew their parting was inevitable. That was a story, but this, my respected readers and victimized brotherhood, is my real-life experience of discovery and loss.

The unwanted political separation in 1947 turned so many of us into beggars, homeless, suffering tragic deaths, a situation I have never been able to accept. I am sharing my small Bangladeshi experience with all of you who have lost everything during the partition, as though we had been in the Holocaust.

LIVING IN HISTORY

Having just delved into my own family history, I was a little perturbed to find that nobody seems to appreciate history as a valuable asset in India.

Study the human past

Working for a for-profit educational institution, I had recently interacted with primary-school and high-school children and their teachers, and to my horror discovered that history was the "boringest of all subjects." Children consider it monotonous and teachers say they are exasperated, as students do not connect to past events.

What is the study of the human past? The Greeks call it *historia* meaning inquiry or knowledge acquired by investigation; in Latin, it is *ēvidēns*, in Italian, vista, and in English, wisdom. The West follows a strict grid for documentation that has become the monument of history. In my experience at seminars, workshops, and forums in the West, to make any point about the present and future, there has to be a connect with history to establish the benchmark. Only then do people connect to the future.

In India, history has been relegated to the neglected, forgotten past, as though it is devoid of value in education or professional areas. Even senior management seems uncomfortable when I include it in my coaching sessions, suspecting it may be "non-actionable." If I show black-and-white pictures as authentic historical testimony, they ask for color pictures to "make it exciting." It is difficult to explain that being true to history, when only black-and-white gravure existed as in this case, is important.

Why documentation is required

We need disciplined documentation to ensure the wheel is not reinvented. Has India mined and stored our rich ancient heritage of habits and practices from different centuries as a repertoire that anyone can dip into? The West follows a strict grid for documentation. People still play Handel's 17th-century or Mozart's 18th-century music compositions using modern instruments, sound and interpretation as the written notation is unchallenged in posterity. In Indian music's guru–*shisya* (teacher–pupil) tradition the finer points or melody may get altered or fade out with multiple non-grid interpretation, depending on how the disciple captures it.

Historical data, facts, and figures in human or natural evolution, sociocultural, technical, or entertainment areas define how society's emulsion in every epoch generates incredible invention. I have heard stories here of people who considered their work to be invention, but when the patent or intellectual propery recognition was refused, discovering that the invention had occured earlier. To prevent waste of time and energy, its important to search a subject in the global field; this can turn out to be very inspiring too.

Inventions close to us

Let us look at a few examples of how and why certain inventions took place and became a part of our daily lives.

Nestlé

The early, mid-1860s' history of the Nestlé company was Henri Nestlé's search for a healthy, economical alternative to breastfeeding for mothers who could not breastfeed their infants. This trained Swiss pharmacist's first customer was a premature infant whom physicians had given up for lost as he could not tolerate his mother's milk or conventional substitutes. After Nestlé's new formula saved the child's life, people quickly recognized the new product's value. Mr Nestlé's ultimate goal was to help combat the problem of infant mortality due to malnutrition. The Nestle company's focus today is on responsible nutrition and promoting health and wellness.

Pasteur

As a youngster Louis Pasteur showed no special ability, but in high school became interested in science. He had five children, three of whom died of typhoid fever. This motivated him to develop the germ theory of disease to save people from diseases. Eventually Pasteur solved scientific mysteries such as a generation of ailments like rabies, anthrax, and chicken cholera, and contributed to the world's first and most significant vaccines. He died a national hero in 1895, and his remains are at the Pasteur Institute, Paris.

Bose

"Research fuels technology and superior technology leads to superior performance," was the philosophy of Amar Bose, founder of Bose speakers. As an MIT graduate student in 1956, Bose bought a high-end stereo system but was disappointed when it failed to meet his expectations. He later began extensive research to fix the fundamental weakness plaguing high-end audio systems. Today, the Bose brand that stands for "Better Sound through Research" has become the most respected name in sound, from the Olympic Games to the Sistine Chapel, from NASA space shuttles to the Japan National Theatre.

Internet

The Internet was designed 1973, and was up and running by 1983. Developed by Vinton Cerf and others, this international network of computers delivers information "packets" such as email from one "address" to another. Tim Berners-Lee became a part of the Internet's complex history of innovation by inventing the World Wide Web in 1989–1991. With mathematicians as parents who worked on the first commercial computer, Berners-Lee used the Internet to provide universal access to a comprehensive collection of information in word, sound, and image, each discretely identified by universal document identifiers (UDIs), also known as uniform resource locators (URLs) and interconnected by hypertext links.

Berners-Lee made it really easy for people with Internet access to contribute and collect information when he gave specifications for HyperText Markup Language (HTML, the code in which websites are written), HyperText Transfer Protocol (HTTP, the code by which sites are moved in and out of the web), and URLs. He continues to promote the web as an open, accessible, interactive, and universal community, and his book *Weaving the Web* is about his creation's past, present, and future vision.

Universal Studios

American Caucasian history is recent compared to Europe, but they have meticulously preserved it to cultivate the cultural aspect. Take the film industry. Aside from the entertainment value of cinema and television, you can experience how films are made at the entertainment park of Universal Studios in Hollywood. The real atmosphere is recreated here, from cinematography to acting and editing. You can enjoy how different scenes of the film *Psycho* were shot, and feel that you are directing the film along with Alfred Hitchcock. This is an outstanding way of bringing back a sense of history by making people experience it.

I would love to hear from you about how we in India can bring living substance into history. Write to me at shombit@shiningconsulting.com. Let us drive the knowledge grid to help future generations benefit from history, so tomorrow prospers through invention.

LOYAL GAY LIBERTINES

Take a look at the history of free expression. Catholicism took 17 centuries to grant liberty of expression. Thereafter, science, invention, art, and literature flourished. An American president took just over four years into his term to set a precedent by endorsing homosexual marriage. That has bubbled up wide-ranging, negative–positive views across the world. Being black, did Barack Obama empathize more with the discrimination that non-mainstream people are subjected to? Experience of such prejudice could be on account of race, color, caste, gender, and same-sex marriage, among others.

My first gay encounter

Pede comme un phoque, meaning gay like a seal is how my colleagues had cautioned me when I was assigned to assist Maitre Arte, Russian-born French art deco artist. I had to clean scratches in his lithographic prints on paper in a closed room. That was my first brush with the concept of homosexuality. As a 20-year-old sweeper in a lithography paint shop near Paris in 1974, I did not understand their warning as I still could not speak French.

I deeply revered this first art master I met, a gracious, creative, and humble person who treated me as an equal artist, saying, "Art is a silent giant that stays, it's never obsolete." Arte trained me that, "Art does not sell by itself. It's not like physics or chemistry with the intrinsic ability to move. As an artist you have to make art go places." After he had migrated to the US and become a famous designer in many fields including fashion, jewelry, graphic arts, costume, and set design for theater, film, opera, and interior décor, I came to know he was a homosexual. Because the first homosexual I had ever met was Arte, whose talent, passion, and love for human beings is etched in my mind, I have become a supporter of the gay community.

Unparalleled intellectual connect

Jean Francois Trouve, a most talented business principal in my Paris office who had worked 10 years with me, makes no bones about his being gay. I will never forget his elegance, extravagant knowledge, and perceptive behavior. He loves to drive my Mercedes, and being of short stature, pulls the seat up front. But when he returns the car, he has never failed to leave the seat exactly the way he found it. I have met his boyfriend Bertrand several times; they have lived together for over 25 years now. This exceptional couple's intellectual connect with me is unparalleled.

The 1980s AIDS propaganda in Europe was that all homosexuals are in trouble. I was very scared for them, but Jean Francois explained:

> AIDS has obliged gays to re-invent a new sexuality, more sensual, more based on sharing moments. The fear of the damaged condom is always present in our mind. AIDS actually reinforced links in gay couples, there's more fidelity now, less sexual partners! Sexuality will always be important for us, but in a bit different way.

While writing this, I gave Jean Francois a call and found him in his country house. He and Bertrand had taken his father for a vacation there.

Theatrics at a gay café in Paris

Jean Francois introduced me to the famous gay café in Le Marais district, Paris' legendary gay quarter. It is a place to become drugged by creativity. Nothing can replace for me this most fashionable district of incredible creativity because I am forever looking out for new ideas for corporate work or my own paintings. Alone one day in this gay café, I was concentrating on some writing when a little drama unfolded. I may have been the only non-gay person at the café so I tried not to give any false impression.

Seated at the next table was a gay couple, one dressed in a manly fashion reading a newspaper, while his partner with female mannerisms was holding his hand, looking up to his face lovingly. But the newspaper reader paid scant attention.

Upset or perhaps bored by this lack of response, the partner's eyes strayed to a nearby table. The man there turned an expressive face, making inviting eyes. It was an amazing experience watching this fabulous romantic adventure in such an open space. Contact of four eyes, interlocked in fascinating gestures that even a man–woman couple cannot craft. Slowly the partner released the newspaper reader's hand and went toward the toilet, making a wonderful body movement like a woman. The man making eyes followed him.

When his partner returned talking animatedly to the other guy, the newspaper reader looked annoyed, put down his paper. But tantalizingly ignoring him, his partner continued to chat away with the other guy, but took stealthy sideways glances at the newspaper reader. In one such look their eyes suddenly locked and stayed hooked for a while. Then the partner hissed the word, "Jealous!" to the newspaper reader. Theatrically the newspaper reader threw his paper and stormed angrily out of the café at high speed. Immediately, the partner ran behind him in utter despair, calling out in a shrill voice, "Pierre! Pierre! *Je t'aime mon amour…*" (Pierre, I love you…).

Gays hate hypocrites

The Paris gay circuit may not be as effusive today, but gays hate hypocrites and are extremely sensitive. My creative route led me to many genuine friendships. From them I have discovered intra-gender nuances of the "active gay," with the male role, and "passive," the woman's role. Normally the roles do not change, but there is total democracy to switch as per the couple's choice.

Among my gay women friends in Europe, many had heterosexual marriages that broke up because they were frustrated over men's attempts to dominate them. They subsequently became gay, and explain how lesbianism is very different. According to them, both women are at the same level, with a comfortable, acceptable hint of dominance and submission. Their emotional and sexual pleasures are different from men so their harmony is a win–win game. They will never return to the man–woman liaison.

In today's democratic world we still find opponents of homosexuality becoming incensed when two men or two women kiss before a marriage judge. However, let us hope that Barack Obama's support of gay rights signals a positive change of wind across different cultures and countries.

OOZING CREATIVITY

Is there a link between homosexuality and creativity? This intriguing subject is recognized and debated in the West. Heightened gay creativity, it is reasoned, comes from exceptional coping skills as gays traverse tremendous societal pressures and so they become super inventive. Initially when gay feelings emerge, young people experience confusion about their sexuality. Feeling isolated even from the family, they become adept at creative expressions.

Incredibly crafted David

Gay creativity is spontaneous, vibrant, deep, intelligent, and soaked in sentiment, with a soft corner for human society. Let me illustrate. I often go to Italy's Accademia di Belle Arti Gallery in Florence to see a 5.17 m (17 ft) piece of marble weighing over six tons. The emotion of the man who sculpted this colossal single marble with an extraordinary expression of a Biblical man never fails to amaze me. You can still see its original uneven marble remaining as the pedestal. Most people would evenly cut Italian marble of this size as slabs of flooring for luxurious homes, but Michelangelo crafted the incredible David, a standing male nude.

When studying in Kolkata's Government College of Art & Craft before leaving India, I had become familiar with David, imagining it to be 5–6 ft high. The first time I stood in front of this Renaissance masterpiece created in 1501–1504, I was shell-shocked, not just from its size, but the perfect anatomy of the whole body. This was the masterstroke of a homosexual genius. Such unparalleled artistic skill I find only in another gay artist, Leonardo da Vinci.

The only Indian-origin global rock star

In 1980s, I was among those millions who worshipped that rare, four-octave-spanning, Western opera-type voice of my rock-star hero. I would follow him from London to Buenos Aires to New York just to hear him belt out super-hit songs. Thousands of crazed spectators would swoon and screech with excruciating joy at his powerful, pulsating stage presence. Even his vulgar gestures looked like visual art. This was Freddie Mercury, a pseudonym for Farrokh Bulsara, a Zanzibar-born Parsi Indian. He was Asia's and India's first mega rock star, songwriter, and composer, voted in polls by several Western magazines, radio, and TV channels to be the world's all-time greatest singer or second-greatest entertainer after Michael Jackson.

Freddie Mercury's is a story of another homosexual who died of severe AIDs. His band, Queen, sold over 300 million records; sales continue unabated even after his 1991 death at the age of 45. His tremendous talent combined all musical genres, revolutionizing music for millions of fans world-wide. Huge Freddie Mercury sculptures have been erected in Montreux, Switzerland and London. In 1999, British Royal Mail issued a postage stamp of him in performance.

In the way Charles Chaplin is considered British, although he gained fame in the US and spent his last years in Switzerland, Freddie is a Gujarati who studied in India. What is regrettable is that India never did recognize Freddie Mercury. Bollywood songs, many copied from Western tunes and genres, have made celebrities of playback singers known through cinema actors. Apart from Oscar or Nobel winners, globally reputed winners created by the masses like Freddie Mercury also deserve our acknowledgment. He is an inspiration for young Indians who want to excel at the performing arts beyond Bollywood's boundaries.

Gay creativity overflows in Paris

When a city brims with love and sexuality, creativity also reigns. Since the 16th century, beautiful Paris has recorded several gays, from writers Théophile de Viau, Marcel Proust, and Jean Cocteau, to composer Jean-Baptiste Lully, poet Paul Verlaine, and fashion designers Jean Paul Gaultier, Karl Lagerfeld, and others.

Meeting the creator of the YSL brand

In Montparnasse, I had often frequented Lutetia Hotel for a cup of coffee. On weekend afternoons, two men, one tall, the other short, would come in with a small dog. Their elegance was a pleasure to watch. This was Yves Saint Laurent and his companion, brilliant intellectual Pierre Bergé, who together created the luxury fashion brand YSL. The creative St Laurent is no more with us, but I can still visualize this gay couple's artistic rapport.

In 1991 I had made a drastic change in Danone's brand Taillefine, internationally called Vitalinea. Bringing the concept of 0 percent fat and "*cosmetique qui se mange*" (cosmetics you can eat), I introduced violet color in yogurt branding. That shocked France. I had explained to Danone that L'Oréal products are for surface beauty, but bacteria-based Danone yogurt acts inside the body to keep real beauty intact.

Pierre Bergé read my revolutionary idea in the newspaper. Before launching YSL skin-care products, he called me. We spent some time on cosmetique qui se mange. He wanted to hear me talk about the latent trends among women. Most spectacularly, he surprised me with his eloquence on Bengali culture, including writer Sarat Chatterjee.

Brilliant gay intellectuals

The universal intellectual brilliance of homosexual writers have shaped timeless ideas in millions of readers. Among gay authors are Oscar Wilde, Christopher Marlowe, Ralph Waldo Emerson, Tennessee Williams, Truman Capote, Walt Whitman, W.H. Auden, Gertrude Stein, André Gide, Arthur Rimbaud, E.M. Forster, and Hans Christian Andersen. Performing gay entertainers who have dented our imagination include George Michael, Elton John, Lady Gaga, Rudolf Nureyez, and composers Tchaikovsky, Leonard Bernstein among many more.

Ethical cosmetics turning gay

San Francisco's Castro Street with multicolored flags is a manifestation of hardcore gay culture. I saw gay customers making eyes at one another in the large mirrors of a 1930s-style art deco barbershop. What startled me was Body Shop, seller of "ethical" cosmetics, completely customizing the outlet to welcome gays. The shop's entry picture had a man's nude buttock with words conveying that it was the best cream for sexual pleasure.

Early record

Existence of homosexuality has been recorded since 2300 BC in ancient Egypt, but its public acceptance took several centuries. Did you know that Greek philosophers from Zeno in 500 BC to Socrates, Aristotle, even Macedonian ruler Alexander the Great were all gays, also Roman emperor Julius Caesar? There is a contemporary LGBT culture for the lesbian, gay, bisexual, and transgender community, although not everyone subscribes to this reference term. Without differentiation among human beings will not the world become boring?

REIGNING OF CONSISTENCY

I am a great lover of consistency, which I have learnt from different experiences in life such as business, painters, singers, entertainers, and LGBT culture, among others.

In the business domain, big objectives applied consistently leads to sustainability, the capacity to endure the market to overcome competition. Even brands that are consistent have become sustainable in business over time. An example among others is Nike. From its inception, Nike has shifted its business approach from the language of footwear to another experience of human life, the sporty character that eggs people on to "Just do it." In this way Nike has the power to control the consumer in the highly commoditized footwear market .

Picasso & Marceau

Somewhere that consistency or coherence is important for it brings a comfort feeling, which is predictability. Picasso changed his painting style many times in his 92 years of artistic life, but even without his signature there is always something you can recognize in his paintings that identifies it to be his genius. All-time mime king Marcel Marceau, my very close friend, confided in me that he had to maintain consistency in style through his different performances across time. This way he endorsed his technique to his faithful fans from his young age, midlife, and later career mime shows.

Shakira

Another outstanding example of consistency is from Colombian singer Shakira with her song "Ojos Asi" (Eyes like yours). I have seen her in at least five different concerts, from MTV Unplugged to shows in Dubai, Amsterdam, and others, with different makeup, hair color and bitsy outfits, very different ambience in terms stage sets and spectators, but every time, her belly dance, performance steps with the mike stand, and body movements were always exactly the same.

I have even used this consistency example in different workshops I have conducted for my corporate clients in India and abroad. And invariably all the participants want to better understand how Shakira has achieved sustainability as a star performer by demanding to watch, over and over again, how she is consistent in her dance!

Paris

The city of Paris, my home since 1973, displays sustainability like no other. Under Napoleon III, between 1852 and 1870, Paris was transformed by his préfect, Baron Georges-Eugène Haussmann. Haussmann's plan to modernize Paris leveled the narrow, winding medieval streets to create a network of wide avenues and neoclassical façades that still make up much of modern Paris. It encompassed all aspects of urban planning, from regulations imposed on façades of buildings, streets, public parks, sewers, water works, city facilities, and public monuments. Disease epidemics ceased, traffic circulation improved, trees were planted. Cleaning up living areas implied better air circulation, provision of water, and evacuation of waste.

A new water provisioning system led to the construction of 600 km of aqueduct between 1865 and 1900. These aqueducts discharged water in a newly built city reservoir, the largest in the world. Haussmann's 19th-century urban scenario has, until the 21st century, sustained a profound positive influence on the everyday lives of Parisians.

Acropolis

On a visit to Greece I was suddenly sparked by another European example of consistency. ESOMAR, the global research organization, had invited me to deliver a keynote address to their 1,000-peopled congress in Greece. I spoke on "Disrupt to Connect to 21st Century's Digital Zappers." The sharp contrast of this contemporary subject in front of the Acropolis (from the fifth century BC) of Athens felt uncanny.

I have often been to Greece on work since 1985. But this time, dining with my Greek friends overlooking the ancient Parthenon and watching everybody busy with modern mobile phones, the European consistency of carefully sustaining their heritage became very stark. You will not enjoy such unique disparity between the ancient and contemporary times in a young civilization like the US. The Acropolis and its monuments are universal symbols of the classical spirit and civilization bequeathed by Greek antiquity to the world.

Consistency maintained very strongly year after year, generation after generation, century after century becomes an icon of symbolic expression. Picasso was consistent over 92 years, but consistency can be momentous even in shorter life spans. Raphael, the 16th-century painter, and the 18th-century music composer, Wolfgang Amadeus Mozart, both died in their 30s. But the magnificent artistic works they left behind have become references of classicism that we follow till today.

Sustainability has become a buzzword in the business world to satisfy shareholders in quarter-to-quarter results. The impact of the last recession has made business houses co-opt this word vigorously, and also use it for being politically correct in the environmental sphere. Sustainability is also related to a community's quality of life, whether the social, economic, and environmental systems that make it up are providing a healthy, productive, meaningful life for all residents of the community, present and future.

Nuclear tests

The devil's work can also be consistent. By official count, about 2010 nuclear bombs have been consistently tested by mostly developed nations. The environmental destruction is both short- and long-term, triggering landslides, tsunamis, fish poisoning, earthquakes, and severe atmospheric pollution. Ironically, these developed countries are now asking for sustainability from the rest of the world.

Is it a farce when they meet at world environment summits? Surely the scientists knew the damage all these nuclear tests would cause to our planet, yet for about 50 years they continued their devil-like nuclear programs. Consciously, if we can be positively consistent about whatever we do now to protect the planet, it will result in environmental sustainability for future generations.

21ST CENTURY DISRUPTS AND CONVERGES

Are we ready for the new departure that the 21st century's digital era is bringing to human society? Change, after all, is the only consistent permanence.

21st-century diversity

The innovation explosion, which now comes every 20 days, as opposed to every 20 years in the 20th century has brought center-stage the role of psycho-socio diversity.

To understand and measure this 21st-century diversity, we have found yesterday's effective tools to be quite inadequate. Let me take you through our psycho-socio-behavioral discoveries with new codifications.

Our global business interactions for different brands have shown us that living in this disruptive century are three distinct generations in eight socio-behavioral clusters. We have already touched upon the three generations, the tech-born Digital Zap, Compromise, and Retro generations.

The eight socio-behavioral clusters (as seen in the Chapter 2 mini-tale slice called *Art of mass connect*) we have identified are: (*a*) low key (*b*) value seeker, who gets involved only when a worthwhile payoff is seen, (*c*) sober, who goes about things with quiet efficiency, (*d*) flamboyant, who is an exhibitionist, (*e*) critical, who is a perfectionist, (*f*) novelty seeker (*g*) techy, who goes for the digital mode, and (*h*) gizmo lover. These clusters were spun off from Digital Zap, but are common to Compromise and Retro generations too.

Connecting to Digital Zap

When I ventured into Paris at age 19, I found myself hugely different from other 19-year-olds. That was in 1973. As I was poor and came from a refugee colony in West Bengal, it was natural that I did not connect with them. But I later discovered that even among people of the same generation in Europe and America, there was disconnect.

Winston Churchill once said it was not easy to get European and American youth in the Allied nations to join World War II. In contrast, the leaders of the enemy Axis powers had ignited passion in their youth to fight for their newfound ideologies. So, only by carefully crafting communication, the Allies managed to align their youth to go to war against the enemy.

My business travels to different continents has now made me realize that the youth today in every country, more or less, have similar ideas on how to live life. This is the real globalization, the globalization of the mind. But management decisions in corporate houses across the globe are often made by the Retro and Compromise generations. That is why Digital Zap has a huge disconnect to many industries today. A few exceptions would be Google, Apple, Nike, and Cisco among others, companies that Digital Zap connects to.

Change to disruption and convergence

The process of change from 19th (mechanical era) to 20th century (electronic era) was big, but evolutionary. For example, there is no radical difference in the looks, mechanism, or functioning of a mechanical gramophone and electronic modern turntable. But in the 21st century came the iPod, breaking every known system for operating a musical player. iPod and MP3 players are disruptive in every sense. The change they have rushed in is entirely revolutionary.

Convergence is the name of the game now. The iPhone incorporates several industries and functions—it is a camera and a photo album, a bank and a data bank, a post and telegraph office, a writing pad and a pen, an audio and a video player, a calculator and an alarm clock, and much more. Do you know how to grab this diverse world of disruption and convergence in the 21st century?

Revolutionary change in the 21st century

Using the music player, let us illustrate 20th century's innovation, from the invention of the tape recorder to about 20 years later when the Walkman hit the market. In comparison, 21st century's innovation every 20 days is represented by newer versions of mobile phones, software, and digital products. Even the fashion industry has experienced last century's unsettling detonation but the flow of change was harmonious.

Then bang comes 21st century's fashion communication. The brand Diesel says, "Smart has the brains, Stupid has the balls. Be stupid." In one of their ads, a boy almost tumbles over a bus window to kiss a girl on the street. Dolce & Gabana shows a woman on the floor, body arched, and four men around her, suggesting group sex. An Emanuel Ungaro woman is sensually enjoying hedonistic pleasure. Tom Ford has two nude couples lying on the floor. Calvin Klein jeans portrays an orgy. Such distractions pervade almost every aspect of life globally. What was considered appropriate to be hidden yesterday is out in the open today.

Digital Zap at the cusp of the century

I consider every one below 30 to be Digital Zappers as they are fully conversant with digital technology.

Tomorrow there may not be Compromise or Retro generations because Digital Zap will continue to drive future generations. It may become Digital Zap Mature, Digital Zap Ripened, and Digital Zap Youth. A century storm is what Digital Zap represents. Engulfed in 21st century's rapid change, they have no attachment to anything in any sustaining way.

Differences in attitude are clearly visible

To get the news, Retro reads a newspaper at home, Compromise uses the Internet at office, while Digital Zap stays in touch with an iPad or smart mobile phone while on the go. To communicate, Retro writes letters, Compromise phones, and Digital Zapper just texts. The more you think, act, and align with youth, the more you connect to the happenings in the world. Irrespective of whether they are spenders, Zappers influence purchases in the family. They are a new civilization of digital connectors.

The way the baby-boomer generation dominated the second part of the 20th century, Digital Zap is set to revolutionize the 21st century. They are dictating terms in every sphere, are in tune with the world's diverse ways in every aspect. I salute Digital Zap, the future of business, and the way we will live.

SOCIETAL AND BUSINESS CONVERGENCE

Connecting to India's billion plus, extremely heterogeneous, people would perhaps be among the world's biggest challenges. When you are able to do so, the scope for business would be humungous. In their Global Market Forecast for 2032, Airbus has predicted the Indian sky will have the world's fastest growing domestic aviation route, and low-cost carriers (LCC) will grow the fastest. Asia Pacific will witness a fourfold growth of middle classes, rising from being 32 percent to 62 percent of the world, and emerging regions will contribute 70 percent of the economic growth between 2027 and 2032.

So to understand the behavior of India's diversity, you need to bite multiple times into the fabulous Indian jalebi. Most sweets in the world are made in a mould so there's a form of homogeneity. Jalebis may be the only universally popular sweet in the world where every jalebi form is different while having an archetype. This metaphor corresponds to India's heterogeneous society where complexity reigns and homogeneity does not exist. As all jalebis are different, the behavior, skills, and outlook of all Indians are different.

In my observations from Indiscope, My Political Whiff to being a Globetrotter, and looking at the historical perspective, I find human behavioral change to be society's most dynamic fireball. Feudal and monarchical society has always wanted to retain tradition and the supremacy they enjoyed, so the people they subjugated had little scope for change. Agrarian society followed Nature's cycle where people adapted to seasons without considering behavior change. From 17th century Catholic reforms onwards, the arts, science, literature, and philosophy were liberated from the religious code. Before this, even imaging something beyond the obvious was like a crime. With the evolution of science, people went against nature to control it, thereby disproportionately changing behavior. Science pushed people toward nonstop imagination so the unobvious has become the obvious today and will continue to be tomorrow.

ALTER BEHAVIOR, BECOME ICONIC

Agents that play a critical role in changing behavior are culture, food, and human touch devices, that is, the ergonomic relationships between people and machines.

Culture

Nowhere is culture changing behavior more visible than in China. When Deng Xiaoping led the country after Mao Zedong, he introduced reforms from 1978 with his slogan of "To get rich is glorious." This inspired private enterprises to grow. His de-collectivized communes shifted to the household responsibility system which made millions of peasants return to family farming. Village and town industries responded to the market. Shenzhen, a little village near

Hongkong became a special economic zone (SEZ) in 1979; today it's the world's largest manufacturing hub.

Opening up to international trade made Western influences enter politics, culture, the economy, challenging official values and moving beyond urban to rural areas. Dramatic culture change included family woes like broken homes. As incomes grew so did adultery. Divorce cases rose from 341,000 in 1980 to 2.2 million in 2013. Suspicious wives are resorting to private detectives who use secretive measures like attaching GPS trackers to their suspects' cars or monitoring their calls. Such spying services are illegal but continue as privately collected evidence has been permitted in civil law suits. So, traditional Chinese culture is undergoing changes akin to capitalistic societies.

Religion is not necessarily a part of culture

Cultural attributes that change behavior are basic functioning of day-to-day family life, health, education, economic conditions, lifestyle, and livelihood generation. Religion is not part of it unless the society is monatomic with one religion driving the socio-eco-political spectrum. Culture started before religion or civilization where people discovered how to make fire, find food for survival, or draw cave pictures.

It's evident that materialism brings behavioral change. Take material comforts that Indian Godmen enjoy such as air-conditioned rooms and cars, first or business class air travel instead of meditation under the trees. Their disciples may have thrust these comforts upon them, but it's obvious these disciples have managed to change the habits of Godmen. In the West, economic capitalism has changed deep-rooted religious practice with modern life when people say, "I'm Catholic but not practicing."

Food

Food is the behavior changer. For example, immigrant children pick up the new country's eating routine, although their parents may take time to change because they entered the foreign country at an older age. On the other hand when food is designed with strong universal appeal, it can change behavior beyond any frontier. The world's mass-level people can never accept French style rare mincemeat beefsteak, but a well-done beef patty covered with salad, cheese, and sauce within a bun becomes the familiar, favored McDonald's. Change beef to chicken, it even works with heterogeneous Indians who have heterogeneous food habits. Rarely in India will you find a traditional Indian food restaurant chain across the country. Every state will have different restaurants with local cuisine. Even the Chinese devour burgers, abandoning their centuries-old noodles habit.

Behavioral change from convenience

Successful packaged food companies in developed countries have remarkably turned people from handmade to readymade food. Without laborious work you just microwave an enjoyable dinner of varied dishes. Europe's recent trend is frozen bakery and dessert, unheard of 20 years earlier as freshness found in specialized shops or home baking was always valued. Today companies have converted consumers to buy frozen stone-like mousse from supermarkets.

When heated this soft product tastes incredibly good, so there's no more hesitation to consume elaborate premade pastries.

Fast food is snowballing

"Eat slowly" is India's social nicety when hosting a meal for invited guests. Yet along with 118 countries worldwide, India has abandoned specific, food-related cultural nuances to embrace typical American fast food like McDonald's. Europeans hated this "time is money" fast food concept, resisting its entry, but when at midnight you don't find any restaurant open in rural Europe, a McDonald's welcomes you. In fact McDonald's has democratized society globally. A low-economic strata family now dares to eat at the extremely expensive Champs Elysees high street of Paris because affordable McDonald's is there. Also, tourists amidst alien ways and food habits make a beeline for the predictably familiar McDonald's.

In places famous for gastronomy like France and Italy, McDonald's tweaks its menu and décor to attract localites. In Milan's 14th-century Piazza del Duomo with Galleria Vittorio Emanuele II, the world's oldest and beautiful shopping mall, there's luxury brand Prada on the left, Louis Vuitton on the right, Cartier, Gucci, Ferragamo all within eye view jostling for prominence. I was amused to see the bright yellow M twinkling at the edge, saying "I'm lovin' it" and attracting heavy traffic in total defiance of the dissonance traditionalists feel. The only food connecting poor, rich, old and young across heterogeneous India is the jalebi, which is the idea of my *Jalebi Trilogy* because jalebis represent everyone. India's traditional food habit is different every

500 km, but McDonald's with the same veg and nonveg menu is mesmerizing all age groups across south, east, north, and west. This is the US$28 billion McDonald's incredible spirit of changing the eating behavior of Indians.

Ergonomical behavioral change

Physical instruments that humans touch for playing, working, or entertaining can disruptively change behavior. Just imagine, before Thomas Edison there was no repeated listening to music, sound, or voice. The gramophone entirely modified our approach to entertainment. After Graham Bell's telephone invention our primary communication style changed from using the pigeon, horse rider, or cycling postman as messengers. People held two instruments with both hands to talk and listen; then landline phones became one instrument; now the mobile phone is a single device you keep in your pocket. This behavior-changing evolution spans from the mechanical, electric, and electronic to the digi-tech age.

Products that changed behavior

Making money by selling a product or service in any industry is routine. Innovation that changes the end-user's behavior is the real breakthrough, the pull of a brand's lasting edge in society.

How and why do people change their behavior to use one product rather than the other? Historical trend is a great source to understand this. Enterprises that contributed toward human behavioral change have always provided some extra benefit and mileage in their products and critical uncommon drive at the social level which the masses were sensitive to perceive.

Inventing the jeans

Let's take the birth of jeans, the most popular garment worldwide. Blue jeans have changed the way we want to look and feel—casual, comfortable, and fashionable. In a town called Nîmes in the south of France, there were monks in the 19th century who used strong material to make protective clothing to shield poor people from winter's cold. This was the origin and invention of jeans, the practical clothing for multiple and long-term usage. In the 1870s, a Bavarian immigrant to the US called Levi Strauss imported this cloth to make trousers for people going out to explore the American Wild West. He supposedly made them in Genoa that's the origin of the word "jeans." The cloth came to be known as denim from "*de Nîmes*" which in English means "from Nimes." And so the denim culture started for the masses. While American cowboys used jeans as rugged wear, the category was called by its original denim name to make it more authentic. This shows us how Americans are loyal to authenticity.

France, among the first in the world to revolt against monarchy in 1789, took *liberté* very seriously, one of the three social values of liberty, fraternity, and equality. So it is normal that France gifted the Statue of Liberty to the US which has since then become the symbol of America in New York. You'll find its smaller scale model on River Seine in Paris. This American symbol of liberty transcended to the casual denim. The initiative that Levi's brand took was an incredible contribution to the world. Wearing jeans made people change their behavior. Now you can do any job with just one style of dressing, the jeans, and feel at home in all the jobs.

Since the 1920s, Americans invented the idea of casual dressing. The lavish European dressing style started to see difficulties after World War I. Then the Great American Depression in the 1930s made clothing more somber and requiring less dress material. This led to sportswear becoming fashion, the start of the denim culture. In fact in 1992 the Levi's company gave it another push by publishing a manual called *A Guide to Casual Businesswear*. This was sent to 25,000 Human Resources Managers across the US and it set the tone for business casuals. So casual dressing is not just a dress, it is a radical change of behavior.

Changing role of innerwear for women

Changing the behavior of women wearing innerwear is said to have started in ancient Egypt 3000 BC. Its purpose was to alter a woman's shape to preserve her modesty. Later came the French name lingerie, originating from *linge* meaning linen which first referred to undergarments as scandalous. During the French Revolution, women's lingerie was revolutionized. Women discarded all symbols of French aristocracy including their conforming underwear such as petticoats, corsets, and camisoles, and panties first appeared.

From 1890 the brassiere had begun to replace corsets as women started to participate more in sports and energetic dancing. The bra changed women's looks from flattening breasts to accentuating them. In 1935 Warner Brothers labeled the "alphabet bra" with four cup sizes: A, B, C, and D used even today. During World War II, when materials such as steel and rubber were in short supply, synthetic materials such as lycra, rayon, and lastex were used to make undergarments.

Designer contribution

In 1948 Monsieur Christian Dior invented "hourglass" innerwear fashion. From the 1968 French Student's Revolution highlighting freedom and nonconformity, the expression of women's liberation was strengthened. Women publicly burnt bras in protest. The garter, made for sex workers to hypnotize their customers, was made the trend in 1980 by French brand Dim. In 1990 Calvin Klein's advertisement had men and women wearing underwear with branded waistband. It was showing above jeans for the man, the woman wore nothing but panties. These are all attempts by designers and industrialized brands to change human behavior. The way Victoria's Secret, the world's biggest lingerie seller, presents its wares in London's famous high fashion Bond Street store is as though it's the Louvre Museum's painting presentation. In multiple niches there are outstanding colorful carnival-like displays of women posing with innerwear.

Such examples show how creative people and industries have changed women's behavior. You can as well ask why women spend so much money for innerwear that's not publicly visible. Not only that, men's attitude toward women has changed; they have understood that women can be socially exuberant with their body because it's their self-liberty.

Historically, the shift has been from corsets that squeezed the waist during Elizabethan times to the Wonderbra that highlighted the breasts to create a definite cleavage. In essence, lingerie has defined the meaning of beauty of women's bodies during different eras and so reveals the changing role of women in society.

CREATE ADDICTION, TRANSFORM HABITS

Behavioral change is extremely physical. There's got to be some bodily object that interacts with people for behavior to change, no intangible theory can do this job at the mass level.

Evolutionary stages of shaving

The straight razor where the blade folds into its handle, what roadside barber shops still use, was invented in 1680s. In 1901, Gillette initiated the double-edged safety razor with replaceable blades. To modernize men's shaving habit, Gillette invented the single side razor. Introducing the "razor and blades business model" or inexpensive razor with disposable blades, Gillette grew its business tremendously. The beauty here is the high-tech blade; it's expensive but gives a large number of shaves, the razor picks it up from its packaging socket, men don't touch it. It's so efficacious, simple, and safe that women are attracted to use it.

So year after year with single focus Gillette follows every generation, social trend, state-of-the-art engineering with precision manufacturing to innovate and revolutionize the way the world shaves. The Fusion ProGlide with FlexBall Technology has a maneuverable handle that moves, adjusts, pivots across a man's facial contours to allow capturing every facial hair. This is a grand example of Gillette's drive for world leadership by constantly changing men's practical behavior.

Walkman was a visibly dynamic behavior changer

History shows that Philips, the fundamental inventor of many products, could barely get registered in people's minds as a behavior changing agent, whereas newcomer Sony, not a fundamental inventor, successfully did so with the Walkman in 1979. The behavioral change Walkman established was phenomenal; people moved around with little earphones, hands-free, enjoying music with a personal device.

Being able to transform habits often comes from single focused, creative entrepreneurial challenge. Sony masterminded entertainment devices with the Walkman, but it diversified, then ran into losses. Sony lost focus on entertainment devices for the digi-tech generation when it de-rooted its creative ingenuity into too many directions. The big behavioral change Sony Walkman introduced has shifted to Apple.

Roller-coastering with the smartphone

Changing people's habit and behavior through the smart mobile phone, Apple dynamized the finger touch. Monopolistic Microsoft missed the boat with people shifting from laptop to mobile phone. Till a few years ago I was comfortable with my Blackberry, the typewriter replica. The day my IT engineer changed my dumb phone to a smartphone, I was lost as in an Indian crossroads junction where you don't know where to go. But just a few days usage changed my habit.

I could never imagine I'd write articles and books on the touch screen. Just look at how these industries have not only innovated but contaminated people to change their product usage behavior.

Product changing behavior is never so easy

Behavior change through product usage is not always easy. Take the e-cigarette that's trying so hard to shift smokers. The response is minimal as e-cigarettes merely give flavored vapor that simulates tobacco smoking. Actually the main question is, "Do cigarette companies really want their business model to change?" Is the e-cigarette an eye-wash to fool the public and regulators that people's health is not being damaged? As the e-cigarette is not addictive it doesn't work toward behavioral change. So will smokers and cigarette companies forget about changing behavior and continue to injure health?

Behavior changing task for Indian companies

Are Indian companies ready to take global leadership by driving to change customer behavior? India's demand-led market is growing. When the demand is there, just supply; why ideate more? But actually, changing the behavior of a product's end-user does not happen by chance, nor is it a miracle. Only an enterprise with special motivation can make it happen. There are so many areas where industry in developed countries has changed the behavior of people.

We can expect tremendous change in future from India's Zap generation born after 1986. India needs creative business people and creative entrepreneurs to innovate the change in people's usage and behavior. This behavior changing industrialization should travel the world so that India's products and services can achieve high aspiration along with commercial business success globally.

On demand, IT services changed India's corporate work culture

When the West defined their work discipline to inject IT at every function, they hired Indian companies for their IT servicing requirement. What's radically changed India's working culture is servicing the global IT needs. That reigns in about US$80 billion every year to the country. The work culture change includes Indian service providers sitting at client locations abroad or servicing them from development centers in India while adjusting to different time zones across the world.

Also, young boys and girls in India work together in call centers. At age 18 in their first job after school these youngsters can earn up to ₹18,000 per month, whereas if their father was a simple worker he'd be earning that amount perhaps after 25 years. So father–child cultural behavior cannot be the same. News stories abound about condoms clogging call center drains. Employees also become disoriented and need counseling. That's because their speech has become American English at work where they respond to American names they use to talk to American customers. With friends they speak Indian English, and with the family, their native language. Their odd working hours make them miss all family functions and social contact outside office.

CHANGING BEHAVIOR IS A TASK OF PASSION

The substance of changing customer behavior always requires a distinct spark. The product or service has to be extremely humane and uplift routine to an ideal habit. Society's drivers may start the change in a small way, but if it's really scientific it quickly shapes up to addict the masses who are the followers in society.

Enterprises become iconic by winning the ultimate challenge of altering people's habits. Behavior change comes in two ways: at the basic level, all enterprises follow the same obvious route of avoiding product obsolescence; the other unobvious way is to spectacularly step forward toward making a distinct change.

The enterprise needs an ingenious mindset

It's the ingenuity of the enterprise that drives new behavior creation. Before the digital age crept up on us, human behavior took time to change. Digi-tech now helps speed up innovation for industrial production to surprise human needs up to desire. Another quick turnaround in the digi-tech age is desire transforming to need. Corporate ideation for changing and sustaining the customer's behavior tomorrow will be very different and challenging because of fast changing digi-trends. An innovative but traditional mindset company can make profitable growth, but when it can command the mechanism of changing behavior, it enters a higher league and metaphor. So without changing the behavior of employees, you cannot enter this league to command that industry as a leader.

Designer of any industry needs to bathe in contemporary insights

Children's physical attachment to Barbie, Lego, or Mechano sets has shifted to digitally driven games. If as a product designer you don't follow children's changing behavior with games or the education system, you won't be designing any saleable instrument for work, play, or entertainment tomorrow. I've seen my 9-year-old granddaughter Sreeya who lives in London, return from school at 4 pm, then rush to the computer at a prefixed time to work online on mathematics with her classmates for the next day's test. Their regular practice is to connect to the Internet for doing school homework together. Just imagine how digi-tech is changing children's behavior, Sreeya often takes up a challenge against any child who's online anywhere in the world. Even at office, digi-tech is infusing every domain with radical transformation, from HR recruitment to production to supply chain. Instead of spending time and money traveling, you conduct a multiple country meetings through tele-presence.

Creative entrepreneur

Changing the behavior of the masses through marketing and R&D activities is very different from traditional marketing and R&D. This behavior changing factor does not happen from the user only. It requires another dimension, that of becoming a creative entrepreneur. There has to be an osmosis between the willingness of an enterprise to change the public's behavior and the logic perceived by the public to go for that change. In the gene of the developed Western society, I have observed a strong tendency to innovate in order to change people's behavior. When they started to shift from being an agrarian society to becoming an industrialized consuming one, the ability to change the behavior of the masses became evident and one of the tasks to perform.

The way we worked 10 years ago is not the same now, but our attitude in certain areas will never change. Fashion is cyclic, something new comes, vanishes, returns and we knowingly ride that cycle happily. Whether you're an entrepreneur, a politician, or a philosopher, try enlisting culture, food, and our ergonomic relationship with devices, the agents that change human behavior, to really become iconic, capture mindshare, and sell your product or ideology across the world.

Customer centricity is the crux of business

Since 1984 when I founded Shining Consulting in Paris, I've been an entrepreneur consultant. In all these years I've had the opportunity of sitting with senior management teams from enterprises in diverse industries to infuse customer centricity into their products and services. This has been both a pleasurable experience and the toughest job in my business life.

I've always faced two types of clients: those interested in achieving customer centricity and the large section that's quite indifferent. The interested ones put tremendous effort to understand how core the customer is. They drive hard to inject this core inside their organization, facing the difficult job of changing employee behavior. The second type of clients enters the comfort zone of ad hoc adaptability. They deliver what's feasible as per their backend capability and act as though customers will accept it. This is the trouble-free route of changing the bottle, not the wine, and hoping against hope that customers will not notice.

Without end-customers, where is business? Enterprises agree to this, but miss out on driving it seriously as business truth. It makes me very uncomfortable when management-level people barely put in effort to understand the end-customer's subconscious mind where buying motivation resides. I cannot fathom why trying to own the end-customer's mindshare is not the first priority of every enterprise. After all if an enterprise can find out what to do to change the end-customer's behavior toward favoring its product or service that enterprise can smile all the way to the bank.

Learning from the source of business

I believe in nonstop enterprise learning using customers as teachers and insight dispensers for business improvement. The ability to absorb human culture and behavior, anticipate economic and political phenomena in advance, co-opt technology advancement and dig deep into the social and psychological aspects are all necessary at this level to know how to respond to the market. However, industrial heaviness sometimes becomes so overpowering that managers get waylaid from the track of discovering and satisfying an end-customer's need or desire. In India in particular, it's a huge dilemma.

Because managers do not always live in the end-customer's domain, it becomes difficult to make them understand the micro layers of end-customer centricity. I very often become stubborn in defending the value that end-customers should legitimately be receiving. It's become my passion and obsession to add end-customer benefit in any enterprise I work for.

To tell you the truth, I'm addicted to observing human behavior. Wherever I am, with the family, in the sports ground, entertainment or working environment, seminars, condolence visits, while traveling, watching television, Internet surfing, visiting painting museums, or receiving response from my readers, my eye turns to watch behavioral traits and reactions. The rapport between people of any age and economic stratum, their relationship with some product or service, are indeed very telling.

No matter where and in which country I am, I don't hesitate to ask if something raises my curiosity. "Why" something I never ask as the person gets intimidated; it's the "how" I enquire and learn about the purpose. Learning can never be achieved when you are in the challenger mode. Rather I try to make learning conducive for both of us, me the learner and the end-customer as a teacher. These ingredients have helped me understand the end-customers in every industry wherever I have entered because no industry can run without an end-customer. Challenging a learning seed is totally destructive, as is the preconceived notion, which intellectuals and professionals are said to be guilty of. Preconception actually kills unearthing the new.

Corporate transformation is a mere jargon

It's true that behavioral change cannot be an easy job in a company aligned to market dynamics. You can transform a material in a machine to make products; iron ore can become steel. But human beings cannot be transformed like that. Actually changing employee behavior can be a nightmare in our country's multi-behavioral heterogeneity, because people work and interpret the same subject very differently inside an enterprise. When they go into social and family life, it's diametrically different. That's why a huge drive from management is required to thoroughly educate employees on the purpose and objective of internal behavioral change according to the changing end-customer trends.

The company has to patiently work to make employees understand the benefits of end-customer centricity. Not only will the enterprise get better returns, but employee skills will improve, careers will get furthered, which in turn will impact the enterprise. It's a very painstaking task. Unfortunately, most enterprises would rather spend money buying hallucinating capital assets than training human capital.

Need to deal with new market realities

Indian enterprises are largely growing in a demand-led market. Just to illustrate, look at the contrast. Organized retails in Western countries have captured more than 50 percent market share in every FMCG category. They sell high-quality private label products at 30 percent lower price than national brands. So most manufacturing company brands are in a tight situation. Indian manufacturers are likely to face this condition too when this market matures.

But managers today mistakenly believe that once they've performed in their key result areas, they've achieved the business strategically. In reality they have merely supplied to the existing demand. They have not worked to sustain their business, make it long-term sticky nor worked to deliver differently to get end-customer mindshare for repeat purchase consistently today and tomorrow.

Having brought end-customer centricity into several Indian enterprises in 15 years, I've seen growth happen when the end-customer centricity is tightened, and slacken when corporates get diverted to make easy money trading in diverse categories. When they lose sharp competency focus and capability, they become like conglomerates selling products in different categories wherever there is demand. With complacency and routine comfort, they bring products from China or cut price to make volume. They've still not taken seriously the global predator-competitors ready to kill, to grab market opportunity.

To capture local and global markets with sustainability, enterprises need to cultivate the passion for end-customer centric drive and change employee behavior to align with that. The best way to do so is to grab the changing behavior of the end-customers.

CONNECTING CHANGING BEHAVIOR TO BRAND FRIENDSHIP

Jalebi has a huge power of friendship. All Indians connect to it due to its dynamic character.

In today's dynamic changing world, digital technology is driving human behavior in all aspects of society across the globe. It's making ours a frontierless world. Merely the transactional act of selling brands will not be sufficient in tomorrow's business culture. Nor will excellence of engineering, good-looking products, big advertising budgets, or even highly skilled employees be enough for business success. Being constantly connected through real-time digitech, the customers' purchase and repurchase motivations, decision, and pattern have been revolutionized.

The industry needs to establish a relationship with customers beyond business by creating Brand Friendship. This is a new idea I'm presenting on why and what to create for Brand Friendship to become obvious, from the product/service to the brand, from the point of purchase into social communication. The extent of Brand Friendship can be measured. Respecting cultural nuances of different countries, how the brand is embraced in day-to-day social context and its resultant business growth can be evaluated through a pre-formulated assessment system.

Brand Emerged as Inventors' Bequest

Religion, it can be argued, is the origin of branding. All religions had intangible ideology but they created a physical manifestation with tangible architecture and collaterals. This comprised the genesis of branding but with no commercial give and take. I'm naming this sanctified unification through fraternal relationships as Brand Friendship. For example, The Early Christian Church adopted "INRI" (in Latin, Iēsus Nazarēnus, Rēx Iūdaeōrum; in English Jesus the Nazarene, King of the Jews) as a symbol which appeared in many paintings of the crucifixion.

Similarly, when formal monarchies emerged, the monarch's emblem was the brand that symbolized his power when conquering lands and making people subservient to him. Initially, flags with heraldic symbols created brand identities and statements. For example, *Dieu et mon droit* (divine right to govern) is the British monarch's motto, inscribed below the British coat of arms.

Historical perspective of the brand

The era of commercial branding started in Europe through inventors after the 17th century when the Age of Enlightenment made Christianity liberalize the pursuit of literature, science, art, and technology. Commercial branding timeline has two points of inflection. The first is when mechanization launched the Industrial Revolution, and the second is the onset of assembly line industrialization pioneered in/by the US (see Figure 4.1).

After Britain's Industrial Revolution from 1760, from previously handcrafted products, small-scale mechanized

Figure 4.1 Invention Chart

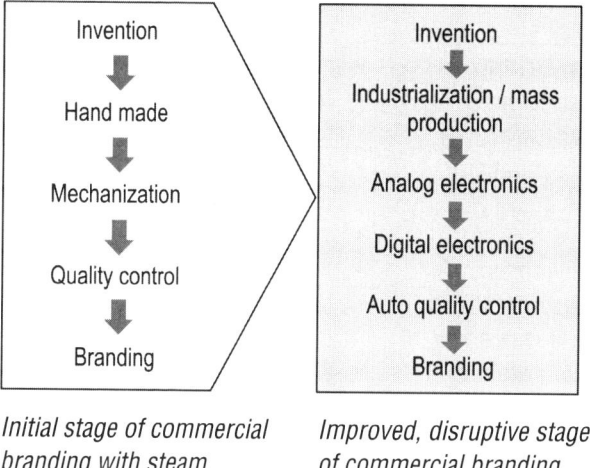

Initial stage of commercial branding with steam mechanization after 1760

Improved, disruptive stage of commercial branding with industrialization, end 19th century and onwards

Source: Author.

reproduction was made for selling. In time this led to commercial branding. Mechanization led to the shift from agrarian to industrial society. Its big impact was on transportation of goods and mass mobility.

In parallel, this started the big wave of migration; people started moving from one place to another on their own volition. Further improvement came with industrialization which helped to eventually reduce drudgery and increase productivity, slashing the number of hours worked. By the end of the 19th century–beginning 20th century, industrialization led to mass production and large-scale improvement in the wealth of society. For example, with Henry Ford's initiative, the Taylor system for mass production was introduced in the automobile industry. This was the beginning of modern Capitalism (Table 4.1).

Table 4.1 History of Branding: From Seals to the Arrival of Brand Friendship

1760–1850	**First British Industrial Revolution** (mechanization): From artisanal products to machine made products— *Branding through seals more for local sales*	• Hand production to machines made. • New chemical and ferrous production processes. • Improved efficiency of power from water and steam. • The development of machine tools. • From wood and other bio-fuels to coal-centered on textiles, iron and steam engine technologies. • Creation of turbines.
1867–1914	**Second Industrial Revolution** (USA centered): Mass production— *Start of commercial trademark & regional competition*	• Early factory electrification, mass production. • Building of railroads. • Large-scale iron and steel production. • Widespread use of machinery in manufacturing, start of assembly line. • Greatly increased use of steam power. • Electrical communications. • Revolved around steel, railroads, electricity, & chemicals.
1930–1956 / **Jet Age**	**Large-scale production & sophisticated technologies—**	• Hydrocarbon revolution. • Defined by the advent of aircraft powered by turbine engines. • Making transcontinental and intercontinental travel considerably faster and easier.
1957 onwards / **Space age**	*Start of commercial branding & heavy global competition*	• Rapid advances were made in rocketry, materials science, & computers.

(Table 4.1 Contd)

(Table 4.1 Contd)

1950–1970	Start of Electronic Revolution		• Change from analog, mechanical, and electronic technology to digital technology. • Mass production and widespread use of digital logic circuits. • Derived technologies, including the computer, digital cellular phone, and the Internet.
1970s onwards	**Information Age (Computer/Digital/ New Media Age):** Internet sales without country barrier, aside from heavy global commerce—***Start of digi-tech branding for individuals in the social context***		• Advances in computer microminiaturization. • Internet reaches a critical mass. • Information storage & retrieval (cloud computing is now the way to go). • Electronic data interchange. • Automation through robotics. • Mobile phone is becoming an essential commodity. • Arrival of Brand Friendship

Source: Author.

European inventors such as Louis Vuitton and Cartier among others, from bespoke became brands with logos, just like the medieval coat of arms that symbolized luxury. It is possible that the luxury category emerged from Europe because there was a distinctive royal society and aristocracy that craved premium and privileged products as necessary to display status.

Precision engineering pioneered by Karl Benz, Ettore Bugatti, among others, was another manifestation in the automobile industry. Henri Nestle created milk powder and condensed milk for infants as a substitute for breast milk. It is evident that due to the constraint of being in small independent nations where scale was not initially a consideration, brand creators in Europe historically made their brands more known globally in luxury and sophisticated engineering categories, but not in mass-scale production.

Branding in North America

North America, however, turned to a cowboy branding culture with no monarchical influence.

The hot stamping of American Wild West farm animals was simply to identify their different owners and not as statement. The 19th and 20th centuries saw an American shift toward inventive power of distinctive inventors such as Henry Ford (Ford Motors), Thomas Edison (GE), Graham Bell (telephone), George Eastman (Kodak), Procter & Gamble (P&G), James Casey (UPS), Charles Flint (IBM) among others. They started the culture of the commercial trademark.

After the trademark age which ended with World War I and II and right up to the end-1960s, the German Bauhaus school of design and Frenchman Raymond Leowy in the US among others extended branding philosophy with clean designs. These extremely stylized graphic concepts emphasized on strong typographic grammar. They brought a new style of branding.

In parallel, large American companies established their power through brand recognition symbols. Over time, Americans have mastered mass market production and perfected the religion of commercial branding with large-scale industrialization. They have provided affordable pricing to customers through inventive mass production processes. Ironically, the two World Wars helped American business to penetrate their brands globally.

Inventors created branding culture

It's very clear that both in Europe and America, the commercial branding culture originated with inventors who wanted to protect their inventions and hence they used trademark as a commercial weapon. The history of branding shows that it's only when customers experience enough distinction in the knowhow of a product or service, will they pay a premium for the brand.

Such a brand delivers better profit for the company with sustaining focus in the market.

In today's world, trading of available products from the market and stamping them as brands is not at all considered branding. Stamping a brand on traded products makes the brand quotient vulnerable and short lived.

Birth of the supermarket for self-help grocery shopping

With the birth of King Kullen in 1930s, the world's first supermarket invented by American Michael Cullen, branding underwent another stage. The self-help purchase pattern of supermarkets brought disruption worldwide. Behavioral and consuming pattern changed with the joy of shopping freedom. The brand had to become a self-selling provocation at the point-of-purchase.

As no retailer was behind the counter to advice on buying the product, the packaging itself had to have all details written on it. Customers now have the choice of multiple brands in the same category. So in any category, the brand has to perform from innovation to quality distinction translated as brand communication because customers make their choice in a matter of a few seconds. This liberalized shopping behavior of customers necessitated the creation of another kind of commercial self-help branding.

1970s was the departure of the digital technology era

From 1970s entrepreneurs such as Bill Gates and Steve Jobs among others, started the digital interface with customers. That stretched branding toward a new dimension continuing into the 1990s which saw a totally new digi-tech interface begin with Google, Facebook, Twitter, YouTube amongst others.

Japanese and Korean brand power

After World War II, countries such as Japan and Korea understood the meaning and power of the brand. Without tinkering with the fundamental invention of the Western world, they brought in refinement to make the delivery of existing invention extremely customer friendly both in terms of experience and in cost. This proves that without being a fundamental inventor, you can be an innovator through high-class refinement and by executing perfectly.

Digi-tech started the uncontrollable mass production of digitally driven products and services with cost reduction and without any industrial frontier. These digi-tech happenings created a huge disruption of absolute behavioral change in the human being.

In Today's Frontierless Global Paradigm, Business Requires the Brand in a Different Context

Summary of the brand's historical background

In nearly 300 years of invention, failure, and fine-tuning, the brand has placed the real value in products and services for customers. But the way the world has changed in the last 20 years has been exceptional and quite incomparable to the last three centuries.

The biggest disruption has been the breaking of frontiers among countries, enabled by digital technology. This phenomenon brought in a new language in the social context in total discord with the preceding 300 years. We cannot look at the brand today as we did traditionally. Its most critical aspect now is to deliver the quality that customers want. This creates a "friendship" between the brand and customer.

The customer is in command today

Digital technology's biggest contribution to the world is bringing extreme proximity among human beings. No longer can corporations have commanding power over their customers.

Previously, the distance between a company's boardroom and its customers was wide and cold. If your company was expanding locally or globally, you were advised to invest a percentage of your revenue in brand-building. You listened as though it's a ritual you cannot ignore. But did you check how efficacious your brand investment was?

Today, in spite of heavy investment, your customers can make you miserable through criticism in the social media that you cannot control.

Your customers can shift their purchase from your company's product to another company's because there is a huge choice in every given segment and in an instant. In India, I call the generation born after 1986 into a liberalized economy as Zappers who flit without loyalty to acquire the quality they want. Your internal industry actions no longer drive customers who are defining QCW (quality customers want). Only if you have the art of listening with process and passion can you address and convert customers of all age groups.

Otherwise like inward-looking Kodak, you will be out. By not anticipating human behavioral change, even Microsoft is experiencing a business descent. Usage of desktop computers is drastically falling in the market by 6 percent annually because people are moving to the smart mobile phone interface.

The digi-tech smartphone has made another sweeping change in human behavior. Several industries have been converged into the mobile phone. This, I'd say, makes the phone become more than a staple food. Nothing today can beat the innumerable things you can address in your daily life through the mobile phone. So if your business action is not instantaneously smart mobile phone centric, you will be left out in the customer's consideration.

Relationships that human beings desire

By nature, human desire has a cyclic logic of friendship. It is surrounded with trust, functional need, and emotion. These drive an orbit which cannot be dislocated in the human

Figure 4.2   Human Friendship Quadra Orbit

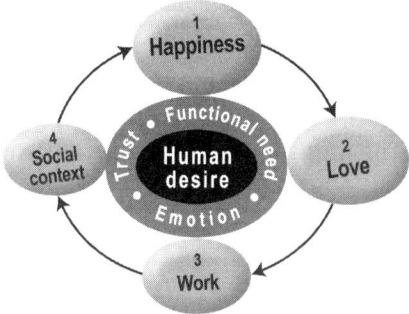

Source: Author.

paradigm. Happiness is the factor that's most desired in life at any age of an individual. It extends to love in multiple senses (see Figure 4.2).

From livelihood to lifestyle, human life is embedded with work, the struggle to achieve that elevates to happiness. All of this happens in a cocooning social context of collective life of caring, sharing, and understanding which translates to working in an environment of shared trust.

The social aspect is driven by friendship

Marriage is mere social recognition. If there's no friendship between a couple, infidelity starts and leads to the hide and seek game. After every deceptive trick is exhausted, it may translate to divorce or living together in cold war. "No friendship" between children and parents translates to "no trust." Children nowadays live the way they want, while playacting in front of parents.

If you spy on why your adult child did not return home last night, your friendship will definitely disappear even as the child gives a big lie and you want to believe it, although you know it's absolutely not true.

In this contemporary world, is there much meaning between being a minor and adult? How can you stop your minor child from not googling the porn website in your absence? So the definition of minor and adults needs a re-look.

On one hand, the social system is getting molded with friendship and on the other, the urge to possess is diminishing. For example, possessing a musical record, CD, DVD, or book is not the trend anymore. The physical points-of-purchase of all these products is closing. Everything is getting cloud driven for the purpose of using and sharing, but often by paying for it. Without this desire to possess at the individual level, it is evident that the brand can stick to the customer's mind like a friend socially does only through Brand Friendship. It follows the quadra orbit of human friendship.

The Disruptive Dimension to Create Brand Friendship

Brand is the first connection medium in business

As the brand is your first medium to connect to customers, the big question is how to drive it in this digi-tech, social zigzag world. Traditional marketing ideas of getting brand pull and emotional connect by hiring a recognized brand ambassador and spending heavily on a media blitzkrieg is not valid any more. International statistics show that 70–76 percent of purchase decisions happen at the point of purchase.

So you cannot buy society's emotion with money through media. Your only choice is to create Brand Friendship which is beyond the brand's monetary transactions.

What exactly is Brand Friendship?

The product experience and usage are the key engagements with the brand which happen over a period of time, built up by awareness. The sustained engagement with the brand has to produce a smile.

You'd be sorry if you believe a brand is merely a selling procedure with give-and-take transactions with customers to make your profit. The serious fact is that everything in every industry needs to start from product performance that has distinction and is better than competitors within a price band. So product seriousness is Brand Friendship's key engagement. You have to smile to create friendship between the customer and brand in a social context because your brand's sustaining success depends on it.

Brand Friendship as human resource driver

Development of human capital at the workplace is the key to talent creation for expanding, stabilizing, and sustaining business. Whether you are the boss or a subordinate, unless a certain employee Brand Friendship is created, the delivery you get will be basic, without that extra mile of passion. To deliver Brand Friendship to customers, it's extremely important for any corporation to first create employee Brand Friendship for tomorrow, not just with customers but to develop friendship with employees.

Real friendship develops not only in school or college, but at any age, time, or with any person when a spiritual connect of the anti-hate religion happens. My Brand Friendship idea creates strong proximity with social relevance between the brand and its varied stakeholders.

Often not all customers understand the meaning of sustainability, the way it is used as a jargon in corporations. You need to tangibly prove your company's friendship with the environment through your corporate social responsibility activities.

Customers will then better appreciate your respect for social causes which is priceless and understand it's not just a public relations (PR) exercise to hide something or promote the company, but something more profound. I call such healthy corporate social responsibility (CSR) as Brand Friendship with the environment and society.

Match it with corporate culture

Brand Friendship strategy requires an enterprise culture that's favorable for its seamless implementation. After a certain time of existence, every company develops its own culture. In this culture and vision, its people, processes, and IT systems have to work with coherence and consistency. When the total enterprise buys-in to the Brand Friendship strategy, we can expect excellence in execution.

In case the company's culture needs to change due to pressures from diametrical change in the marketplace, it should be within a timeframe. Moreover, it's essential that the enterprise culture remains conducive for Brand Friendship. As it is people who drive an enterprise, choosing the right operational leaders is critical. Every candidate cannot fit every enterprise. There has to be a professional match of the candidate's aptitude to the enterprise culture when that enterprise is implementing its Brand Friendship strategy with customers.

Brand friendship in B2B business

One-to-one relationship with customers is the key to business to business (B2B) business discipline. This is included in the Brand Friendship strategy facilitated by five aspects.

1. How you understand your customer's business in the customer's competitive environment,
2. Which industry pain areas you need to highlight to your customer,
3. How do you portray the future of your customer's industry,
4. How do you help your customer shape business strategy and execute as per the requirement of the customer's customers,
5. How do you align your enterprise to the culture of your customer's industry and its local culture.

Very often B2B business leaders say the end-customer domain is not their sphere of activity. This is a monumental mistake. No business in the world exists without end-customers.

B2B business has to polish these five elements to create relationships that reflect Brand Friendship.

QCW is quality customers want

Continuous creation of Brand Friendship with customers can emerge if the brand delivers substance that's unobvious, distinct, and trendy from competitors.

Customers don't understand technical quality processes that your company uses, such as International Organization for Standardization (ISO) certifications, among others. They go for looks, how relevant, adjustable, and friendly it is for their different usage needs, and whether it's reliable and affordable.

These attributes build QCW to consistently deliver the brand's repeat purchase. QCW better defines your company's quality parameters. Its three strategic attributes reside in the customer's subconscious and conscious mind, and blend seamlessly to establish QCW:

"It looks good" (emotion)
"It works well for me" (usability)
"I believe in it" (trust).

Only the seamless blend in high ground elevation of these three attributes can establish QCW.

Incredible approach by an organized retailer on QCW

In my book *Art of the Brand* (1994), I'd written that brands have a role to act as social beings. In the French countryside, I recently experienced exactly how a brand can become social.

Opposite the entrance of a hypermarket called Super U, I saw a life-size sculpture of a cow with an indication arrow saying, "Get fresh cow milk."

There was an automatic milk vending machine outside the retail store where fresh milk is available 24 hours/7 days a week. The milk comes from cows who graze in nearby village fields. To ensure it is fresh, it is replenished twice a day. You can pick up the milk in an empty bottle that's available in an adjacent machine that vends different sizes of bottles for holding quantities of 20 cl, 1/2 liter, 1, and 2 liters. Everything is automated and hygienically superior. You put a coin to get the bottle for the quantity you require, and then hold the bottle to get the milk.

With modern digital technology, you now get cow's milk the way a milkman used to bring it fresh from the farm, not industrially processed as milk generally is in developed countries. I found this was Super U's superb way of developing QCW with a brand. It's not about differentiation, rather it is brand distinction. This experience portrays how the platform of Brand Friendship can be created even by offering four quantity options.

This is also an example of how the power of digi-tech can silently enable the customer to enjoy a genuine, fresh, and local farmland experience.

Brand-friendship-building Strategy Through Quadra Orbit Function of QCW

We can draw a parallel between the quadra orbit of human friendship and Brand Friendship with customers. By its very nature, industry requires product/service, brand, point of purchase, and communication to connect with customers.

Creating these four Brand Friendship attributes as in the cow's milk example given earlier is akin to the human friendship quadra orbit. In essence, Brand Friendship delivers quality that customers want (QCW), amounting to a disruptive way for your enterprise to increase its profitable business. It's essential to add tangible and intangible elements to the four areas of Brand Friendship. Tangible elements will physically connect while intangible elements can be built upon continuously.

The quadra effect orbit around QCW cannot be dislocated. If this quadra effect orbit is executed minutely, your brand will create continuous friendship with customers which unquestionably would result in continuous growth and profit for your enterprise. The quadra effect attributes of Brand Friendship are:

1. Product/service distinction surpassing competitors;
2. Transmitted through humanized branding;
3. Continuous magnetic activity at the point-of-purchase;
4. Continuous, unconventional, sociable communication activity.

To elaborate the quadra effect of Brand Friendship (Figure 4.3) let's look at the previous example of Super U retail dispensing fresh local milk 24 hours a day. Here is how Brand Friendship was created:

ACTION TAKEN BY THE RETAILER	BRAND FRIENDSHIP THROUGH THIS QUADRA-EFFECT
Fresh cow milk available with glass bottles holding different quantity	Product and service distinction surpassing competitor
Mega size sculpture of cow as branding	Transmitting through humanized branding
24 hours availability of the milk	Magnetic power at the point of purchase
Milk from local village	Sociability factor

Figure 4.3   Quadra Orbit of Brand Friendship with Customers

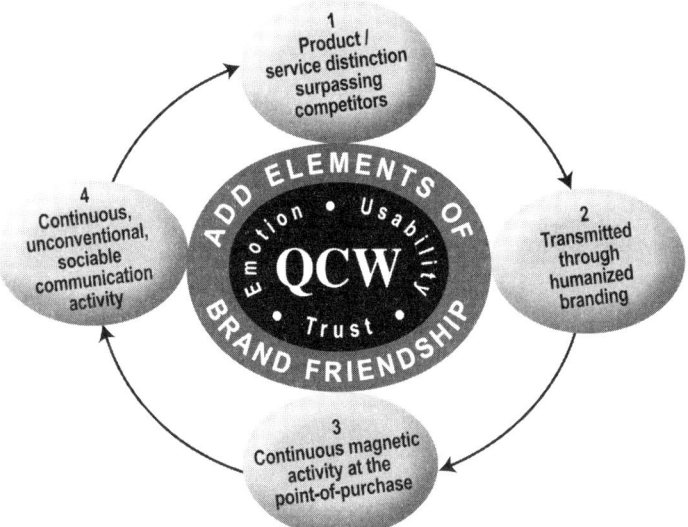

Source: Author.

1. **Product/service distinction surpassing competitors**

   At inception, the product/service has to have some perceptible element of Brand Friendship. That means its functionality has to help create friendship with the customer which is tangible.

   For example, Ilkone has designed a mobile phone for the Middle East market which has a special application that points devout users in the direction of Mecca. Then there's Toyota that has designed the welcab category car that has a flexible chair system with easy ingress and egress for disabled people.

2. **Transmitted through humanized branding**
   Trademark

   The beginning of the 20th century saw the emergence of the etching style trademark such as Brooklyn

Cloth, Continental Watch Co., Julien Gallet & CIE, and International Business Machines as shown in Figure 4.4.

Figure 4.4 Etching Style Trademark Branding from 20th Century

Source: Collated by author. Brand logos are for representative purpose only and are solely owned by the respective copyright owners.

Graphic centric branding

The old geometrical school branding then changed to become more stylized graphic design as used by Nabisco, Philips, De Dietrich, Chase, AEG, or Exxon up to 1960s (see Figure 4.5).

Digi-tech ear branding

From 1970s onwards, digital technology has literally changed the branding rule. A totally new domain of digital companies such as Google, Facebook, Twitter, and YouTube has created an industry dimension not dreamt of or predicted earlier.

Apple's identity of a bitten apple is symbolic of lust at the Garden of Eden, also knowledge, hope,

Figure 4.5 Graphic Centric Branding upto 1960s

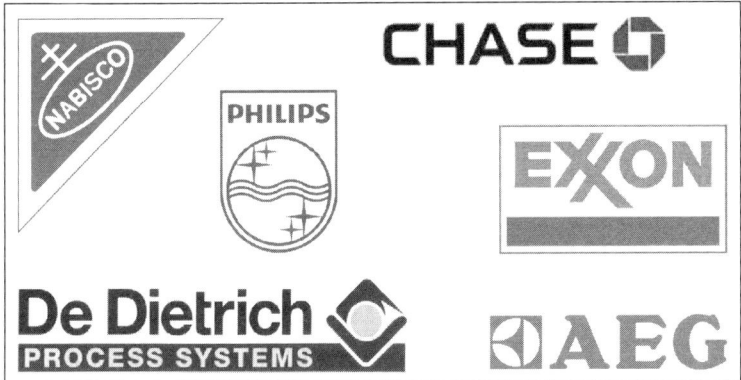

health, products for good living, the new yuppie life-style of quality, and perfection. Another example is Nike's "swoosh" logo. It symbolizes the wing of the Greek Goddess of Victory called Nike who largely influenced countless brave warriors (see Figure 4.6).

To establish Brand Friendship, tomorrow's branding has to have some perceptible friendship element that's precise.

Figure 4.6 Digi-tech Branding Style from 1970s

3. Continuous magnetic activity at the point-of-purchase

You may have created Brand Friendship from product development up to branding, but unless you create the same friendship at the retail point, everything will be lost.

Creating Brand Friendship with customers in the retail is another science that has to have some perceptible element. The distribution machinery is often not under the company's control; in fact, it is totally in an uncontrollable external environment. Here the presence of your brand needs to be bigger than its real form to be noticed among competitors. This will help customers navigate toward your brand.

Only when the brand can display magnetic power to tantalize customers at the retail outlet can instant Brand Friendship be created. So if the trade lacks in friendship with your brand, your brand will not succeed. Similarly, if you as a theater director have not created a strong friendship with the light man of the stage, you can be sure that your show will go awry.

Here are two examples. At the retail, Gillette set up a winner's podium indicating first, second, and third prize winners. Gillette displayed its products at a great height and engaged customers to step up to first position to take the product as a winner. In a bike store in Barcelona, the bikes were displayed as if they were paintings in a gallery. A large central space was created inside the store for the shoppers' experiential trail of different bike before purchase.

As in these examples, the brand's strong friendship with its distributors will give it the right light at the retail. If you can create strong friendship of your brand in the trade, then it will obviously have a rub-off effect on Brand Friendship with the customer.

4. **Continuous, unconventional, sociable communication activity**

A brand has to have some perceptible element and the power to create friendship to connect to customers in the social context. Most customers know that TV advertising makes a hallucinating story to entertain on the virtual screen. But in today's world, a brand cannot remain a cinema image or be magical because cinema is ephemera and hence, cannot be touched, and when the magician is no longer on stage the subject will disappear. Communicating in the traditional way will not get the brand's credibility factor. Taking peer effect in an unconventional way similar to documentary films will create better Brand Friendship.

The brand has to play a role in a customer's body and mind, in the family, at school, college, and workspace with a social element that creates a peer effect. For example, Apple inspires people to dress their heads with hair-embossing that creates the Apple logo.

Sociable communication should not seem like traditional-doctrine-driven advertising. For example, real friendship encompasses multiple phases of participation at both difficult and enjoyable times. Similarly, the customers must experience sociable communication that appears to be part of their life including both their ups and downs.

Metaphoric device to create Brand Friendship—
microscope, binoculars, telescope
Past centuries have not faced the everyday changing phenomenon. This social context has radically shifted from the last decade as people have changed beyond imagination. Only the social aspect can shape your business now, nothing exists outside social magnification. So, you simultaneously need the microscope, binoculars, and telescope. Looking through the microscope will reduce your risks to achieve your short-term goal as it shows you a magnified, detailed direction from what is actuality.

In fact, the microscope reveals the incoherence at the interface between your enterprise brand and your customer in the competitive environment. At the same time you will need to use the binoculars to see the mid-term. Forget about your vision in the long term if you consider carrying the telescope is too cumbersome.

So the microscope magnifies the short-term perspective, binoculars helps you see beyond the naked eyeview to address mid-term planning, and the telescope brings the long-term vision nearer to start planning and execution. These three magnifying instruments bring you closer to society and customers in the social context from where you can create durable Brand Friendship for short term, mid-term and long term.

Connect to Brand Friendship all day long
Once you implement Brand Friendship strategy and execution, you can measure it with the measuring system given in Figure 4.7.

Figure 4.7 Areas of Measuring the Quadra Orbit of Brand Friendship with Customers

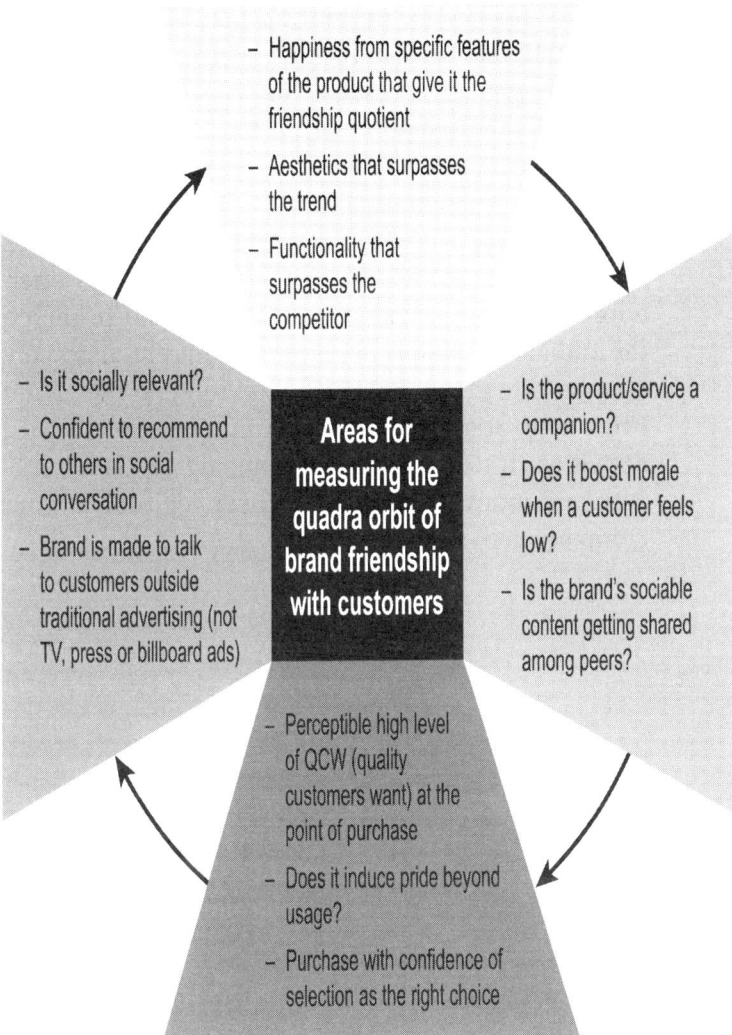

Source: Author.

As a business enterprise leader, you will have to connect seamlessly to the Brand Friendship strategy through the quadra orbit while respecting its additional tangible and intangible elements. Individual elements can give results, but when you combine all the elements mentioned in this, you will get the wholesome benefit of Brand Friendship.

Whether in manufacturing, service, or retailing, your real mandate is profitable growth. This describes how to absorb and action business operations from the backend to the front end to match the radical behavioral change of today's customers all over the world. You just need to keep the Brand Friendship idea in your mind in all your day-long activities. It will enormously impact to both renovate and innovate product and service brands your company delivers.

POSTFACE
Actioning
the Jalebi

So this is the end of my *Jalebi Trilogy*. After so many years of global experience, that is, 3 years of sweeping in a lithography studio, 8 years of professional working experience in design, and 30 years of running my company Shining Consulting in the global arena, and simultaneously working for 15 years in India, the jalebi has caught my head. It is embedded in there so deeply as the glue that binds India that I had to use it to write this trilogy. Initially, when writing the first book in this trilogy, it was to be named "Managing Displacement." But I did not find the sense and sensibility of India there so *Jalebi Management* was the name I found most appropriate. In my entire global expertise, looking through the window of India was most important for me.

In my profession I had to learn how to work in different countries by learning and understanding the nuances of their different behavior patterns. That gave me a huge scope to comprehend the world in a very creative and empathetic way. When I came to India to start work, the plethora of different behavior samples in one country mesmerized me. I found this diversity in behavior to be the ideal bedrock for creative people in the industry to form different design styles that can change behavior. From here you can ignite many new things. So I continue to be very passionate about discovering the different behavior of people in different countries.

Summing up my *Jalebi Trilogy*, the call of action is at three levels—country, enterprise, and individual.

The agenda for the country is indeed mammoth. At all times, high magnification is required with the microscope for the short-term, binoculars for the midterm, and the telescope for pressing long-term projects such as cleaning up rivers, countrywide focus on infrastructure, and growth of industry. At the enterprise level, are we sensitive to the customer? Is our product or service portfolio centered on what the market requires? Tightening up our enterprises with discipline to deliver QCW is the biggest schema. Jalebi action for the individual is clearly to sharpen our aptitude to build capability and skills for leadership.

The social jalebi is an expanding landscape with far-reaching nuances because slowly but surely the world is turning towards globalized interdependency. We have become aware that we globally trade and transact, invest, migrate, or travel everywhere, share common environmental challenges, knowledge, and expertise. Look at new dimensions such as mobile phones and electronic goods, and services such as travel and the Internet, which have brought us together.

Yet there are humungous social differences when it comes to culture and food that are never ever going to completely converge. *Corrugated Slices: The Social Jalebi* revels in these differences and has brought you many, many mini tales to savor, to change your mood through a variety of reading to deployment experiences. The ups and downs of corrugation describe the positive and negative aspects of the jalebi.

This third book of *The Jalebi Trilogy* weaves a kind of togetherness that aims to tie people to one another at a social level. An emotional bond is conjured up when fresh jalebis are being fried and laid in sugar syrup. You cannot stop admiring the skill required to design the jalebis in hot oil and take them out at just the right time. The jalebi retains its crunchy exterior, while light, warm syrup oozes into your mouth and rolls around your tongue.

In an analogy, society needs the scrumptiousness that jalebis offer. At the same time let us recognize, acknowledge, and enjoy the mischievousness that cooks in the social cauldron. It proves that you can seek perfection, but you will always experience life in *Corrugated Slices: The Social Jalebi*.